Soft Spots

I WISH I WAS VIOLENT SARCASTIC OBNOXIOUS

I WISH I COULD RAISE MY VOICE WHEN I TALK

AND RECLAIM

(MY SPACE)

I WISH I WAS READY
TO TELL YOU

TO SHUT UP

NOW I AM MY OWN GOAL
AND I AM ABOUT TO CLIMB

THE HIGHEST MOUNTAIN
AND TO BE A FEARLESS

DRAGON

Foreword

I am writing these lines as the unprecedented armed aggression of the Putin regime is raging in and against Ukraine. The war is destroying the country, terrorizing its people, trying to break their morale and their bodies. Within a few days, it shifted the political and personal paradigm we used to live in.

First of all, I would like to express my solidarity with the people of Ukraine. Our thoughts are with our friends and colleagues from the Kyiv Biennale.

Our collective strongly condemns the invasion, acknowledging the bravery of the Ukrainian people fighting for freedom and independence. We are standing with you.

> "Everything that happened at the time has left its mark in the cells of my body. Not in my memory. The body's cells seem to remember better than the memory which is intended for it."[1]

The experiences we take from the world and recorded memories are deeply imprinted in our minds and bodies—they make us who we are. Gloomy times wreak havoc on peoples, the angst that obliterates our spirit, with long-lasting effects on our health, becomes engraved in our souls. Distressing events, be it the struggle against oppressive regimes, racism, class violence, or the loss of loved ones, are causing trauma as emotional and physical response. It affects our lives in various ways, stretches into multiple forms and layers. One cannot put trauma on a scale—when it hurts it hurts.

The current war against Ukraine comes just after two years of living in a pandemic, another global disaster that has brought us face to face with uncertainty, the horrors of the unknown. In a blink of an eye the constellations we were at home with fell apart. It exposed those sores and wounds that are long lasting and deeply rooted, revealing historical and political traumas. They lay bare the damage, uncover the already harmed that was lying beneath, invisible,

1 Jewish writer and holocaust survivor Aharon Appelfeld in Thomas Fuchs, "Body Memory and the Unconscious," *Founding Psychoanalysis Phenomenologically: Phenomenological Theory of Subjectivity and the Psychoanalytic Experience*, ed. D. Lohmar et al. (Dordrecht: Springer, 2011): 69–82.

ignored or repressed. It has been a time of dealing with these ruins. In a way we are always standing on ruins of the world that used to be. The ruins as haunting testimonies of broken relationships, be it with ourselves, with others, with nature. But what if there is nothing left to break and there is only a void?

Pain and trauma make one disconnected and alienated from others, from the world. The mind oscillates between the nightmares and glimpses of the real world that is hard to hold on to. Where to look for the escape roads to exit the multiple crises we are in? Is there a recovery from the grief? And where does the pain go, does it just hurt away? We tend to think that the best response to trauma is to pursue the path of the fastest healing and recovery, and as quickly as possible return back to "normal" and move on. But the stress stays with us, imprints in the fabric of our flesh, is recorded in our bones and movements.

How to live on together? How to be in solidarity with others in their pain, in their situation that I haven't experienced?

We cannot command the pain away. But we can give ourselves and each other space to be with the pain. We can relate to, gesture to, and hear each other. Stillness can be an action. Listening is an action. Active listening can be a way to overcome. Acknowledging my own vulnerability and letting others stand by me is to produce a WE as resistance. By reconsidering the narratives and the status quo we emphasize the tension between the contingency of radical historical change and the efforts to represent this change. Representations are fixed in time, fixing time, whereas history and our experience is always changing in the becoming.

This book is the mental map of trajectories of thoughts that staged the vantage point of the second edition of the Biennale Matter of Art 2022. We grew together in the process of dwelling with the questions while deprived from sharing a physical space with each other. In the long zoom talks, based in different places and time zones, we have established the online practice invested in scrutinizing the familiar. The collection of essays and artistic interventions is based on long-term research and experience; resulting from conversations and brainstorming sessions, the conceptual birth of this anthology and the biennale brought together the curatorial approaches of Rado Ištok, Renan Laru-an, Piotr Sikora, and the tranzit.cz collective.

Gratitude to all the friends, colleagues and partners who have supported us and made this book possible.

Soft and Weak.

Introduction

Rado Ištok
Renan Laru-an
Piotr Sikora
(tranzit.cz) Tereza Stejskalová

We are all born with soft spots on our heads; these are called fontanelles. They symbolize the extreme vulnerability with which we enter this world, and that this vulnerability remains with us as long as we live no matter how healthy, strong and self-sufficient we may appear to be. To have a soft spot for something or someone means to have a particular fondness for someone regardless of his or her shortcomings, to suspend one's guard in the presence of someone or something. We have chosen such particular vulnerability, weakness and defenselessness as the central perspective and intellectual and affective point of departure for this publication, which accompanies and complements the exhibition and the public program of the 2nd edition of the Biennale Matter of Art.

This publication brings together new as well as existing essays, interviews, short stories, and reports from different fields, geographies, and issues, composing a constellation of sparse clouds, where every contribution is a departing point rather than a complete story. The contributions often start from the point of exhaustion—mental exhaustion, cultural exhaustion, material, and economic exhaustion—and the ensuing strategic position of weakness or softness. Many contributions map the space of Eastern Europe so that even in the case of texts referring to other cultural contexts, the latter can always be seen as having implications for the region and vice versa. Indeed, the texts refer to the East European context and beyond with a special emphasis on the preposition. Thus situated, they address a variety of topics: racialization, the decolonization of museums and museology, intricacies of cultural exchange or implications of radical modernist traditions of thought and aesthetics. They are accompanied by artistic interventions by Dorota Brázdovičová, Tarek Lakhrissi, and Markéta Soukupová. Included are also excerpts from *Pižmo, the Independent Magazine for Strengthening Cultural Diversity*, a zine published by the SAM83 gallery collective in Česká Bříza.

As a heterogeneous curatorial group, we decided to work on the reader outside of common pedagogical principles and to turn towards more elemental features of language. For after critique, there comes a second stage, that can be described as criticality. It inclines to question the methods, motifs, limitations, and biases we operate within when attempting to translate thoughts, emotions, or experiences into words or images. We have therefore decided to drop the usual practice of arranging thematic groups into chapters, which often tend to cause disappointment by reducing the possibilities of reading and understanding, instead of serving as a fruitful guidance. This step was driven by a growingly urgent feeling that something has to be unlearned from the legacy of editorial orthodoxies and the impositions of comprehensibility stemming from the tradition of literacy and explanation. Although burning editorial bridges might lead to confusion, we are taking this risk in order to give the text the freedom to float and live its own life, co-create a spectrum of meanings, questions and possibilities in conjunction with the words and sentences that precede and follow, together with the readers, or possibly onlookers. We encourage you to set out on a journey through the cadency of words and flow of sentences in the following essays, which deliberate among each other, open up for new methodologies, and enable encounters that create platforms for new understandings of the topics at hand.

The opening text takes us into the midst of a women's prison in mid-1960s Czechoslovakia. Following the everyday life of the inhabitants of Pardubice penitentiary, the short stories *Soul Prints* were partly written in the prison where Jana Krejcarová—a young outstanding writer, drug addict, and mother of five kids—was taken due to the neglect of parental care. The redemption song she has put together in five chapters has a heavy beat, a slightly naive plot, and heroines that struggle with day-to-day problems. As the short texts unravel their life and crime stories, their near future is defined by deficiency and absence. What brings them together is the time spent waiting for something (someone?) to come and save them from the boredom of punishment.

The complicated and ambivalent relationship between the renowned African American musician and Communist Paul Robeson and the Czechoslovak cultural elites is the subject of Františka Schormová's contribution. While Robeson's political and musical trajectory has brought him well-deserved fame and it belongs to the histories of leftist antiracist and anti-imperialist struggles, in the Czech milieu he is mainly known as a symbol of state socialist propaganda.

Yet, the reality of contacts and exchanges between Czechoslovak culture and Robeson was more complex. The essay shows how that exchange was defined by internationalist radical leftist culture or the surprising ways in which Robeson's music became, in the hands of politically dissenting musicians, a strategy to push against the censorship. Paradoxically, Robeson's spirituals influenced the musical group Spiritual Kvintet who used the songs to fight against the system Robeson himself defended.

It is a little-known fact that the Náprstek Museum in Prague, the main ethnographic museum in the Czech Republic, was originally conceived as an industrial museum, with the collections from Asia, Africa and the Americas gathered by Czech explorers playing a secondary role. This double origin of the museum serves as a point of departure for Anna Remešová to untangle the knot of the 19th-century Czech national emancipation and its intimate relationship with free-market capitalism, reliant on the extraction of resources and unequal distribution of power between the Global North and South. Today, the museum has initiated its own transformation in response to discussions on decolonization. Yet, as Remešová shows through her explorations of 19th century Czech industrialism, this troublesome kinship between Czechoslovak statehood and European imperialism and economic liberalism should be the starting point of these discussions.

Decidedly distant from Prague's discursive community, Filipina artist-educator Brenda Fajardo's texts come in contact with the Eastern European art historical and cultural milieu today through two terms that may have been the cord that ties Southeast Asia and East-Central Europe together: "decolonization" and "poverty." Almost monographic in focus with a clarity that is inherently pedagogical, Fajardo permanently theorized the subjects of decoloniality and poverty to be interwoven realities in artistic practice. *Decolonization Through People's Art* (1985/1992) and *The Aesthetics of Poverty* (1982/2010) are republished in a new language and offered to new publics who are effectively reading Fajardo's notes on how to live and work artistically in the perpetual states of postponement and development. Her honesty in discursifying material conditions together with the tenderness that is executed in her understanding of education form a modest yet fundamental replacement to autonomy as the primordial power of artists. In her newly written essay, the curator Amanda Carneiro raises the question of what decolonizing an art museum really means. She cautions us not to equal decolonization with a mere pluralization or diversification of the museum's collections and programs, which appears to respond to social demands while operating within the extractive and neoliberal managerial policies. In other words, the mere inclusion of artists from historically subjugated and marginalized social groups into institutions built on colonial classificatory categories and power hierarchies is not sufficient for decolonization. What is more, it often leads to tokenization and "folklorization" in which non-white artists and curators can only act in the international scene as long as they meet the colonial institutions' expectations on representing their places of origin, communities and identities.

Three voices chasing one another, speaking over each other, finishing each other's sentences. The pace of this conversation is rapid. The stakes are high. The artist Robert Gabris is in conversation with Jana Horváthová, the director of the Roma Museum in Brno, and Ábel Ravasz, the former Plenipotentiary of the Government of the Slovak Republic for Roma Communities, discussing the topic of the Roma queer community in a Czech and Slovak context. The first question posed by Robert Gabris fast-forwards us into the future three hundred years from now. This sets a pace for the triangular conversation where each question is immediately followed by a crossfire of energizing answers. We are late and as we realize it in the course of this conversation, there is absolutely no time for hesitation when it comes to giving voice to and supporting communities and minorities that are still being harassed, objectified, racialized and even killed in Eastern Europe just based on the color of their skin.

Prompted by the impact of the widespread racialization of the Covid-19 pandemic, the artist Zai Xu reflects on his experience of growing up and coming of age in the predominantly white Czech society as a child of Chinese migrants. While the childhood experiences of difference and bullying resulted in his attempt to forget and distance himself from everything that could link him to his skin color, as Xu realizes in hindsight, these attempts led in turn to alienation and internalized racism. The new wave of stigmatization at the onset of the pandemic has, in his view, only highlighted the already existing racial stereotyping, ranging from bullying to sexual objectification, and the feeling of second-class citizenship passed from the non-white migrant parents on their children.

The fantasy of diplomacy retools the imperial romance that particularly the international artworld enjoys in its soft-loaning of "basic human rights" from politics to poetics and across infrastructures and rhetoric. One of the many historical examples that we included in the publication is what Robin Hartanto called the "architecture of nationalism" in Indonesia's Gelora Bung Karno Stadium, initially named the Asian Games Complex, which was built for the Fourth Asian Games in 1962. The readily available analysis in Hartanto's essay emphasizes the perverse nature of internationalism whose dysfunctional output reorganizes different scales and imaginations of the local. This fragment of archipelagic Indonesia's relationship with the Cold War protagonists, the USSR and the United States, figures an opportunism or even a managerialism of indigenous diplomacy that demands, manipulates, and retorts to the world stage with an alternative: plan, method, platform or lie.

The problem of heritage—a line that also initiates Ramon Guillermo's argument on comparative social realism—suddenly rouses the filiation of aesthetic concepts in the wake of content-based moral panic. Guillermo abandons the genealogy of the Lukacsian formulation of realism, grafting other formations and qualities that approximate the "representation" and "content" of reality. The cross-citation that occurs in Guillermo's essay, a Maoist injunction to a Eurocentric Marxism elaborated by specific intellectual traditions and cultural practices, situates the publication's suggestion on reading as a continuous experience of discontinuities. Especially in the territory of Marxist interpretation, reading the inadequate articulation of comparison delivers the reader to a history of disappointments.

The term "homo sovieticus" encompasses all of the post-soviet stigmas. It expresses the incompatibility of finding your path in the bright scenarios of end-of-history time and inability to adapt in the rising capitalism. This way soviet being is a leftover from the former regime and a bad penny between the letters of the success story of transformation. The term itself was somehow lost in the abyss of the nineties and now, as happens with many phenomena from that era, it comes back to haunt us in a new context. In her essay, Dorota Michalska took a chance to look at this term from the lens of racialization and by this way to juxtapose two different realms and knot them together. Introducing the category of race into the studies of post-Soviet Eastern Europe she made an attempt to re-inscribe this part of the world onto the global map of racial relations.

The text by Olúfẹ́mi O. Táíwò circles around two neuralgic points of current debates on the left: the issue of representation and the issue of trauma. It revolves around the absence of a necessary link between those who represent marginalized groups in elite spaces and the emancipation of those marginalized groups. Táíwò calls on us to leave elite spaces and start to build new ones together with those who will for various reasons never make it to the privileged spaces. Also, he questions trauma as a useful guide for politics. As he writes: "Contra the old expression, pain—whether borne of oppression or not—is a poor teacher. Suffering is partial, short-sighted, and self-absorbed. We shouldn't have a politics that expects different: oppression is not a prep school."

Colonial complicity and exceptionalism of the Czech lands are the two key terms addressed by Filip Herza's overview of the history of colonial interventions and unfulfilled colonial ambitions of Czech elites. While the Czech lands, first as a part of Habsburg Monarchy and later as Czechoslovakia, played only a marginal role in the global trade reliant on resource extraction and enslavement, they shared the ideas of the superiority of Western civilization which was reflected in their oftentimes problematic treatment of inhabitants of Carpathian Ruthenia, a part of Czechoslovakia in the interwar period, or Slovakia for that matter. The refusal to come to terms with this past is echoed in today's reluctance on the part of Czechs to accept responsibility for their role in global conflicts and crises or global climate change.

The human rights activist Gwendolyn Albert outlines the history and current state of forced sterilization of marginalized communities in various parts of the world on the case studies from the former Czechoslovakia—where Romani women were particularly affected, the USA, Sweden, Japan, Bangladesh, China and Peru. Promoted and perpetrated by the local political elites, the ongoing forced sterilizations can be traced to the early 20th century eugenics movement and its attempt to eliminate traits perceived as undesirable, including poverty, and promote desirable ones. What the given examples from around theworld share is, in Albert's view, the disregard for violations of the justice system and the sustained investment of energy and resources into forced sterilizations as part of state policy regardless of authoritarian or democratic governmental rule.

In the previously unpublished conversation with the writer Giulia Loi, the artist Hamja Ahsan provides an insight into Shy Radicals, a fictional movement of liberation and a coalition of shy, quiet, awkward, introverted and neurodivergent people, which materialized in an eponymous book and as an art project. Ahsan and Loi discuss questions ranging from historical anti-colonial and liberation movements and their relation to violence, the impact of neoliberalism and its war against public ownership on our sensitivity, to the impact of mental health diagnoses, therapy and medication, and its relation to work and productivity. As Hamja reminds us, since the structure of the work day doesn't allow time for healing or processing, staring into space or at the sea can be a powerful act of resistance.

Enclosed in the book is a letter. It is prefaced with the question "Who are we writing for?" The weight and exhaustion of this interrogation is even more unbearable when the action of "counter" is invoked in a coupling with feminism, public intimacy, and unalienable privacy. Whoever carries this epistolary must be tired now. When Brigitta Isabella proposed to revisit a letter published in a newspaper, she continued a correspondence between two female artists in 1960s Indonesian art ecology. She assumes the role of companion, someone who walks with us in the spell of solidarity and collectivity. This gesture shares the task of carrying a burden that is always a shared responsibility. A task dogged by the schedule of commitments, frustrations and promises that delay resolutions to federal questions, like "Should Female Artists Separate Themselves from Male Artists?" Forty years since the letter was first read, Brigitta wrote that perhaps we can be feminist readers now. She creatively asks a new question out of older questions: when is it timeliest to read this publication?

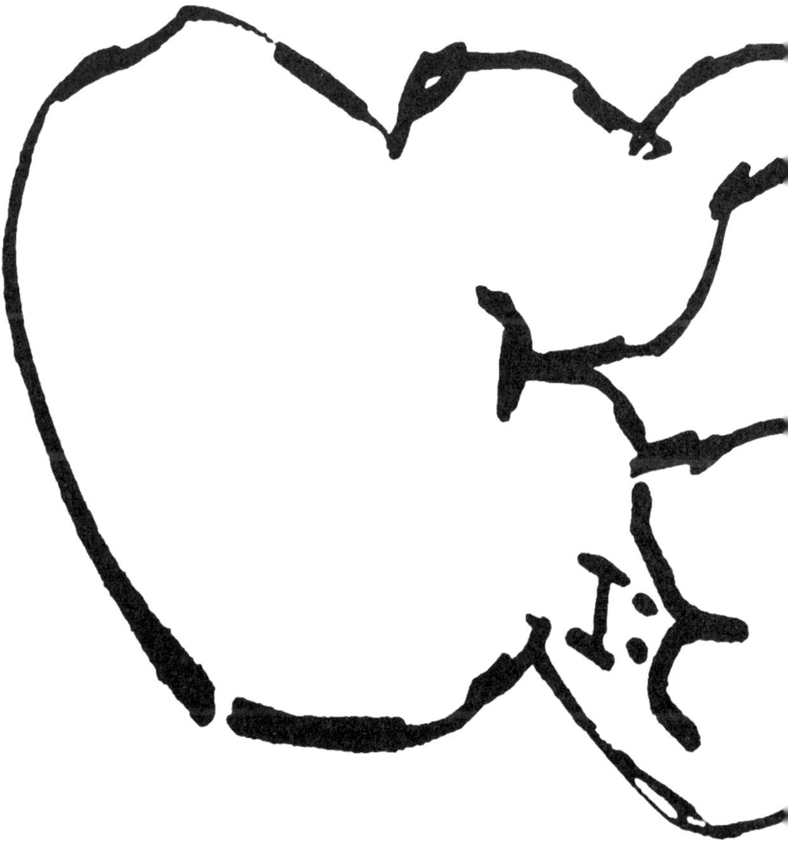

T

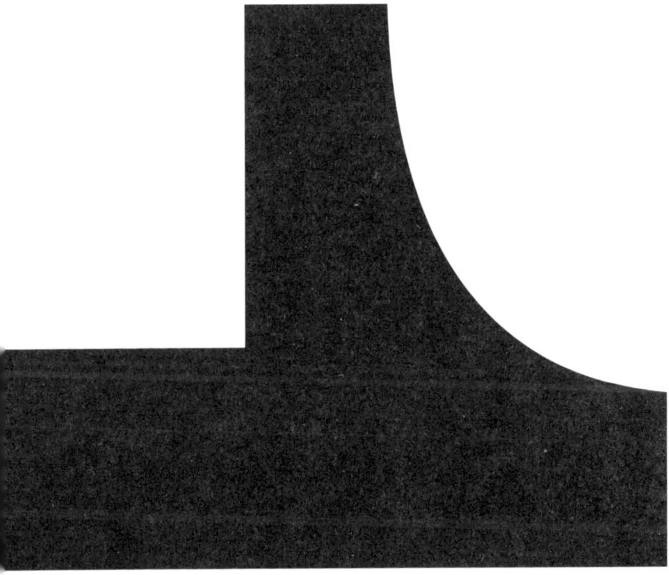

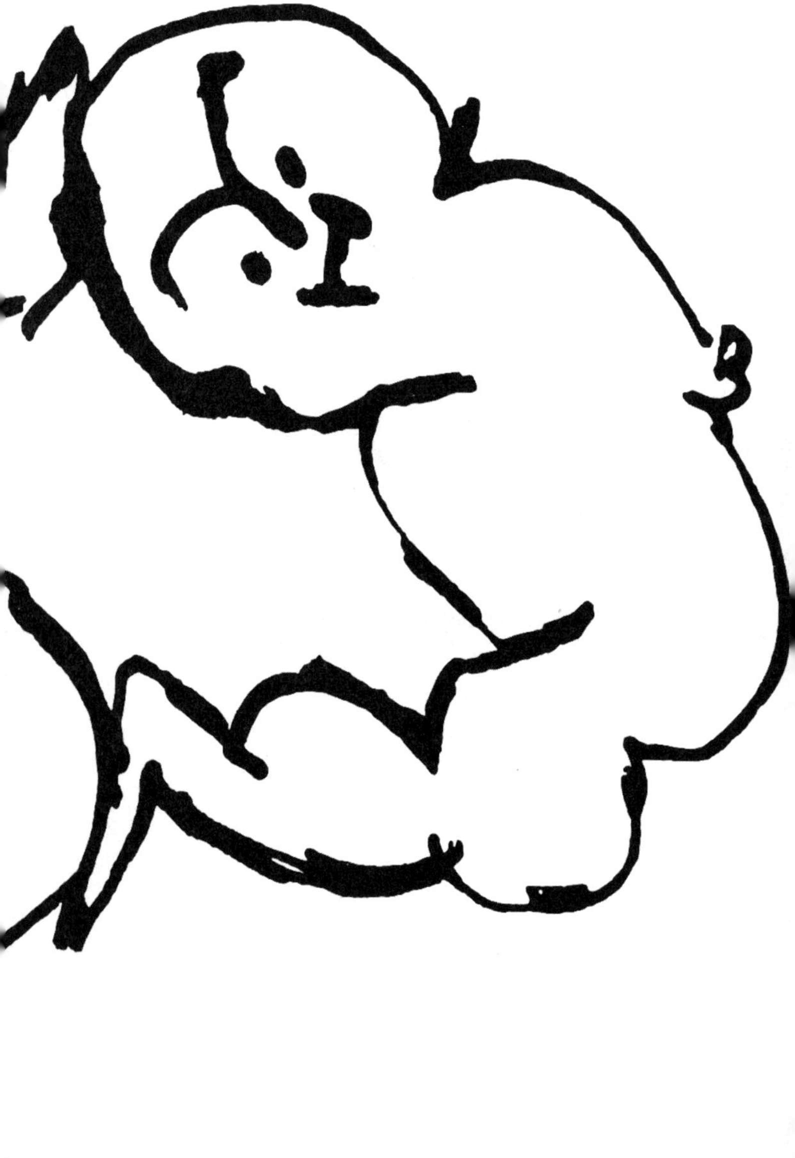

Soul Prints

Jana
Krejcarová-Černá

The check-out period is from three o'clock to six o'clock on Mondays, Wednesdays, and Fridays. On these three days, roughly a hundred readers take turns in the library. Of them, two know what they want, eight browse the shelves, ten want "something romantic," and the remaining eighty all insistently ask for fairy tales. Eighty out of a hundred women convicted of various criminal offenses. That is—eighty out of the hundred women who read while serving their sentences. Women, each of whom has committed some criminal act, from murder to social parasitism, including theft, disturbing the peace, assaulting a public servant, and sexual deviance. The scant few copies of fairy tale books that the prison library possesses pass from hand to hand, with worn spines, loose, dog-eared pages, and soiled dust jackets. The pages printed with stories of unreal magic and non-existent princes become a perfect collection of the fingerprints of real and existent criminals.

The convicts' theater group has prepared a premiere for their fellow inmates. For talent does not preclude the commission of a criminal offense, and vice versa—committing a crime does not divest an offender of their innate talent.

They're putting on Tyl's *The Stubborn Woman*, a fairy tale about Zlatohlav and the lord of the Giant Mountains, about a stubborn miller's wife and a meek but relentlessly enamored schoolboy. A fairy tale with forest spirits and a happy ending.

The culture room where the performance is taking place is packed. The space is completely silent, and even the biggest troublemakers, ceremonially dressed in their Sunday uniforms, follow what is happening on stage with rapt attention.

Right in the front row, up by the stage, two inseparable girlfriends sit next to each other. One of them raped her ward, a five-year-old girl, causing the child such grievous bodily harm that she had to be taken to the hospital. The second is here for drunkenly inciting a brawl in which she nearly killed a rival. Now they're holding hands, not even breathing, and one can tell from their faces what disgust the schemes of the philandering lord baron arouse in them, how they tremble in fear for Tereza and admire Zlatohlav, who punishes evil and rewards the schoolboy's enduring love. The story is nearing its end. Good and evil are getting what they rightly deserve, and Zlatohlav is once again returning to the mountains. Both women, tears in their eyes, go out to the courtyard of the prison block. Everything turned out okay… Touched and weepy, they hold hands all the way back to their quarters.

A roughly thirty-year-old woman waits in the corridor in front of the doctor's office. Obviously a repeat offender, according to her clothes, she's from the second correctional group. She waits patiently, pacing back and forth holding a matchbox in the palm of her hand, all the time uttering tender words into it. In response to the puzzled question, "What do you have there?" she first covers her palm mistrustfully, opening her hand again after a moment to display a cotton-lined matchbox in which lies a tiny baby mouse. With a careful tenderness, she strokes its belly with her index finger. The little animal doesn't even take up half the space in the matchbox. The woman, who has been convicted multiple times, is obviously embarrassed—being caught in a moment of tenderness has made her feel awkward… "Well, after all, I gotta have something alive in here!" she explains.

It would certainly be an explanation—if she weren't residing with nineteen other living women in her quarters and a hundred living women in the block.

The quarters must be kept tidy, and this is very categorically demanded of the inmates. Every Saturday, there is a big clean, which the women perform in turns as it falls to them. No one has the right to an exception. When one's Saturday comes, one must clean, scrub the floors, and wash the windows and furniture. Only exceptions do exist… A strong, robust woman in her fifties, sentenced for the murder of her husband, is cleaning two Saturdays in a row. She doesn't talk much—she can only express herself with considerable difficulty. She is Polish by birth, her vocabulary is very limited, and moreover, she is quite simple-minded. But hardworking and very cleanly. She is doing the second cleanup for a young worker who she has grown fond of and whose notorious messiness she forgives in exchange for her drawings.

And after the cleaning is finished, she sits with the girl at a freshly scrubbed table in the quarters and selects, from among the kitschy little doodles of kitties and dollies, the image she would like to have drawn on a letter to her adult son. When she has picked out the sweetest and most colorful one, she brings writing paper and watches, with the tip of her tongue protruding, as a sketch of two kittens with big bows begins to take shape on the letterhead. “He’ll know I didn’t draw it, but he’ll like it.”

These are the things that inspire awe. The things that inspire fear or sadness are far greater in number. And those that inspire hope or joy are perhaps the rarest. But a person who is capable of brutal murder but whose face also lights up like a child’s when listening to fairy tales, a person who is incapable of rudimentary communication with human society and yet, with a nervous tenderness, keeps a baby mouse alive—all of this inspires mainly awe in me. Awe of the fact itself and awe of the mistake that happened somewhere, which—I’m afraid—cannot be corrected, even by a correctional facility. One Soviet statesman once said that there are problems even communism won’t rid us of, because even under communism, one person can kill another out of jealousy or because they have stopped loving each other. But I don’t know anyone who could tell me why this same person would be capable of sacrificing for someone who draws pictures they like. Or why someone would devote all the affection they can muster to a mouse. And mainly I don’t know anyone who could tell me where that mistake lies—the one so vigorously corrected in correctional facilities, mostly in vain. Perhaps a doctor, perhaps a psychologist, perhaps a sociologist...

FEAR

A woman was brought in to serve a sentence of several years. Her carelessness caused the deaths of several young people, nineteen-year-old students, whose school bus she allowed to collide with a train because she didn’t lower the crossing gate in time. It is her first day, she’s getting acquainted, and in her first moments she too—like most—confides: “It’s a shame. They locked me up just when we were finally about to buy a car...”

A woman convicted of child abuse. The child, after constant, repeated blows to the head, was left brain-damaged. After a year, she is called before the judge again because the child has died. She reacts to his death with a monstrously clear logic: “It’s a good thing he died. After all, if he would’ve had to live as a retard...”

A bald-headed convict who has permission to wear a wig. She brushes it at night in the shower room so that no one will see her bald head. She constantly writes letters to the office of the President in which she tries to explain that she must be pardoned for the remainder of her sentence, even though she committed the crime she was convicted of, because, due to her baldness, the execution of her sentence demeans her human dignity, which, as Mr. President surely understands, is against the law.

A witless mother of several children, convicted of prostitution and social parasitism. She writes letters to her partner, and when, after three months in prison, she starts to grow noticeably fat, she has herself scheduled for an appointment with the gynecologist at the earliest opportunity. She carries herself proudly around the camp and joyfully announces to everyone: "I think I'm gonna have a little baby. I've already got four, and two are pretty normal."

A woman who rather late in life married a widower who already had a young son. After many years of marriage and many fights and blows, one day she killed him with a knife in self-defense. Only that in her anger, she dealt the already dead man several unnecessary extra blows, which made her self-defense excessive, and so she was given a sentence of several years. And now from here, from prison, she is litigating with her stepson—about the inheritance left by his father, her husband. "After all, I can't lose the house. Where would I go when they let me out? I already had to pay twenty thousand for the autopsy and the doctors..."

A woman who was given a long sentence and therefore needs to earn a favorable position in the camp in order to make the years she has to spend here easier. She gets herself onto the inmates' council, and she has several functions and a certain, not so small amount of power. Evening after evening in the quarters, she grows sad and reminisces about the good old days when she lived with her partner, a commissioned officer of the SS. The war was the most beautiful time of her life: "If only he had survived, he'd be surprised to see me in here! But if he were alive, I would never have ended up here, I guarantee you that!" she says wistfully and sentimentally into the darkness. In the morning she's once again the self-confident functionary of the council, a dangerous enemy of all of the inmates.

An underage girl who was convicted of burglarizing apartments. She is a notorious alcoholic, a lesbian, and an addict, and she attempts to hide none of these things. She's friendly, used to living in a group, and has her own quite clear ideas about morality. She has authority among the younger girls and a number of lovers. She constantly sabotages her work, she's honest, she can be left alone in the quarters indefinitely, and nothing goes missing. She usually has something to smoke, even though she doesn't get an allowance—she gets tobacco from her girlfriends. But she's never friends with anyone for self-serving reasons—she has an innate and violent abhorrence for prostitution. She doesn't hide her relationships, nor does she hide her crimes. If she is attributed a lover with whom she has not had an affair, she replies matter-of-factly either: "No, I haven't slept with her yet," or, "I wouldn't sleep with her. I don't fancy her." "Once I get out? What else would I do? I'll burgle apartments again. I'll just be careful not to get caught. I don't want to do anything else. It's great fun. I never know what I'm going to find in such-and-such apartment. But a lot of times, it's not even worth the effort. It's just about the thrill of what might be there."

A woman whose age is impossible to estimate. Certainly more than thirty, certainly less than fifty. She murdered her child and threw the body into the sewer. She is immensely hardworking and cleanly. (For that matter, hardest working and tidiest women here are the ones who are in for murder.) She's always cleaning something in the block, washing windows or tidying the quarters, workshop, and office. She doesn't talk to anyone, and she never smiles. One day, she is sitting in the sun in the courtyard holding a kitten in her arms and gently—almost lovingly torturing it. The animal has bristly fur, and it is meowing in terror. And the murderess smiles kindly, sweetly...

The wife of a man who was a member of the secret police and had access to money which he systematically embezzled. Over several years, the embezzlement amounted to a few hundred thousand crowns. He was sentenced to ten years, and she, because she knew about his actions, was sentenced to two. She's in the prison office all the time, reporting the inmates' every transgression, no matter how small. Smoking in the quarters, saying bad things about the correctional officers—anything she hears about. "I have to get out on parole after half my sentence. I have children at home. And we were wronged. We didn't take the money for ourselves. My husband used the money to fund subversive activities on May Day," is the version she tells fellow inmates. The version for the correctional officers is: "As soon as I tell them my husband supported subversive activities, they're instantly nice to me. If they could, they'd have a coup!"

A girl just barely of adult age. She is slender, with a delicate face, dark eyes, and dark hair. She was originally given a six-month suspended sentence for social parasitism. Only after her conviction, she was living with her mother, who wanted to remarry, but the daughter was in the way. One day, the mother reported the girl for taking some food at home. Because she was already of age and was not entitled to be supported by her mother, she was sentenced to two months, this time not suspended. She even has to serve her first sentence as well.

When she came to serve her sentence, she spent all of her free time sitting in the quarters with both her index fingers in her ears and a book of poetry in front of her. After a month, she had a lover, an older woman who washed her shoes, did her cleaning for her, and gave her tobacco. After three months, she'd tell off anyone not to her liking, including the old grannies, and instead of in the quarters, she spent her time in the common bathroom. After eight months she was released, and three months later she was back, serving another sentence for social parasitism, disturbing the peace, and fighting. After commencing her second sentence, she once again started sitting in the quarters with her book of poetry and her fingers in her ears. Actually, she initially wanted to recite poetry, and she thought she could make a living with it...

Sunday afternoon. It's the most unpleasant time at the camp. No one works on Sunday, lunch is earlier, and from yard time until the evening roll call, time drags endlessly. The block is overcrowded. During the week, the morning and afternoon shifts alternate, so the only time everyone is in the block together is at night. You can't even move in the building on Sundays. Forty girls sit on the floor in the common bathroom from three o'clock to seven. They beat on the doors and walls with their hands and feet, singing a song with a chorus that goes: "Banjo, my banjo, I'm lucky to have you." Four hours. In one go. The same song. Non-stop. At seven, they go for the evening roll call.

Extremely reluctantly, because it means interrupting the only thing they really enjoy here. They leave behind battered toilet doors, black shoe marks on the walls, and an almost tangible silence.

It's the evening roll call. The women have to be arranged in groups of five in order for it to be possible to count them. One of the inmates is lining them up. She walks around the crowd and shouts: "Get in groups of five!" She jostles the ones who aren't in file and transfers the ones who have more than five in a group. "Can't you count to five?" she shrieks. She's going mad with the effort of preparing a perfect formation for the correctional officer who will come to count. "No smoking during roll call!" she shouts hoarsely. Her moment has finally come. The officer arrives. She stands at attention and roars at the entire courtyard: "Women, attention!" She gives the account: "Such and such number of women are standing in the line-up." And she waits with her chest stuck out until the correctional officer checks her count. Then she gives the command to disperse, drops her shoulders, lets her chest sink, and goes to join the line in front of the kitchen. She waits in line to get her dinner like all the others. Only a slight trace of importance remains on her face—and a trace of inferiority on the others' faces. After all, she has a function. She stands out in some way from the crowd of a hundred drab faces.

The cafeteria. Dinner time. In the indescribable turmoil among the tables, the women sit spooning food out of their mess kits, shouting at each other across the tables, and throwing bread. There are puddles of spilled soup and trampled potatoes on the floor. There is a line at the troughs of warm water. The faces are almost indistinguishable from each other, all of them equally gray and framed by the same bandanas. The din is so loud that you can't hear your own words.

An old, gray-haired woman sits in the corner of the cafeteria. She has her mess kit laid out on a napkin. She cuts thin slices of bread with a knife and scoops up small mouthfuls of soup with a spoon, which she slowly, neatly transports to her mouth. Someone bumps into her, spilling her soup. With a smile and without a single unpleasant word, the old woman wipes the table and continues eating. The one who bumped into her mumbles an apology. From the next table over, someone says, "Forget about her, she's a nun. She's in here for being too holy." Perhaps there's someone who wouldn't be frightened by all of this. But I wouldn't like to meet him. I think I would be afraid of him...

SADNESS

Lights-out is at nine. Then the entire block goes dark, save the corridor and very dim lighting in the bathrooms. At half past eleven, in the poor light and in spite of the prohibition against working after lights-out, a thirty-year-old woman with a face slightly different from the usual faces here sits on a toilet in the bathroom with a notebook on her knees, drawing. A commission. For the camp magazine. The drawing is well-rendered, though her subject is somewhat unsophisticated: two women, one wicked, who is leaning against a machine and smoking, and one good, who is hard at work, the graph above her machine displaying the quotas she has met. And in a bubble, of the kind which in comic books usually contains words like "I've got you, you scoundrel!" is a sweetly baroque child's face. The drawing was supposed to be finished before lights-out, but one also needs to do their personal laundry, wash up after work, and read for a little while too. The artist is thus finishing her work in secret at night. She is in the correctional facility because she drunkenly insulted a public official. She drunkenly insulted the public official because he refused to recognize her right to do and paint what she pleases. "And now I do commissions—and not even for money. If I had just done this on the outside, I wouldn't be in here now, and I could have done what I wanted. That is, I could have done something they would have paid me for, you know. You could say that there's hardly any difference if I'm locked up or if I'm free..."

The drawing is technically very well-rendered. The child in the bubble looks alive...

Every evening—or almost every evening—the mail is handed out. Some women receive letters daily. Some almost never. Of those who don't receive letters, one group doesn't expect to hear their names. While the names are being called, they watch the correctional officer, look around the room, shove each other, and behave altogether naturally. The second group waits. They can even be subdivided into two categories. The first type stare intently at the person handing out the letters, never taking their eyes off of him and shouting impatiently at anyone talking: "Quiet! I can't hear!" The second type act indifferent, but they jump a little bit when names similar to theirs are called, and when the last letter is distributed, their faces dim slightly, and their shoulders slump.

To this group belongs one woman, roughly forty-five years old, tall and beautiful, even in her uniform. She read the tarot, and because she lived near the uranium mines, the "uranians" paid her a tidy sum for her prophecies. She made sixty thousand crowns with her fortune telling. She's smart, she studied medicine for a few semesters, and she could easily imagine what was in store for her customers—what would not pass them by and where they might go wrong. With the money she made, she paid for her son's wedding, arranged an apartment for him, and furnished it with the kinds of things even rich brides can't dream of. And now her son doesn't write to her. For several months, he hasn't sent so much as a sentence. In the evening, after the mail is distributed, she sits in the bathroom, smoking her evening cigarette with her two closest girlfriends, whom she reassures in a voice all but frozen: "I can pretty easily forget my own child. It's not that hard. I've lost all connection to him. If he was dying, I could walk right past him, and I wouldn't even know he was my son. I stopped caring about him. I was sorry at first, but now all day long I never even think about him. I only write to my mother now, but that babushka doesn't like to write, so I don't get many letters..."

Both women nod like people who have no argument with which to counter. There's also nothing else they can do. All too often in the quarters they find half-written letters to the mother: "Write to me. I'm doing fine. I don't need anything. Just tell me, for God's sake, what's going on with Pavel?"

The letters are strewn about her nightstand—there's almost no privacy here—but neither of the girlfriends lets her know they've seen the letters. In some cases, you have to at least pretend the missing privacy.

A young woman with a not too pleasant face and equally unpleasant, impudent behavior. She's pregnant. Despite receiving extra food, she has unbelievable cravings for snacks. She sometimes pilfers treats from other women's nightstands—things sent in the mail or brought by visitors. She soon turns the majority of her fellow inmates against her, and her peers begin to poke fun at her for her pregnancy. “So you’re gonna have a bastard, eh? Don’t tell me you’re married. Who’d want to get hitched to a pig like you?” At first, she defends herself by assuring everyone she has a husband, but when that doesn’t help, she steals a photograph from someone’s nightstand and passes it off as a picture of her hubby. It has an inscription: “To my little star. Popík.” When her fraud is discovered, she is obstinately silent. She refuses to explain anything, and what’s more—she refuses to return the photo. Nothing can compel her to give up the photo of the pimply, twenty-year-old youth. She sleeps with it under her pillow, and sometimes, at night, in the light that falls into the quarters from outside, she softly pronounces each syllable: “To my lit-tle star...”

It’s after dinner—a moment of relative calm before lights-out. Two women stand in the corner of the corridor, and it appears that they are conversing. But what they’re sharing is not a dialogue—it’s two completely independent monologues. When one is speaking, the second indifferently looks around at her surroundings. And as soon as she sees the opportunity to interrupt the speaker, she jumps in and starts speaking herself. At that moment, a completely detached look comes across the first speaker’s face, and she begins looking around the corridor. Only that she can’t find the right moment to jump in again, and so she interrupts her comrade mid-sentence. The second speaker protests: “You’re not listening to me, are you?” And then the first one begins zealously feigning interest: “I’m listening. Of course I’m listening to you. Go on. Something just popped into my head. So, what were you saying?” And for a moment, she listens with her eyes fixed on the speaker’s face. Interest has to be bought. Everyone has the need to tell someone about herself, but there’s a fee that has to be paid. And the only currency is tobacco or attention repaid. For either, you can talk to your heart’s content.

The days are no different from one another. The morning wake-up call, then the workshop, then lunch, yard time, afternoon free time, roll call, dinner, another period of free time, and lights-out. One day is the same as the next. The same faces in the same uniforms, penal or service. The same voices on the camp PA announcing the wake-up call, the time to go to the workshops, or the evening roll call. The same furniture in the quarters, the same path to the workshops. The same voices, the same arguments, the same stories. Each day divided in the same way between several cigarettes and worrying about what you will smoke tomorrow. Tedious, paralyzing monotony. During roll call, a fairly recent arrival suddenly announces in a quiet voice: "Girls, you know, I haven't seen a living child in three months!"

But living children can be seen. It's visiting day. The women—except those whose visitation papers came back from home with a note stating that it is not convenient for their family members to visit at the indicated time or those whose papers did not come back at all, without even a word of explanation—are gathered in the large culture room, from where they are called one by one as the visitors arrive. Some of the inmates are holding packages. Gingerbread hedgehogs, cottages, or little men, wrapped in cellophane. These women's children are visiting, and they have saved up their allowance to buy gifts for the little ones. They are confident of their visits. Not one of those who is holding a package is disappointed. Or perhaps it's the other way around: none of the women who might be disappointed would risk wasting money from their allowance on a gift when they could otherwise spend it on tobacco. And then those who are sure of their visits risk nothing: the package they receive in return will make up for the expense. And all those who do not receive visits will look at them covetously and beg for cigarettes or sweets if they're humble or plunder their nightstands if they're rebellious and full of class hatred. Because in reality, this is the worst place to try to eradicate class differences. Despite all the efforts at sameness, despite the uniformity, and despite not making distinctions, there are rich inmates and paupers. And the rich ones buy power and services and attention, while the paupers obey, fear, and pay attention—except for the few rebellious ones who fight, are rude and spiteful, and are condemned in advance by the rich, the poor, and the correctional officers alike. Because no one is as troublesome as a rebellious pauper.

There are also a lot of gypsy women in the camp. They are loud, quarrelsome, and boisterous, some of them are beautiful, and almost all of them steal without shame or remorse. It is as if they were collecting a compulsory tax from the whites for their oppression.

They fight with each other, and they fight with the whites. They stick together and speak in a gibberish composed of Czech, Slovak, Hungarian, and slang, the harsh dissonance of which grates on the ear.

But once in a while, one of them starts singing a drawn-out song in a minor key, like a psalm, a few endlessly repeating measures of some old gypsy song. The others slowly join in, and in half a day, the psalm has spread throughout the entire camp. There's nowhere to escape the desperate, mournful melody which creeps under the clothes and under the skin, worms its way into the brain, and doesn't allow you to think of anything other than those few endlessly repeating measures. You can't shut them up or otherwise get them to stop, they simply can't be held back, the melody must come out of them—perhaps they would die if they had to stop singing. There is no place in the entire camp that their howl-like psalm doesn't penetrate. At the same time, they don't cause any trouble, and they keep to the daily routine. They sing on the way to the workshop and on the way to lunch, they sing in the quarters and while washing up, they sing till they're blue in the face. And then some of them fall silent. The howl slowly subsides, interrupted by occasional quarrels and shouting, and eventually ceases altogether. And for a while, the gypsies turn back into normal inmates, screaming, communicating in their shrill language, and threatening everything around them with their boisterous solidarity. Until one of them again launches into that heart-rending, wordless psalm, whose infinity is as unchanging as their longing for freedom and the sense of injustice under their dark skin.

The cultural program for the inmates in the camp is led by a forty-six-year-old woman—a tiny, extremely sprightly and nimble creature whose energy is—seemingly—inexhaustible. She is the soul of every enterprise the inmates undertake within the scope of their cultural activities. Her distinctive handwriting is on all of the notice boards and charts. She chooses and directs all of the plays put on by the theater group, and she is in the corridor at lights-out working on the notice boards and posting the roles.

She has been here for several years. For fraud and illegal business practices. She published translations under her own name which she did not write herself, and she collected a part of the translators' fee for it. Here, her dedication to a field that used to be a source of profit for her has become almost dangerous for her. This incomprehensible energy of hers arouses a bit of suspicion in everyone, inmates and correctional officers alike. After all, everyone here is looking to just meet their work quotas and be left alone. Most break the rules by sleeping when it is forbidden, but she breaks them by not being in bed even when sleep is mandated… "You're insubordinate, you don't follow the rules!" the correctional officers rebuke her. "You know very well why you do it, right? You think they'll let you out on parole," the inmates tell her suspiciously. And she sits alone in the dressing room after the performance, tired, with circles under her eyes: "They liked it. A lot of them cried. And how they applauded… Maybe next week we could start rehearsing *A Doll's House*…"

The vast majority of women here believe in God. Some simply pray that they'll go home soon, that their husband hasn't been unfaithful, that their children are healthy, or that they'll receive a letter from home. For others, faith is just a superstition—if I do this or that, God will help me. They don't usually talk about it with each other. Only sometimes. They stand in the courtyard and quietly confide the experiences they've had with God. The wrongs they have suffered at his hands. And their hopes for his wonted and proverbial slowly grinding mills. Only one of them has the courage to admit her lack of faith: "What a God. Take a look at yourselves, at the state of us. If this is supposed to be the image of God…"

At times, almost everyone has a fit of longing, crying, and uncontrollable sadness. The restriction of freedom is too great, the separation from one's people sometimes too much to bear.

Sadness comes at the most unusual times. This time it has struck one of the women in the workshop. She has left work for a while, and she's sitting in the bathroom smoking and sobbing fitfully. Two of her girlfriends are consoling her, doing what they always do in these situations. They point out to her that her husband is at home waiting for her and that crying will only wreck her nerves and that she won't be here all that long and that there's another visiting day in a couple weeks and that her family's sure to come. The one crying doesn't speak, just smokes feverishly until she finally cries out: "But I'll never be able to talk to anyone again. I'll never be able to talk to people who haven't seen it. I'll never be able to, do you understand me? I'll never be able to talk to anyone. I can't explain it to anyone, do you understand?" They've stopped consoling her. I suppose they do understand.

There is too much sadness. It's the dominant feeling that takes over a person here. It affects us all, everyone in a different way, and everyone for a different reason. But no one is spared. The prison is the saddest place in this country. It's sadder than the cemetery because there are living people here, sadder than the hospital because there are people here who have a sickness in their souls, and sadder than a psychiatric ward because there are people here who are responsible for their own sickness, and they know it.

JOY

It would seem to be difficult to draw a line between what inspires fear or sadness or between what brings joy or hope. In reality, it's impossible to separate joy from sadness or fear from hope. Or more precisely—one can find moments of pure sadness or those that only cause horror. But not a single moment of joy remains untarnished. In these places, there is never—and can never be—joy without sadness, and there exists no hope for which one mustn't also fear. I suppose it comes with the territory—after all, there is nothing joyful in crime, and the women here haven't been sentenced to spend time rejoicing and jubilating. Perhaps then this is why there is such joyless joy here...

New arrivals have it the worst. Usually, if they're here for the first time, they don't have enough tobacco on them, and so they have to wait for their allowance or their first visit. Of course, they always find someone who will lend them enough to roll a cigarette or even offer them a pre-rolled Partyzánka. But when it comes to heavy smokers, even these loans aren't enough. It takes quite a while for them to get to know the others—it's not at all easy to forge relationships here—and so they quite often find themselves searching in vain for just a few drags. Otherwise, if they do get anything, it's a loan which they will have to pay back out of a package yet to arrive from home.

Coming to the correctional facility affects everyone differently—but almost everyone, at least in the beginning, falls into a rather nasty depression. And in this situation, the newcomer will find a pinch of tobacco and two rolling papers wrapped up in toilet paper in their nightstand. The next day, it's a Partyzánka in their pocket and another bit of tobacco with papers on their work table. No one ever mentions the perpetrator of this friendly little joy. And the perpetrator herself never confesses. It is a gift, not a loan. It can't be reproached or reclaimed, and it is unburdened by gratitude or thanks. It is not clear whether it is given from an excess or a shortage. And it is the first friendly expression that cannot be suspected of anything, neither self-interest nor ostentation.

Violation of the disciplinary code results in disciplinary action. If the infraction is of a repeated or more serious nature, the punishment is usually several days in the isolation ward. In a large cell with wooden bunks, the biggest "numbers" of the camp are brought together. It's usually the young girls—they're the hardest to handle. And in isolation, you won't hear a sentence that doesn't contain a few words that aren't in the dictionary. The lesbians here have no qualms about partaking in their fornication in the presence of others, accompanied by sticky, gag-inducing profanity. It is unbearable.

A forty-six-year-old woman is sent to isolation. It's her first time, and she breaks down crying after two hours. One of the girls shouts at the others: "Girls, stop it! She really can't take it!" And until the next day, when the older inmate is sent back to the block, everyone sits in a circle, talking in almost human language about all sorts of things, and the loving couples chastely hold hands...

The culture club for the juveniles is run by the older inmates, though they don't otherwise come into contact with each other. Running the culture club here is no easy task. The girls are totally wild, and it would be a difficult job even for a correctional officer who has all the benefit of his authority, including recourse to disciplinary actions. The girls are also mistrustful. First they try to impress with the size of their crimes: "I'm in for murder." "Freeloading and thieving for me—but the big kind." In that case, the club leader displays neither outrage nor astonishment. The girls get embarrassed, slowly grow more trusting, and after a while, one announces: "I write poems. Want to read one?" She does. The girl runs off and returns a moment later with a packet of papers torn out of a notebook. "Not this one. But read this one here." While the club leader reads, no one breathes.

One has to praise carefully so that they trust that the praise is sincere. And in a moment, there's a stack of papers on the table filled with poems. Some have grammatical mistakes, some are written in beautiful handwriting, some have things crossed out, and others have so many ink blots and smudges all over the pages that they're barely legible.

God knows why no one has published a volume of these poems. It's a document that would be hard to replace with an extensive sociological study. Only it would probably have to include photos. Photos of the authors taken at that moment when they're waiting for their work to be judged...

It's the night shift. It's not compulsory, but because an order needs to be filled, the workshop has approved this shift so that the finished products can be shipped from the camp in the morning. And suddenly the atmosphere in the workshop is completely different from normal. No one is arguing, no one is shouting. The women smoke together—no one is enviously eying the bathroom door to see if someone has smoked a couple of cigarettes more. The workshop's output increases. More gets done in the eight hours of the night shift than would otherwise be done in two normal day shifts.

The explanation is simple: They're doing something that no one has forced them to do.

People steal often, and people steal everything. Tobacco, writing paper with stamps, food from parcels, and items of state-issued clothing. People steal anything they lack. There really isn't anything joyful about it—except for one important thing: you never—or almost never—steal when you don't need to. On the day you buy tobacco, you only have to watch it around the ones who don't have any more money to buy their own. Nothing would be easier than to calculate how long your allowance will last and then steal tobacco while you still have some of your own. It would arouse less suspicion, and it would also be safer because during a search of personal effects, which is sometimes made in cases of theft, it would make it easier to explain where the tobacco came from. But no one ever thinks of stealing until their own packet runs out. Only then do they start looking around to see where they could get their next smoke. They are as lacking in subtlety as most of their crimes. They have as much in common with children as children have with criminals. One of the inmates always helps the censor unseal and reseal the letters. She's not allowed to read the letters, and she wouldn't even have time, but she can see who has received a letter or who is sending one. She is the head of the quarters where another inmate has been waiting in vain for months for a letter from her husband. This kind of waiting can't be hidden—the entire block knows about it because everyone is present when the letters are handed out, and everyone knows who is not receiving any news from home. And one afternoon, the censor's assistant is running around camp looking for her fellow resident. "Do you know if she's in the workshop? Did you see if she maybe went to the club meeting? Is she in the laundry? Has she been to lunch yet?" She finally finds her in the library. "There's a letter from your husband. I don't know what's in it, but it ends, 'Only yours...'"

If someone were to learn that she had divulged this information, she would certainly lose her position with the censor immediately, and moreover she'd probably face disciplinary action. But it's Saturday, and the letters won't be handed out until Monday...

Even here, crime is romanticized. But the crime itself is not romantic. There is nothing exciting about social parasitism or misappropriation of state property. And someone who lives in a block with fifteen murderesses won't feel that same chill go down their spine like when they read a mystery novel, because most murders are usually committed for very unromantic reasons and under very prosaic circumstances. For a small apartment, in self-defense against a drunk husband, or because one needs to get rid of an unwanted child from an unwanted relationship, and it's clear the abortion commission would never give their permission. Exciting crimes simply can't be found here. One has to invent them:

"There was one old lady here, and for a long time we didn't know what she was in for, but then we figured it out. It's like this: She had a girlfriend who she really loved, and who she'd lived with since they were young. They lived together, and neither of them ever got married. They were faithful their whole lives. And then her girlfriend found somebody new, and she didn't treat her the same anymore. And then the girlfriend just disappeared. For a long time, the cops couldn't find anything. They even searched their apartment, but they didn't find a thing. Supposedly she took off somewhere and didn't even tell her girlfriend where. Until one day, the scrapyard reported something—supposedly an old lady wanted to sell them some bones, but something seemed off about them. And they were right—they turned out to be human. And the girlfriend of the missing woman was the one selling the bones. So they took her into custody, but they couldn't get anything out of her. She claimed she'd found the bones and went to sell them because she was broke. So they hit a dead end with her. And then one day, when the old lady was still in custody, she was sitting next to the stove—in jail they have heating in the corridor, but there are stoves in the cells—and the wind was howling outside. And she was listening to it, and she was already going completely nuts from the investigation, which is no surprise since it had been going on for months and they wouldn't let her out—and as she was sitting there listening to the wind, out of nowhere she said: 'Jolanka's probably not happy in the chimney there, and that's why she's crying!' The girl who was living in the cell with her reported it, and because the missing girlfriend's name was Jolanka, the cops searched the apartment again. It turns out she had killed her girlfriend and then smoked her in the chimney, and she was eating her bit by bit. And when they brought her in front of those smoked body parts of dead Jolanka, they say she was crying so hard. Not because she'd killed her, but because they wouldn't let her eat the rest of Jolanka. She thought she had the right because it was her Jolanka and because she'd always been faithful to her."

It has everything. True love, death, horror, and a pleasant chill down the spine. It was told, by the way, by the woman who ran the culture program in the camp. It's not clear who made it up, but everyone listened to it with rapt attention. Their own crimes seemed somehow embarrassing in their mundanity, self-interest, and poverty. This one excited them. All of them. Even the murderesses...

There must be nothing in the quarters that does not belong there. All quarters must be uniform. This means that there can be no photographs on the tables, no pictures on the walls except those hung there with the permission of the corrections officer, and nothing on the tables except glasses of flowers, because that is allowed in all of the quarters in the entire block. It is a necessary regulation. It's hard to imagine how many kitties, doggies, lovers and film stars, moms, dads, children, and Waldemar Matuškas would be found on the walls here if it were allowed and if no one prevented it.

Nevertheless, a flowerpot has appeared in one of the quarters—God knows where it came from—with a half-broken shoot of spiderwort. Slowly, the spiderwort takes hold, puts down roots, and even starts to flower. Only that on Saturdays there is a regular cleanliness inspection, which means that the flowerpot has to be removed somewhere—points would be deducted for it. It is against the rules. It is illicit and therefore illegitimate. Of course, during the inspection, not only the condition of the quarters is checked. The corridors, the showers, and the WCs are also inspected, and so there is nowhere to hide the flowerpot. The head of the quarters goes to see the censor. He can have whatever he wants in his office, and he is not subject to the inspection. It's a slightly risky venture, but the censor likes plants and has a lot of them in his office, so perhaps he'll consent to conceal the incriminating spiderwort.

And since then, every Saturday morning before the big cleaning, the spiderwort makes a pilgrimage to the censor's office, remains there through Sunday, and on Monday afternoon, when the quarters are safe again, it returns home. It grows new shoots, puts out blossoms, and it is clearly doing well. The entire quarters looks after it like their own child. And every Saturday clean-up starts the same way: "Move the spiderwort, it's time to clean..."

In addition to its regular members, the theater group needs a few extra women for each show or premiere. Depending on what is needed: girls who can sing or dance, someone to play a male role, or someone to switch on the phonograph for the show and be the stage manager. Preparations are still underway for the Victory Day production. As it has lots of singing and dancing, they have no choice but to bring in around ten younger performers. It makes everyone a bit nervous—until now there has been an unwritten rule that no one steals in the theater club. But no one in the world could possibly keep close tabs on ten young girls, most of whom don't receive an allowance and all of whom smoke. There are two options: either they start hiding their tobacco and keeping an eye on everything that's left lying out on the tables or they risk it and hope that the girls adapt. Without much debate, they choose the second option. Hiding their tobacco would introduce an unpleasant atmosphere into the group which had never been there before and which, to a great extent, would probably spoil the work for all of them.

The result is beyond all expectations: not only does nothing go missing, but as soon as the tobacco runs out, the girls pull out their own boxes and make them available to all. Just to be safe, no one asks where they got the tobacco. But no matter how they got it, the important thing for this moment is that they have understood why no one steals here and that every last one of them was able to adapt to the atmosphere that makes the culture club a refuge—the only one that exists in the camp. It's best not to ask for any others...

The inmates who do not meet their work quotas for an extended period are put on reduced rations. It's quite understandable. They're not earning their keep, and the camp has to pay for their food. Even so, it is often the case that the camp feeds someone almost for free.

It's usually the young girls who run afoul of this measure. They have a hard time adapting to a regular work tempo, and the quotas are quite high. In order to fill them, you really have to work without a break for the entire workday. You can't go smoke in the bathroom, and you have to really focus your attention only on your work for eight hours.

The reduced ration is a half-sized meal without any meat. This means having the feeling of hunger without any danger to your health.

But oddly enough, most girls who get a meal ticket marked with a capital R are more likely to start gaining weight. And when investigating the causes of this inexplicable phenomenon, one discovers that the girls are in fact consuming several times the normal portion of food. All of the dumplings that would otherwise be used for slop, all of the bread that would either be left unclaimed at the counter or thrown in the garbage, it all goes onto the plates of the girls with reduced rations. Perhaps this is not a good correction for their work ethic. But it is—correction or not—at least one small bit of friendliness. Except that it is not allowed—in fact, it is for correctional reasons that it is prohibited. Fortunately, the small bit of friendliness that people show here cannot be done away with, even for correctional reasons. I don't deny that most of these joys are very questionable. But after all—he who is not content with little is not worthy of more. And even if he were, he'll find no more joy here. Even death cannot take that which does not exist.

HOPE

A person needs hope to live, the same as they need air. As long as they draw breath, they will not give up hope. Or until they give up hope, they will continue breathing. I don't know which. They say that only in hell do souls live eternally without hope, but that's what hell is for, and it only exists after death. It can't be made on this Earth, despite all human efforts, just as it's probably impossible to create heaven on Earth.

Everyone has different hopes, and every woman pins her hopes on something different.

"First, I'll go to the hairdresser. A gal can't get anywhere if she doesn't look presentable. I'm in for six years, but if everything goes well and they let me out after half of it, I'll be forty-nine. After three years in here, I'll look a hundred and twenty. I'll need plastic surgery on my tummy and my tits. A gal's gotta look good naked too. I'll take a job anywhere, at least at first. And I'll find myself a guy—remember, a real guy's gotta have it in the head, in the pocket, and in the pants. What he doesn't have in his pants, he's gotta have in his pocket. The only thing you get from true love is scabies and chicken pox. That much I know, and it's not for me. When I go somewhere with a guy, I don't wanna sip one coffee and wonder if I could maybe order a club soda but have to look around to see how pricy the joint is first. I wanna go to the best restaurants, sit down, read the menu, and then order something that's not even on it, something they'll make special just for me. The more a gal costs a guy, the more he takes her seriously. That much is clear. I treat my stockings from the discount shop differently than my nylons from the Tuzex. When you pay a lot for something, you gotta take care of it. And then I'll start plying my trade again. Carefully, so the cops don't find out. They'll come for me—I have to expect that. For at least half a year, I'll have to watch out.

But don't worry. After a year, I'll have plenty of dough. And money buys you anything in the world. A gal who's got dough is beautiful and beloved, even if she's a hundred years old and looks like an ape. And poor girls go after poetry and true love. I tell you, I'm not built for that. We're gonna get ourselves the kind of life you've never even dreamed of!"

"Me and Danuška will stick together. We've gotten used to each other in here. Danuška will quit drinking beer. I won't let her get drunk, or she'll end up back here in no time. Someone has to watch out for her. We're not together—it's just a kind of pure friendship, but that's what never fails. My kids will live with us. Danuška will like them—she doesn't have kids of her own. We'll raise them together. We'll live at my place, or we'll find something, maybe somewhere with an apartment for at least one of us. I've got some furniture, and if we're both working, we'll just buy what we need. I'll make sure Danuška doesn't drink and doesn't hang out with that girlfriend who lived with her before. That one was nothing but a bad influence. If it wasn't for her, Danuška wouldn't be in here. But she's so attached to me! And I'll get her on the right track. She's never known anything but the pub, but when we have a home, she'll be completely different. And anyway, now that he's been granted the divorce, I'll be alone... And I wouldn't even want another man..."

"I was an idiot. It's clear to me now that I was a fool. But when I go home, things will completely different. I'm going to do commissions. No art. I'm only gonna paint commissions. I'm not even thirty yet. I could maybe find a guy to marry me—some old, rich guy with a car who'd still be glad to have a young gal. I always told off the people who worked in food, said they were whores for sale and not real artists. But they were right: they did commissions, and they could just drink in peace, and nobody berated them, nobody locked them up. And I, idiot that I am, was all art. And now I'm doing kitsch for the camp magazine here, and look how good I am at it. I'm gonna join the Party too. If you're not in the Party, you won't get any commissions, or if you do, they're just tiny ones. Begging for scraps. If I'm going to do something I don't believe in, at least let it pay well. There's money lying in the streets in this country—you just have to know how to pick it up. How illustrious—painting one realistic pile of shit after another... But when

I get out of here, it'll be different. I learned my lesson in here! And I'll quit boozing. I was always at the pub, and that gives people the impression that you're really unreliable. If I do drink, I'll do it at home so nobody sees me. But I'd rather be a teetotaler. When it gets around that I quit drinking, people will trust me more, and it'll just rain commissions!"

"I'll get married to Venca. It doesn't matter that he's a convict. At least he won't hold anything against me. He started writing to me at Pankrác, where they had him working as an orderly in the hospital, and he'd watch us in our cells. He thought I was pretty, so he'd bring me tobacco, and he wrote me a letter. And when he found out I have a little girl, he wrote me that it doesn't matter and that we could get married. He'll be good to her. He only ran off on his first wife because she was a bitch, and anyway, she turned him in to get rid of him. Now we have permission to write each other, and he writes me all the time. Only he hasn't written for a while, since he got released. But as soon as he gets himself sorted on the outside, he'll write me again. And when I come, he'll be waiting for me. He's got an apartment and furnishings. And before he was released, he wrote me that he'll go visit the little one at the children's home so she can get a look at her new dad..."

"As soon as I get out of here, I'll be waiting for that bitch, and she'll see. I want nothing more than to run into her somewhere. And I even told her in court clear as day that when I get out of the clink, she'd better stick to the sewers. She thought they wouldn't let me read her statement, and that was a big mistake. I'm doing two years for her—but she won't get them for free, she can be sure of that. I'm not looking forward to anything else—what could I even look forward to? That shithead divorced me and married that backstabbing bitch. They were in cahoots. But fuck him. He'll come crawling back. He's a weakling, and she'll have him completely wrapped around her little finger. It's her I care about. When I get my hands on her, there'll be nothing left but a greasy spot. I know I'll get sentenced for killing a person, even though it's just slaughtering a pig, but that doesn't matter. Oh, how I look forward to getting my hands on her...!"

"What am I looking forward to? You're like a child—what should I look forward to? Got any ideas? I was a whore during the First Republic, I was a whore during the war, and what do you know, I'm a whore during socialism too. What's there to look forward to—except maybe a beer. I guess I'm looking forward to that. That's what I miss in here..."

"I guess it'll be rough in the beginning. You know, as a teacher who stole. What's more, a college teacher If only it had been the medical school. Doctors are somehow more tolerant, more understanding. And they don't judge it so harshly. But mathematicians are Babbitts—you'd have to know them and I fell from a very great height. I had a lot of functions, I was in the Party—and the thing that counted against me most in court was that I had a high salary plus income on the side. When they read out how much I earned, the chairman of the senate told me he didn't even make half as much. Well, that's all very hard to forgive. I'll have to start from scratch. I won't get out on parole. They already wrote me from the outside that I'm not wanted, that the public would be outraged if got out before finishing my sentence. When I'm released, I'll move somewhere nobody knows me and try to start over. Hopefully I'll manage..."

"I don't want to go home on parole. I've heard they won't give you a passport if you're on parole, and I want to leave. If I get an emigration passport, then I'll leave for good, but if not—well, if not, then we'll see. If I at least got a normal passport to visit Germany, that'd be enough... And if I got an emigration passport, I could leave for good and get a toehold somewhere where people are well-paid, and you can just be a nanny for some kids, and everyone respects you, and you have a car. And once I had American citizenship, I'd come back here to visit again—that'd be great, to be able to come here as a foreign citizen. They'd have no power over me—I didn't actually do anything that bad—social parasitism is such a weird law. I've heard they don't even have it anymore anywhere but here. And I don't do anything else. I've never stolen from anybody or embezzled anything, so what's the problem? When I come to Czechoslovakia as a foreign citizen, I'll parade around the place, and it'll be great! I happen to really like this country, but somehow I don't know how to live here. And all this nonsense that's always getting me into trouble here doesn't apply to foreign citizens..."

"I don't know. Can they take all the property he left behind? After all, we bought it together, and I worked my ass off for it too. And I didn't just kill him for no reason—it was self-defense. I think that if we bought it while we were married, then they can't take it away from me, right? And I'll move back into that house. Nobody really liked him around there, and I've heard they don't even blame me for killing him. My sister wrote me that lots of people said they were surprised I was even convicted, that supposedly everyone would have done the same if they were in my position. And I'm going to raise rabbits. But I don't think I'll get married again—I don't have very good luck..."

"I'm learning to read and write in here, missy. And I'll go into business—that's where you can make a bunch of money. And if you don't think they'll accept a gypsy girl, well they will. Because gypsy, white—nowadays it doesn't matter. There's a lot of money to be made in business. All the better ladies in here, all of them were in business. But they were stupid. You can't be stupid, lady—you gotta be smart. And you better not think that gypsies are stupid. It's just that not many can read and write. But they know how to count. And you better not think anyone's gonna swindle a gypsy girl in business! That's why I'm going to school in here, missy, that's why. So I can get into business. Gypsy, white, everyone can go into business these days. If they don't want to have me, then maybe I'll go to the President, and I'll tell him that. How come they don't want a gypsy in business? And he'll have to make it happen. A gypsy can go into business these days, missy..."

"Lady, are you out of your mind? This is the third regime that's locked me up. Or do you think I should hold out hope for the fourth one?"

"I'll go back to school. When it happened, the school vouched for us, but the court wouldn't acknowledge it. Supposedly our little May Day provocations were too pointed, and people were outraged. I'll go home on parole. My dad is in the diplomatic service, and he's not even in Czechoslovakia right now. I've got an exemplary report from the camp, so I can go finish studying economics. And my dad always sends me beauty products for these pimples. I'll get myself all cleaned up, and then I'll go back to school..."

And finally, one more great hope:

"I'm actually originally an educator, but I can't do much educating here. But we couldn't get by on one salary, and so I'm here. When the little one grows up, I'll find a job somewhere else, but for now there's nothing else I can do."

That is the correctional officer's hope. In the end—everyone wants to get out of here...

So these are the hopes of the people who have been sentenced to stay in the correctional facility. It truly is difficult to distinguish hope from fear...

This text was published in Jana Krejcarová-Černá, *Tohle je skutečnost. Básně, prózy, dopisy* (Prague: Torst, 2016).

Stalin's Black Apostle.

The African American Singer Paul Robeson in Czechoslovakia

František Schormová

Sunday, May 29, 1949, was an unbearably hot day in Prague, writes the British actress and theater critic Marie Seton, who was staying in the Czechoslovak capital at the time. And yet, "people poured into the [Winter Stadium on Štvanice Island] from every corner of Prague. They sat on backless benches fanning themselves and shading their eyes from the sun. Not another person could have found standing room."[1] The crowd had been drawn to the stadium to see a concert by the African American singer Paul Robeson. According to Seton, Robeson was welcomed by the applause of thousands of onlookers.

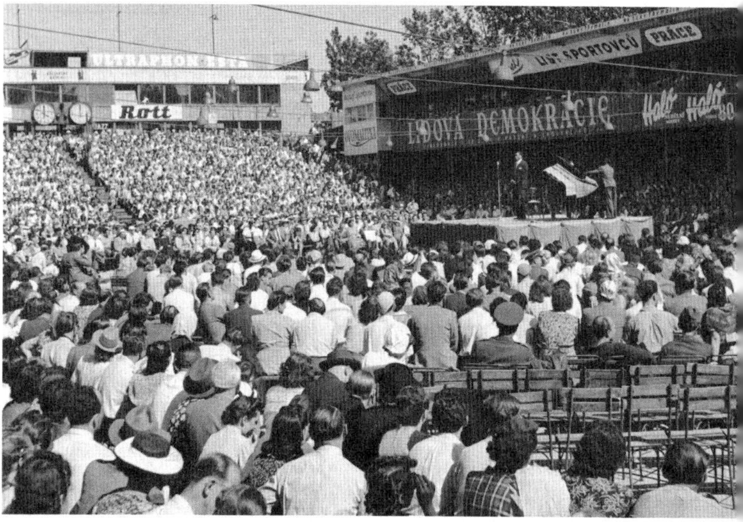

↑ Robeson's concert on May 29, 1949, at the winter stadium on Štvanice Island in Prague. Earnings from the concert were donated to "students of colonial countries" so that they could participate in the International Student Festival in Budapest. © ČTK / Parbus Bohuslav

After giving an introduction in Russian, Robeson began to sing from the part of his repertoire that he was best known for, African American spirituals: "At first the audience were a little puzzled, but as the concert proceeded, the Czechoslovaks, considered by their Slav brothers the most stolid and unemotional of the Slav family, began to expand.

The more Paul Robeson sang the more they understood his art. They grew increasingly excited and responsive until at the end of the concert they rushed down to the floor of the stadium and surrounded him. Finally, they hoisted him on their shoulders and carried him out."[2] But not everyone responded with the enthusiasm described by Marie Seton.

1 Marie Seton, *Paul Robeson* (London: Dobson Books, 1958), 200.
2 Ibid. 201.

As Josef Škvorecký would later write: "Instead of [Stan] Kenton, they pushed Paul Robeson at us, and how we hated that black apostle who sang, of his own free will, at open-air concerts in Prague at a time when they were raising the Socialist leader Milada Horáková to the gallows [...] and at a time when great Czech poets [...] were pining away in jails. Well, maybe it was wrong to hold it against Paul Robeson. No doubt he was acting in good faith, convinced that he was fighting for a good cause. But they kept holding him up to us as an exemplary 'progressive jazzman,' and we hated him. May Go rest his—one hopes—innocent soul."[3]

Škvorecký commented on Robeson's person, career, and political views on a number of occasions. The above excerpt from "Red Music," originally printed in English as the preface to a collection of two short stories published as *The Bass Saxophone* (the title of one of the stories), is also cited by foreign authors in order to underscore the problematic nature of the multifaceted singer's career.[4] Especially in the English-speaking world (but in the German-speaking world as well), the African American athlete, actor, singer, and activist has received much attention in the past decade, mainly in relation to several tendencies: the internationalization of views on the struggle for civil rights in the United States brought by American historian and legal theorist Mary Louise Dudziak's book *Cold War Civil Rights: Race and the Image of American Democracy*,[5] the search for continuity within the African American and radical leftist movements from the 1930s to the 1960s (for instance, in the work of the American cultural and social historian Nikhil Pal Singh),[6] and an interest in leftist transnational solidarity networks that remained independent from (but were still partially limited by) the state structures of the power blocs, as found, for instance, in the work of the American historian Penny Von Eschen.[7]

3 Josef Škvorecký, "Red Music," *The Bass Saxophone* (Toronto: Knopf, 1977), 19. First published in Czech in Škvorecký's book *Dvě legendy* (Toronto: Sixty-Eight Publishers, 1982).

4 According to one of Robeson's biographers, Martin Duberman, Škvorecký later explained (in a letter to Duberman's editor Barbara Bristol dated September 9, 1987) that he was speaking generally, and that Robeson did not perform in Prague at the time of Horáková's execution. See Martin Duberman, *Paul Robeson: A Biography* (New York: Open Road Media, 2014), 861.

5 Mary L. Dudziak, *Cold War Civil Rights: Race and the Image of American Democracy* (Princeton: Princeton University Press, 2011).

6 See Nikhil Pal Singh, *Black Is a Country: Race and the Unfinished Struggle for Democracy* (Cambridge, MA: Harvard University Press, 2004).

7 See, e.g., Penny M. von Eschen, *Satchmo Blows Up the World: Jazz Ambassadors Play the Cold War* (Cambridge, MA: Harvard University Press, 2004).

Within the Czech context, however, Robeson's activities have yet to be properly examined, and so he remains "Stalin's black apostle" or "Stalin's black prophet," as Škvorecký called him.[8] Conversely, there is "Stalin's black son," from a poem by Pavel Kohout published after the death of Stalin. The three stanzas that the enthusiastic communist Kohout dedicated to Robeson deserve to be quoted in full:

Far beyond the reach of good
His black son Paul Robeson
His solemn, gentle giant's head
Raises slowly from the news

His eyes close gently, he begins to sing.
His soft, powerful voice
Flows like the red banner
Over his native father's casket.

"Wide is my motherland..."
He does not cry—he would rather sing!
And into that song he pours
All his sorrow and his hope.[9]

Robeson's contacts with Czechoslovakia relate to several topics currently being studied by Czech historians, such as the role of Czechoslovakia and Prague in the international radical leftist movement during the Cold War (in relation to the so-called "Third World," see for instance Marta Edith Holečková's recently published *Příběh zapomenuté university* (The story of a forgotten university)[10] and the subject of English-speaking visitors to and the life of the English-speaking community in post-1948 Czechoslovakia (see in particular the research of Kathleen Geaney or Doubravka Olšáková). And last but not least, Robeson also represents a kind of complement

8 Cf. Josef Škvorecký, "Domácí fronta, válka, mír a CBC aneb Wie sich die Welt der kleine Moritz vorstellt," in *Nataša, pícníci a jiné eseje* (Prague: Literární akademie, 2006), 99. The text was first published in Czech in Škvorecký's exile collection *Franz Kafka, jazz a jiné marginálie* (Toronto: Sixty-Eight Publishers, 1988) as his own translation of his article "The Home Front: War & Pace at the CBC," published in 1985 in the Canadian magazine *The Idler*. Robeson is sometimes mentioned in Czech journalistic writing; the only more critical assessment of his legacy has appeared in several articles and radio broadcasts by the English section of Czech Radio. See David Vaughan, "Paul Robeson in Prague: Paying homage to Dvořák and socialism," Czech Radio: Radio Prague International, February 4, 2012, https://english.radio.cz/paul-robeson-prague-paying-homage-dvorak-and-socialism-8556902; and David Vaughan, "Paul Robeson in Czechoslovakia: all culture comes from the people," ibid. August 26, 2017, https://www.radio.cz/en/section/books/paul-robeson-in-czechoslovakia-all-culture-comes-from-the-people.

9 Pavel Kohout, "Slovo k bratrům v těžkých dnech," *Rudé právo*, March 10, 1953, 5.

10 Marta Edith Holečková, *Příběh zapomenuté univerzity: Universita 17. listopadu (1961–1974) a její místo v československém vzdělávacím systému a společnosti* (Prague: Filozofická fakulta Univerzity Karlovy, 2019).

to (and antithesis of) Czechoslovak jazz, whose transnational history Petr Vidomus explored several years ago in an article about the bassist Herbert Ward.[11]

The writer Josef Škvorecký, whom Vidomus mentions in the title of his essay, and Škvorecký's friends and collaborators—within the field of music, most notably the musicologist and writer Lubomír Dorůžka—played a fundamental role in the postwar introduction of (African)American literature and music to Czechoslovakia while at the same time giving this cultural transfer its form. This text does not analyze their views or their role as cultural mediators, but it does use Škvorecký's judgments of Robeson as a springboard from which to reassess Robeson's artistic and activist activities. It looks at the American singer's career within the context of the Cold War and the process of decolonization, with a special focus on his contacts with Czechoslovakia and their consequences for Czechoslovak culture. By looking at Robeson and his activities from this perspective, we can enrich the study of Robeson and Czech historiography in general while also highlighting the mechanisms by which individuals, texts, music, and ideas moved about during the Cold War.

THE COLORFUL LIFE OF PAUL ROBESON

Paul Leroy Robeson was born on April 9, 1898, to the family of a former slave and Protestant minister in the small university town of Princeton, New Jersey, in the northeastern United States. He attended Rutgers University in nearby New Brunswick, where he gained fame as an athlete, particularly in American football. After graduation, he left for New York City to study law. In early 1920, he transferred from New York University to Columbia University in the city's Harlem neighborhood. In the 1920s, Harlem was the focal point for a flowering of African American culture known as the Harlem Renaissance, which produced new social and political movements and new forms of art. The educated and successful Robeson seemed to embody its ideal of the new Black man as formulated in the preface to the importantanthology of African American writers *The New Negro*.[12] Robeson began to work as an actor, gaining increasingly more important

11 Petr Vidomus, "Američan—a musí emigrovat do Československa! Škvoreckého jazzman Herbert Ward optikou zpráv FBI," *Soudobé dějiny* 24, no. 1 (2017): 164–206.

12 Alain Locke, ed., *The New Negro: An Interpretation* (New York: Atheneum, 1925).

roles. Widespread fame came when he appeared in works by the era's white modernist playwrights such as Eugene O'Neill. At his first concert, also in Harlem, he sang African American spirituals accompanied on piano and vocals by the jazz musician Lawrence Brown. Their collaboration brought unprecedented success: In 1929, Robeson and Brown went on a European tour during which they also visited Czechoslovakia (when Robeson's singing allegedly delighted President Tomáš Garrigue Masaryk).[13] The tour was organized by Robeson's wife Eslanda Goode Robeson (1895–1965). The first Black woman to hold the position of chief histologist at an American hospital, Eslanda Robeson would later be active as an actress, anthropologist, and African American civil rights activist. She and Robeson met in Harlem, and she would go on to become his manager and the author of his first biography.[14]

Despite his successes, Paul Robeson continued to encounter the limitations imposed by racism and the American system of segregation. He only had limited opportunities as an actor. Many of his film and theater roles were later criticized for their stereotyped depiction of Black characters, and like other African American artists he encountered various aspects of segregation when touring the United States or organizing concerts. When he was offered the chance to appear in an English production of O'Neill's *The Emperor Jones*, Robeson and his family moved to London. In his autobiography *Here I Stand*, Robeson later recalled that "London was the center of the British empire, and it was there that I 'discovered' Africa. That discovery, which has influenced my life ever since, made it clear that I would not live out my life as an adopted Englishman, and I came to consider that I was African."[15] While in London, Robeson began to study African languages at the School of Oriental and African Studies, and he retained his interest in

13 See "Paul Robeson o Československu," *Svobodný směr*, September 4, 1945, 3. According to available sources, Robeson gave two performances in Prague as part of his tour in the spring of 1929: Once on April 10 at the grain exchange building (Plodinová burza) and then again, thanks to that concert's success, on April 19 at the Municipal House's Smetana Hall. See "Černoch v koncertní síni: Basista Paul Robeson," *Expres*, April 11, 1929, 3. The second visit to Prague is described in more detail by his biographer Marie Seton, "Paul Robeson on the English Stage," *Paul Robeson: The Great Forerunner*, ed. Editors of *Freedomways* (New York: International Publishers, 1998), 33.

14 Eslanda Goode Robeson, *Paul Robeson, Negro* (New York: Harper & Brothers, 1930). Interest in this intellectual and Robeson's life partner is reflected in several recent biographies: Barbara Ransby, *Eslanda: The Large and Unconventional Life of Mrs. Paul Robeson* (New Haven: Yale University Press, 2013); and Imaobong D. Umoren, *Race Women Internationalists Activist-Intellectuals and Global Freedom Struggles* (Berkeley: University of California Press, 2018).

15 Paul Robeson, *Here I Stand* (New York: Othello Associates, 1958), 41.

Africa for the rest of his life. Unlike his wife, who visited the continent and wrote a book about her journey,[16] Robeson never made it to Africa, but he took a keen interest in the situation of the colonized and later liberated African nations and in 1937 joined with the sociologist, historian, and writer W. E. B. Du Bois and other African American intellectuals to found the anti-colonialist International Committee on African Affairs, later renamed the Council on African Affairs.

Robeson later wrote: "To the Negro artist, as well as to the Negro spokesman, the 'moral support of England and Europe' has been of great importance and, indeed, the right to travel has been a virtual necessity for the Negro artist."[17] Besides his studies, Robeson was also strongly influenced by his travels, in particular a journey to Spain during the Spanish Civil War and the first of his many visits to the Soviet Union, in 1934, when he accepted an invitation from the director Sergei Eisenstein. There was a tradition of African Americans traveling to the Soviet Union: The country was visited, among others, by the poet and author Langston Hughes, the Jamaican-American writer Claude McKay, and the African-American intellectual W. E. B. Du Bois, often as part of ethnographic or artistic projects.[18] Additionally, Eslanda Robeson's brothers were working in the Soviet Union at the time.[19] Not only was Paul and Eslanda Robeson's visit to the Soviet Union covered by the media, but the Soviet authorities also tried to show themselves in the best possible light: These efforts were highly successful in influencing Robeson, who felt crushed by American racism and by his impressions from the spread of fascism in Europe.[20] In fact, the experience was so strong that Paul Robeson Jr. spent two years attending school in Moscow.

During the Second World War, the family returned to the United States, where Robeson's pro-Soviet rhetoric fit in with the general mood. He also sang several patriotic songs as part of "Ballad for

16 Eslanda Goode Robeson, *African Journey* (New York: John Day, 1945).

17 Robeson, *Here I Stand*, 78.

18 These journeys are most extensively covered by Kate A. Baldwin, *Beyond the Color Line and the Iron Curtain: Reading Encounters between Black and Red, 1922–1963* (Durham, NC: Duke University Press, 2002).

19 The brothers John and Frank Goode traveled to the Soviet Union 1934, several months before the Robesons. John Goode initially worked as a bus driver but returned to the United States several years later. Frank Goode became a Soviet citizen, earned a living as a wrestler, started a family, and remained in the Soviet Union until his death in 1967. See Joy Gleason Carew, *Blacks, Reds, and Russians: Sojourners in Search of the Soviet Promise* (New Brunswick: Rutgers University Press, 2008), 145 and 166–167.

20 One text that analyzes Robeson's first visit to the Soviet Union is Lauren McConnell, "Understanding Paul Robeson's Soviet Experience," *Theatre History Studies* 30, no. 1 (2010): 138–153.

Americans."[21] At the time, he was mainly active as a singer, and after 1942 he rejected all film roles. According to Kate A. Baldwin, his focus on singing and the new, more clearly defined political context of his work helped Robeson to shift the focus away from his body, as represented by his film and theater roles or his appearance in photographs from the 1920s and 1930s.[22] In the spring of 1945, he went on a tour of American forces in Europe. After the liberation of the Czechoslovak spa town of Mariánské Lázně—which served as a center of recreation for American soldiers—he performed at the local municipal theater.[23] He was also increasingly active on the political stage: In the late 1940s, he lent his support for Henry Wallace, who was running for president on the Progressive Party ticket. Eslanda Goode Robeson even appeared as a speaker alongside Wallace.

Also around this time, Paul Robeson strengthened his ties to the jazz scene. In her book on jazz and civil rights during the Cold War, the American musicologist Ingrid Monson writes that "Robeson's prestige cannot be overestimated as an inspiration to many in the entertainment industry."[24] Especially in the 1940s, jazz musicians looked up to Robeson not only as a singer and actor, but also thanks to his political engagement: His interest in Africa in particular inspired many jazz artists. James Donald, for instance, called Robeson a mentor of younger musicians such as Dizzy Gillespie, Harry Belafonte, Sidney Poitier, and Ossie Davis.[25] A concert on the occasion of Robeson's forty-sixth birthday in 1944 featured performances by

21 The patriotic song "Ballad for Americans," originally titled "Ballad for Uncle Sam," was written in 1939 by John La Touche and Earl Robinson. After Robeson, it was also sung by Bing Crosby. A Czech translation was erroneously published as a poem by Langston Hughes (Langston Hughes, "Balada pro Američany," in *O Americe zpívám*, ed. Jaroslav Bouček (Prague: Mladá fronta, 1950), 69–75.

22 Baldwin, *Beyond the Color Line and the Iron Curtain*, 238.

23 Robeson's concert in Mariánské Lázně took place in late August 1945 as part of a cultural program (known as USO camp shows) organized by the United Service Organizations, which provided entertainment for American soldiers. Here, too, Robeson appeared alongside the pianist and composer Lawrence Browne. Besides short mentions—for instance in Lenka Čechová and Marie Plešáková, *Historie orchestru v Mariánských Lázních* (Mariánské Lázně: Městské muzeum Mariánské Lázně, 2012), 60—Robeson's concert is also described in the letters of Julia Mary Hall Baroudi, who was in western Bohemia as a volunteer with the American Red Cross (one of the so-called "donut dollies"). In a letter to her parents dated September 6, 1945, she describes a concert by the African American singer and her astonishment at "the deep-seated discrimination that I have encountered here [in the US Army]." She adds that this discrimination was a reason why some soldiers did not attend the concert. Besides writing about the concert, she also describes a subsequent party at which Robeson sang in Czech (she writes "in Bohemian"). See Kathleen Havens Gezzi, *Journey Between Mountains: A Young Schoolteacher's Experience as a Red Cross Volunteer During WWII and in Post War Europe* (Bloomington, IN: AuthorHouse, 2006), 194.

24 Ingrid T. Monson, *Freedom Sounds: Civil Rights Call out to Jazz and Africa* (Oxford: Oxford University Press, 2007), 36.

25 James Donald: *Some of These Days: Black Stars, Jazz Aesthetics, and Modernist Culture* (Oxford: Oxford University Press, 2015), 216.

Duke Ellington and Count Basie,[26] and Robeson even sang the blues with the latter on a number of occasions, including Basie's musical adaptation of the well-known Black writer Richard Wright's poem "King Joe," written in 1941 after the African American boxer Joe Louis won an important fight.[27]

Paul Robeson's broad popularity in the 1940s was partially due to the fact that the explicit association of anti-colonialism with the struggle against racism in the United States was supported by the mainstream of the movement for African American emancipation that would later give rise to the civil rights movement. But Robeson continued to enjoy support from the jazz scene even in the 1950s, by which time he had become a *persona non grata*. For instance, Ingrid Monson writes that "another enthusiastic admirer of Robeson was Charlie Parker, who was known to go out his way to hear any Robeson performance."[28] Additionally, the pianist Thelonious Monk performed at a concert in 1954 held as part of the campaign for Robeson to have his passport restored, and the saxophonist John Coltrane appeared at another concert in Robeson's honor.[29]

AN EXEMPLARY AFRICAN AMERICA

At the time of his 1949 performance in Prague alluded to in Josef Škvorecký's above-cited text, Robeson was already a legend among jazz musicians and an internationally renowned performer. The fact that he was of use to Soviet and later also Czechoslovak propaganda does not mean that it invented him: The 1940s were the period of Robeson's greatest fame, and the systematic overestimation of his significance found in Czechoslovak reviews from that time do nothing to change Robeson's international popularity or his importance for the American and worldwide music scene. But despite his amicable relationships with jazz musicians, Škvorecký was right in that Robeson's relationship to jazz was complicated. Writing about the persecution of jazz musicians in Czechoslovakia, Škvorecký recalls an article from *Soviet Music* magazine in which Robeson allegedly proclaimed that "the only true Negro music of

26 See Monson, *Freedom Sounds*, 36.

27 Wright was supposedly "proud" of their collaboration. See Hazel Rowley, *Richard Wright: The Life and Times* (Chicago: University of Chicago Press, 2008), 256–257.

28 Monson, *Freedom Sounds*, 109.

29 Monson, *Freedom Sounds*, 156 and 213.

America was vocal, i.e., spirituals and the blues. Instrumental jazz was only played by 'debased Negroes' it 'prostituted and ruthlessly perverted the genuine expression of folk life.'" Škvorecký bitterly remarks that, "with Robeson, science said its last word, and the police took over."[30]

It is unclear whether Škvorecký is citing an original text by Robeson (who was known for his knowledge of Russian) or a translation. Similarly, it is not known when it was originally written.[31] Kate Baldwin has pointed out that translations of Robeson's articles and speeches were often subjected to significant alterations and changes in meaning. It is nevertheless true that Robeson was originally very critical of jazz, a position that was in line with the spirit of the Harlem Renaissance—which may come as a surprise for some people, since the evolution of jazz is associated with this artistic and intellectual movement. Even spirituals were received critically, but much of the Harlem Renaissance was nevertheless founded on a look back at the African American past and on an appreciation of African influences. Robeson's approach to spirituals fit into this vision.[32] Additionally, there existed a more prosaic reason why Robeson later did not sing jazz (nor, except for the example cited above, blues): The genre was not suited to his style and vocal type.

Jazz was not the only musical tradition towards with Robeson's relationship changed over time. The third volume (1935/1936) of *Magazín Družstevní práce* published his article "The Influence of Black Culture," translated by Emanuel Uggé, one of the first people to popularize jazz in Czechoslovakia (criticized by later generation for his preference for traditionals and spirituals). In the article, Robeson describes the decisive and still unrecognized influence that the music of the African diaspora had on classical music.

30 Josef Škvorecký, *Talkin' Moscow Blues* (New York: Ecco Press, 1990), 106. The text was first published as "Talkin' Moscow Blues," in a 1983 edition of The New Republic. He later translated it into Czech for his exile anthology Franz Kafka, jazz a jiné marginálie. Škvorecký was citing Robeson according to the American author Frederick Starr, *Red and Hot: The Fate of Jazz in the Soviet Union, 1917–1980* (New York: Oxford University Press, 1980).

31 Škvorecký is probably referring to Robeson's article "Pesni moego naroda" published in *Sovetskaya muzyka*, no. 7 (July 1949): 100–104. Robeson also influenced German discussions of jazz; see Uta G. Pouger, "Searching for Proper New Music: Jazz in Cold War Germany," *German Pop Culture: How "American" Is It?*, ed. Agnes C. Mueller (Ann Arbor: University of Michigan Press, 2004), 89.

32 For more on the debate surrounding spirituals, see the previously mentioned article by Todd Carmody, "Missing Paul Robeson in East Berlin: The Spirituals and the Empty Archive," *Cultural Critique*, no. 88 (2014): 1–27. The difficult relationship between the representatives of the Harlem Renaissance and jazz music has been studied by a number of authors, including the above cited Ingrid Monson.

At the same time, in accordance with his fundamental views, he emphasizes that "the black soul is inaccessible to all that is artificial and affected. [...] I can never feel a connection with and perform Brahms, Schumann, or Wagner."[33]

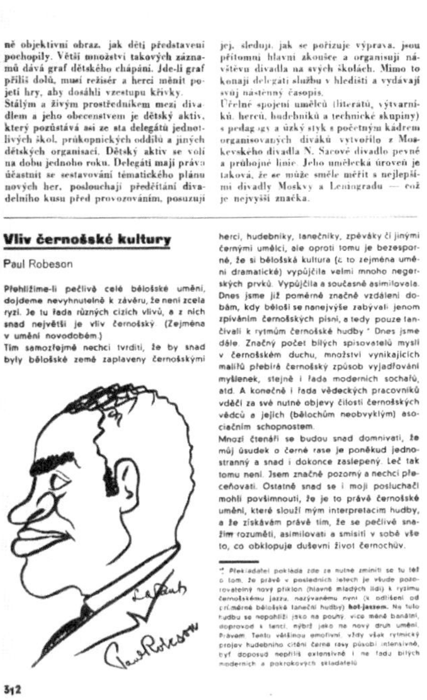

ně objektivní obraz, jak děti představení pochopily. Větší množství takových záznamů dává graf dětského chápání. Jde-li graf příliš dolů, musí režisér a herci měnit pojetí hry, aby dosáhli vzestupu křivky.
Stálým a živým prostředníkem mezi divadlem a jeho obecenstvem je dětský aktiv, který pozůstává asi ze sta delegátů jednotlivých škol, průkopnických oddílů a jiných dětských organisací. Dětský aktiv se volí na dobu jednoho roku. Delegáti mají právo účastnit se sestavování tématického plánu nových her, poslouchají předčítání divadelního kusu před provozováním, posuzují jej, sledují, jak se pořizuje výprava, jsou přítomni hlavní zkoušce a organisují návštěvu divadla na svých školách. Mimo to konají delegáti službu v hledišti a vydávají svůj nástěnný časopis.
Účelné spojení umělců (literátů, výtvarníků, herců, hudebníků a technické skupiny) s pedagogy a úzký styk s početným kádrem organisovaných diváků vytvořilo z Moskevského divadla N. Sacové divadlo pevné a průbojné linie. Jeho umělecká úroveň je taková, že se může směle měřit s nejlepšími divadly Moskvy a Leningradu — což je nejvyšší značka.

Vliv černošské kultury

Paul Robeson

Přehlížíme-li pečlivě celé bělošské umění, dojdeme nevyhnutelně k závěru, že není zcela ryzí. Je tu řada různých cizích vlivů, a z nich snad největší je vliv černošský. (Zejména v umění novodobém.)
Tím samozřejmě nechci tvrditi, že by snad byly bělošské země zaplaveny černošskými herci, hudebníky, tanečníky, zpěváky či jinými černými umělci, ale oproti tomu je bezesporné, že si bělošská kultura (a to zejména umění dramatické) vypůjčila velmi mnoho negerských prvků. Vypůjčila a současně asimilovala. Dnes jsme již poměrně značně vzdáleni dobám, kdy běloši se nanejvýše zabývali jenom zpíváním černošských písní, a tedy pouze tančívali k rytmům černošské hudby.* Dnes jsme dále. Značný počet bílých spisovatelů myslí v černošském duchu, množství vynikajících malířů přebírá černošský způsob vyjadřování myšlenek, stejně i řada moderních sochařů, atd. A konečně i řada vědeckých pracovníků vděčí za své nutné objevy čilosti černošských vědců a jejich (bělochům neobvyklým) asociačním schopnostem.
Mnozí čtenáři se budou snad domnívati, že můj úsudek o černé rase je poněkud jednostranný a snad i dokonce zaslepený. Leč tak tomu není. Jsem značně pozorný a nechci přeceňovati. Ostatně snad se i moji posluchači mohli povšimnouti, že je to právě černošské umění, které slouží mým interpretacím hudby, a že získávám právě tím, že se pečlivě snažím rozuměti, asimilovati a smísiti v sobě vše to, co obklopuje duševní život černochův.

* Překladatel pokládá zde za nutné zmíniti se tu též o tom, že právě v posledních letech je všude pozorovatelný nový příklon (hlavně mladých lidí) k ryzímu černošskému jazzu, nazývanému nyní (k odlišení od průměrné bělošské taneční hudby) **hot-jazzem**. Na tuto hudbu se nepohlíží jako na pouhý, více méně banální, doprovod k tanci, nýbrž jako na nový druh umění. Právem. Tento většinou emotivní, vždy však rytmický projev hudebního cítění černé rasy působí intensivně, byť doposud nepříliš extensivně i na řadu bílých moderních a pokrokových skladatelů.

312

← An article by Paul Robeson in *Magazín družstevní práce*, translated by jazz publicist Emmanuel Uggé. Paul Robeson, "Vliv černošské kultury," *Magazín DP*, no. 3 (1935/36): 312. Photograph © The New York Public Library Digital Collections, General Research Division

It remains unclear when the original text was written: Robeson's relationship to classical music had already improved by the time of his European tour in 1929. At the very least, by 1949 he had sufficiently come to terms with Robert Schumann for him to include the German composer in his repertoire for at the Prague Spring festival.

The excerpt from Škvorecký's "Red Music" cited at the outset of this text can be read not only as an expression of its author's distaste for Robeson and his artistic style, but also as a criticism of the lack of choice. In Czechoslovakia, African American music was represented by Paul Robeson, and there was no room for others within this system of cultural distribution. The American cultural historian Rossen Djagalov analyzed this approach within the entire socialist camp by looking at the example of Howard Fast as a representative of the progressive face of the

33 Paul Robeson, "Vliv černošské kultury," trans. Emanuel Uggé, *Magazín družstevní práce* 3, no. 1 (1935–1936): 314.

United States in the field of literature. According to Djagalov, in the early days of the Cold War the adoption of cultural phenomena across the Iron Curtain followed certain principles, including the canonization of selected individuals and the excommunication of others.[34] Djagalov speaks of a "membrane effect," which he describes as follows: "When only a fraction of the cultural production from one state is allowed to enter another, in the eyes of cultural consumers in the latter, that fraction achieves a truly representative status."[35] The monopoly enjoyed by such individuals was also expressed by adoption of their views.

Robeson's views (at least in the version paraphrased by Škvorecký) did not have much in common with those of the Czech novelist. Škvorecký's generation had been introduced to jazz before the Second World War and during the Protectorate: For this age group, jazz had "naturally become something like a form of religion," as Škvorecký and Lubomír Dorůžka write in the preface to the 1966 anthology of American and Czech poetry *Jazzová inspirace*.[36] For them, Robeson's spirituals represented just a small fraction of the (African)American culture they were interested in, and it was Robeson who symbolized an obstacle that they had to overcome when promoting jazz in Czechoslovakia (although, as we will see later, Robeson was eventually—though unbeknownst to him—helpful in this regard). With Škvorecký, Robeson ends up paying for the role of exemplary African American that haunted him all his life and that he was assigned even within radical leftist cultural circles. The above-outlined principles of this cultural space, its institutions, individual actors, cultural-political awards, and centers of power are today almost entirely forgotten. But it was these networks that brought Robeson to Prague in 1949—twice, in fact, for when the French authorities refused to issue a visa to several participants in the Paris Peace Congress, a parallel event was held in Prague. The famous African American singer came as well.

34 With Howard Fast, the most published American author in Czechoslovakia between 1948 and 1956, this strategy did not bear fruit: Fast left the Communist Party USA in early 1957.

35 Rossen Djagalov, "'I Don't Boast About It, but I'm the Most Widely Read Author of This Century': Howard Fast and International Leftist Literary Culture, ca. Mid-Twentieth Century," *Anthropology of East Europe Review* 27, no. 2 (2009): 48.

36 Lubomír Dorůžka and Josef Škvorecký, eds., *Jazzová inspirace* (Prague: Odeon, 1966), 22.

The program of Robeson's first Prague performance twenty years earlier, in April 1929, consisted mainly of spirituals. Robeson was one of the first to perform these songs associated with the tragic history of African Americans at concert halls throughout Europe. The Fisk Jubilee Singers had toured with spirituals in the late 19th century, but like other African American singers they combined them with other fare.[37] Spirituals remained on Robeson's program during his recital at the Prague Spring festival on May 25, 1949.

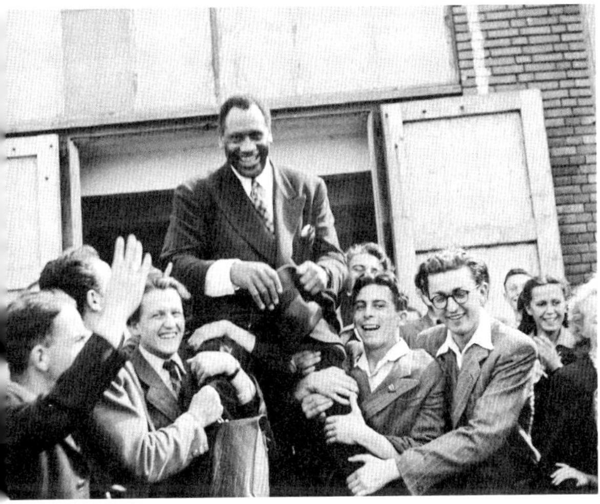

↑ During his visit to Prague in May 1949, Robeson also visited several factories. This photograph comes from Jiří Dmitrov's Čakovice factory (later known as Avia). © ČTK

Specifically, he performed adaptations of the classic spirituals "Waterboy" and "Swing Low, Sweet Chariot." To these, Robeson added the African American musician Harry Burleigh's "Scandalize My Name" and Jerome Kern's "Ol' Man River" from the Broadway musical *Show Boat*, where it is sung by a Black character whom Robeson had portrayed in the past.[38] The song made Robeson famous and was supposedly Stalin's favorite work from Robeson's repertoire. Robeson altered the text from the original version, and so instead of reconciliation with the fate of the American Negro the song now expressed a hope

37 See Irena Přibylová, "Česká stopa: Afroamerické spirituály v koncertní síni," *Od folklor k folkmusic. Hudba a spiritualita. Sborník příspěvků z mezinárodního kolokvia*, ed Irena Přibylová and Lucie Uhlíková (Náměšť nad Oslavou: Městské kulturní středisko, 2019), 156–183.
38 For the concert program, see "Písňový koncert: Paul Robeson," Prague Spring festival website, 2021, https://festival.cz/koncert/pisnovy-koncert-paul-robeson.

for continued struggle. In Prague, he also sang works of classical music (by Georg Friedrich Händel, Robert Schumann, Johannes Brahms, Felix Mendelssohn Bartholdy, Claudio Monteverdi, Frédéric Chopin, Julien Tiersot, and the Russian composers Isaak Dunaevsky and Nikita Bogoslovsky) and several adaptations of old English ("Over the Mountains") and American ("My Curly Headed Baby") folk songs. And he performed Dunaevsky's "Shiroka strana moya rodnaya" in Russian.

The concert took place in the Dvořák Hall of Prague's Rudolfinum. Robeson must have been well aware of the symbolism of performing Burleigh, with whom Antonín Dvořák collaborated while in the United States, and of "Swing Low, Sweet Chariot," which had inspired the second movement of Dvořák's New World Symphony. In fact, Robeson was interested in precisely such forms of cultural mixing, which promoted his notion of the shared foundation of human cultures that had influenced classical music. In the aforementioned autobiography *Here I Stand*, Robeson devotes an entire section to music theory: In his view, the "universal body of music" is based on the pentatonic scale.[39] He allegedly arrived at this idea in Britain upon hearing English, Welsh, and Celtic folk songs, in which he saw "the same soulful quality that I knew in Negro music."[40] His introduction to classical music—among numerous composers, he also mentions Antonín Dvořák and Leoš Janáček—only confirmed his belief in this theory.[41]

According to Robeson, the shared spiritual qualities that reflected this universal foundation were also expressed in people's reactions to the songs he sang. In a 1939 interview, he said: "When I sang my American folk melodies in Budapest, Prague, Tiflis, Moscow, Oslo, the Hebrides or on the Spanish front, the people understood and wept and rejoiced with the spirit of the songs. I found that where forces have been the same, whether people weave, build, pick cotton or dig in the mines, they understand each other in the common language of work, suffering and protest."[42] Robeson believed that there was political potential in connecting various oppressed groups. In the same interview, he added: "When I sing, 'Let my

39 "A Universal Body of Folk Music – A Technical Argument by the Author," Robeson, *Here I Stand*, 123. As some critics have pointed out, however, the idea of the pentatonic scale as universal is distinctly Eurocentric.
40 Ibid. 58.
41 Ibid. 123.
42 Paul Robeson, *Paul Robeson Speaks: Writings, Speeches, and Interviews: A Centennial Celebration*, ed. Philip Sheldon Foner (New York: Citadel Press, 1978), 131.

people go,' I can feel sympathetic vibration."[43] Robeson expressed similar ideas after his return to the United States in the summer of 1949, when his supporters organized an official welcome reception for him. On this occasion, he gave a speech titled "What I Saw in Eastern Europe," in which he talked about how, in Czechoslovakia, Poland, and the Soviet Union, he had met "thousands of people—men, women, children"—who had asked him to express to African Americans not only their love but also "their heart-felt understanding of the suffering of their Negro brothers and sisters."[44]

Robeson's internationalism was essentially romantic in nature, founded on a vision of cultural authenticity and Herderian concepts. At the same time, as Kate Baldwin points out, "Robeson used 'internationalism' as a kind of minority discourse to delineate as points of commonality the political exclusion created by slavery, segregation, and imperialism. [...] His claims suggest the importance of non-oppositional coalitions between multiple outsiderness and enforced non-identities as a basis for the positive transformation of the oppressive effects of Western philosophies of identity."[45]

As the Cold War and decolonization progressed, however, the explicit association between racism, imperialism, and colonialism, as frequently emphasized in the cultural production of the 1930s and 1940s, became increasingly more sensitive. When Robeson sang at Prague Spring, the situation was already changing. His visit in 1949 would be the last for ten years.

AIRING DIRTY LAUNDRY

Robeson's appearance at the first World Peace Congress in Paris in April 1949 would go on to have fateful consequences. Allegedly he gave a speech claiming that America's Blacks would never go to war against the Soviet Union.[46] On the basis of this

43 Ibid.

44 *The New York Public Library Archives and Manuscripts, Schomburg Center for Research in Black Culture*, Paul Robeson Papers, Reel 1/8, ROBESON, Paul: What I Saw in Eastern Europe: For Freedom and Peace. Address by Paul Robeson at Welcome Home Rally, New York, June 19, 1949, 12.

45 Baldwin, *Beyond the Color Line and the Iron Curtain*, 216.

46 According to both Robeson and later research, his proclamation was poorly translated into English. In fact, the Associated Press sent it to the United States before Robeson ever spoke at the Congress. The affair is summarized in, among other sources, Gilbert King, "What Paul Robeson Said," *Smithsonian Magazine*, September 13, 2011, https://www.smithsonianmag.com/history/what-paul-robeson-said-77742433/.

statement, Robeson had his passport revoked. When his lawyer wrote Secretary of State Dean Acheson, the response from the head of the passport office was: "Paul Robeson's travel abroad at this time would be contrary to the best interests of the department."[47] The main context here was the ongoing process of decolonization. The rise of the United States as a world power happened at the same time and in relation to this process; in the struggle for the favor of the newly decolonized states, a Black celebrity that openly spoke about American racism (and, what is more, placed it in association with colonialism) was a problematic figure. In addition, as the American historian Thomas Borstelmann writes, race was "America's greatest weakness in the Cold War."[48] It was also a weakness that the Soviets were unafraid to exploit. As research done by Mary Dudziak and others has shown, these pressures strongly influenced gradual changes in the area of civil rights in the United States.

It was in the interest of the United States government to promote the ongoing process of desegregation as a story with a happy ending—and also as a strictly domestic affair that was in no way related to American foreign policy. African American public figures and intellectuals such as W. E. B. Du Bois, William L. Patterson (an attorney and high-ranking member of the Communist Party USA), and Paul Robeson repeatedly challenged this narrative. For instance, in 1951, they drafted the petition *We Charge Genocide*, which cited hundreds of murders and cases of torture committed against African Americans and tolerated by the government.[49] The petition was delivered to the General Assembly of the United Nations, although in the end it did not receive much attention there. Several prominent African Americans accused Robeson of "airing dirty laundry" on the international scene. During this time of anti-communist trials, a public denunciation of Robeson equaled—in the words of Canadian historian Richard Iton—"the performance of patriotic fidelity."[50] This applied in

47 Jordan Goodman, *Paul Robeson: A Watched Man* (London: Verso, 2013), 195.

48 Thomas Borstelmann, *The Cold War and the Color Line: American Race Relations in the Global Arena* (Cambridge, MA: Harvard University Press, 2001), 133.

49 Among other things, the petition attempted to analyze the causes of structural racism in the United States and elsewhere and contained a list of murdered African Americans. It states, "Once the classic method of lynching was the rope. Now it is the policeman's bullet." The text of the petition gained new life in 2020 in relation to the Black Lives Matter movement. *We Charge Genocide: The Crime of Government Against the Negro People*, Civil Rights Congress/William Patterson, ed., (New York: International Publishers, 1951), 8.

50 Richard Iton, *In Search of the Black Fantastic: Politics and Popular Culture in the Post-Civil Rights Era* (Oxford: Oxford University Press, 2008), 37.

particular to African American public figures and institutions that themselves were often accused of collaborating with the communists.

In the late 1940s and during the 1950s, many African American figures faced such accusations, often based on no more than their interest in African American civil rights or social issues.[51] With Robeson, however, the situation was different. Although opinions differ on whether he was a member of the Communist Party USA or not,[52] Robeson's rhetoric, his visits to the Soviet Union, his friendships with leading American communists such as the African American attorney Ben Davis, and his membership in organizations considered front groups were all difficult to ignore. Robeson's FBI case file contains the suspicion that he used the code name John Thomas,[53] which was also expressed during a hearing of the House Un-American Activities Committee (HUAC) on June 2, 1956, to which Robeson had been summoned as a witness. Invoking the fifth amendment to the United States constitution, he refused to testify, and responding to the question about his code name he replied in his typically dramatic fashion: "My name is Paul Robeson, and anything I have to say, or stand for, I have said in public all over the world, and that is why I am here today."[54] According to some interpretations, Robeson's eloquence helped him to deflect the accusations and to turn the entire situation around—the interrogation ends with him accusing the committee:

51 The FBI had been watching some public African American figures accused of communist sympathies since the 1920s. For more, see, e.g., Kenneth O'Reilly, Black Americans: The FBI Files (New York: Carroll & Graf, 1994). Robeson's files were declassified in 1980 and are available online. They consist of information on his person spanning 2,840 pages, separated into thirty-one sections. Each of his trips, every article, every speech, is carefully documented. There are also records of telephone conversations and private letters. A special genre consists of letters of denunciation. Many of the documents in the files are articles from various media, both foreign and domestic. The FBI's translation services are remarkable: there are texts translated from Hungarian, Polish, Czech, and various Asian languages.

52 Robeson's son Paul Robeson Jr. was a member of the CPUSA for many years (he left the party in the early 1960s) but always denied that his father was a member (cf., e.g., Arnold H. Lubasch, "Paul Robeson Jr. Finding His Own Voice and Learning to Use It," The New York Times, October 21, 1993, 18). On the other hand, longtime General Secretary of the CPUSA Gus Hall claims that Robeson was in the party. See Gus Hall, "Paul Robeson: Artist, Freedom Fighter, Working Class Hero, American Communist," People's Weekly World, June 6, 1998, 8.

53 Report on Eslanda Cardoza Robeson, New Haven, January 11, 1954, page 6. FBI Records: The Vault (website), https://vault.fbi.gov/Paul%20Robeson%2C%20Sr. (file: Paul Robeson, Sr., Part 10 of 31, page 14 in pdf).

54 "Investigation of the Unauthorized Use of U.S. Passports, 84th Congress, Part 3, June 12, 1956," *Thirty Years of Treason: Excerpts from Hearings Before the House Committee on Un-American Activities, 1938–1968*, ed. Eric Bentley (New York: Viking Press, 1971), 770.

"You are the non-patriots, and you are the un-Americans and you ought to be ashamed of yourselves."[55] Nevertheless, by 1956 Robeson had been discredited. Domestically, he could perform very little (in the early 1950s, concert halls and churches where he had previously performed began to refuse him), and he was not allowed on international tours. In 1955, a magazine associated with Robeson, *Freedom*, had to cease publication because of financial difficulties. The magazine frequently wrote about the anti-colonial movement in the world and how it related to the situation faced by African Americans, as articulated by its motto: "Where one is enslaved, all are in chains."

The repercussions for Robeson and other radical critics of America's racial inequality caused international visions and anti-colonial solidarity to disappear from the American movement for civil rights. As Thomas Borstelmann writes: "A credible, coherent black Left sank below the surface of American political life, as the chilly waters of the Cold War closed over it."[56] But it did not sink without a fight, which included attempts at forging alliances with the international community. "The American [communist] party is convinced and calls on you to pay much more attention to the Negro people's struggle in your press and your general propaganda," William L. Patterson stated in Prague in October 1950.[57] It was one of many demands that Patterson made during his meetings with Czechoslovakia officials. He was speaking not only for the Communist Party USA but also as a leading representative of the Civil Rights Congress. Besides seeking closer cooperation between American communists and the Communist Party of Czechoslovakia, he also hoped to strengthen its ties to America's Black community. These ties would be bilateral: For instance, the African American press would, on the basis of information from Czechoslovakia, publish "reports on the immense growth and development of the Czechoslovak People's Democratic Republic."[58]

55 Ibid. The performative aspects of Robeson's hearing before the House Un-American Activities Committee are described in, e.g., Tony Perucci, *Paul Robeson and the Cold War Performance Complex: Race, Madness, Activism* (Ann Arbor: University of Michigan Press, 2012). See also Mark Andrew Thompson, "Now You're Making It up, Brother: Paul Robeson, HUAC, and the Challenge of Institutional Narrative Authority," *Quarterly Journal of Speech*, no. 105 (2019): 156–181.

56 Borstelmann, *The Cold War and the Color Line*, 67.

57 National Archives, Prague (further only "NA"), fonds "ÚV KSČ – Mezinárodní oddělení 1945–1962" (1261/2/4 – previous label 100/3), vol. 5, archival unit 19, memorandum from W. L. Patterson to the Communist Party of Czechoslovakia.

58 Ibid., materials from W. L. Patterson.

Patterson also asked Czechoslovakia for financial support for American friends that (according to the report) "could go via comrade Paul Robeson."[59]

During this visit to Prague, the American communist emissary also discussed several laws back home—the Smith Act and the McCarran Act—that would soon complicate similar contacts. He also correctly anticipated that he would be prevented from leaving the country, and so he sought to prevent the mutual ties from being cut. This would be ensured by the aforementioned exchange between the Czechoslovak and African American press and by inviting important African American figures to visit Czechoslovakia. The Czechoslovak government would send invitations even if they could not be accepted because of government restrictions—such cases would at least serve a propagandistic purpose. Patterson repeatedly asked for financial support, and to this end again met with Czechoslovak representatives in Washington in the early 1960s. By all indications, however, his request was denied, and Czechoslovakia did not become a source of support for the internationalist group of fighters for civil rights in the United States. Paul Robeson thus remained one of just a few connections to this movement.

In America, meanwhile, the new argument that "anti-Communism and civil rights were allies" was a success. The State Department Cultural Presentation Program, which organized so-called "jazz tours," was one of the products of this association.[60] Jazz musicians were now expected to counterbalance similar Soviet projects, present other African Americans to the world (perhaps as a counterbalance to Robeson's popularity), and physically embody the supposed positive evolution of race relations in the United States.

But this does not mean that they always followed this goal and fulfilled official expectations. According to Ingrid Monson, the musicians themselves "did not view their participation in the program as an aspect of Western cultural imperialism but as an alternative to it."[61] Thanks to their representational status, the participating musicians had greater opportunities to speak openly. In her book on the jazz tours, Penny Von

59 Ibid., record of interview with comrade Patterson, October 13, 1950.
60 Monson, *Freedom Sounds,* 110.
61 Ibid. 118. Monson also points out that the program's committee in charge of choosing participants was itself segregated until 1967 (ibid. 119).

Eschen describes the example of Louis Armstrong, who canceled a tour of the Soviet Union in response to the events of September 1957 in Little Rock, when Arkansas Governor Orval Faubus used the Arkansas National Guard to prevent African American students from entering a school: Armstrong accused the government of not acting to defend desegregation. An important factor in this situation was Armstrong's strong negotiating position, recently fortified by a successful tour of Ghana in 1956: "Having visited an African nation on the eve of its independence, and in the wake of the actions of civil rights activists, Armstrong was able to speak out in ways that would have been unthinkable a decade earlier."[62]

CZECHOSLOVAK CONTACTS

But Paul Robeson still could not leave the United States. A campaign for the restoration of his passport launched by his wife Eslanda soon resonated beyond the American continent, particularly in Great Britain. Czechoslovakia also lent its support: At a meeting of the Central Committee of the Communist Party of Czechoslovakia on September 16, 1954, Anežka Hodinová-Spurná, Vice President of the National Assembly and head of the Czechoslovak Committee of Defenders of Peace (the World Peace Council publicly supported Robeson), proposed a seven-point plan.[63] The Central Committee supported her plan in part. It rejected the proposal for important figures to send letters to Paul Robeson, but it agreed to invite Robeson to visit Czechoslovakia. The newspapers would also print his letter to Gusta Fučíková (the relevant document only includes a Czech translation).[64]

62 Penny M. von Eschen, *Satchmo Blows Up the World*, 63. For more on the complicated role of the events in Little Rock in America's foreign and domestic policy, see Mary L. Dudziak, "The Little Rock Crisis and Foreign Affairs: Race, Resistance and the Image of American Democracy," *Southern California Law Review* 70, no. 5 (September 1997): 1641–1712.

63 NA, fonds "ÚV KSČ, Kancelář 1. tajemníka ÚV KSČ Antonína Novotného – II. část" (1261/0/44), inv. no. 431, box 180, campaign for the issuing of a passport to Paul Robeson, September 16, 1954.

64 Ibid. The original letter, stored 4,000 miles away at the New York Public Library, differs in its wording. A comparison of the two versions shows that the Czech translation is missing the introductory salutation "Dear Friends." Additionally, the use of an uppercase initial letter for the personal pronoun "Vy" (you) gives the impression that the letter is addressed to a single person (an uppercase "Vy" in a letter indicates the formal form of the second person singular, a lowercase "vy" indicates the second person plural). The Czech translation sounds more personal, more heartfelt, than the English original. Was it a conscious attempt at giving the impression of more personal ties between Gusta Fučíková and Robeson? Cf. *The New York Public Library Archives and Manuscripts, Schomburg Center for Research in Black Culture*, Paul Robeson Papers, Passport Case, Correspondence, Reel 6/1, letter from Paul Robeson to Gusta Fučíková dated July 26, 1954.

Repeated invitations form a large part of the written communication between Robeson and his Czechoslovak contacts from the 1950s, but it would not be until 1959—ten years after his previous visit—that the famous American singer would again be able to visit. The invitations were either sent directly or via the Czechoslovak embassy in Washington, where representatives from Prague met with Robeson, his son Paul Jr., and his wife Eslanda, with whom they, among other things, discussed an interview with Robeson published in the African American magazine *Ebony* in which Robeson referred to his invitation to the Prague Spring festival.[65] Invitations to this annual event form the largest portion of this correspondence, but as a strategy they were not just limited to Robeson. For instance, the list of musicians for 1955 includes a note that "even if the festival committee and the Ministry of Culture believe that few of the artists will accept the invitation, it is a good idea to issue it."[66] Robeson was nevertheless the only one who could influence his invitation. Czechoslovak officials regularly consulted him on issues such as whether it was wise to invite him officially. They also inquired about his efforts to have his passport returned. During the planning of the Prague Spring festival in the autumn of 1952, it was decided not to invite Robeson after the matter was discussed with him. Nevertheless, a note in the related documents expresses the hope that, should Robeson be allowed to travel to Moscow after all in order to accept the International Stalin Award, "his inclusion in the [Prague Spring] program would cause no difficulties."[67]

Prague also tried to provide Robeson with material support: Cut off from his international audience and with limited opportunities on the domestic scene, Robeson's income had declined drastically, as numerous sources pointed out in Czechoslovakia.[68] Most Czechoslovak aid was mediated by the Artia foreign trade company, through which Robeson distributed his recordings for the Czechoslovak and international market—his collaboration with the company yielded eight records. Besides correspondence of a business

65 Archives of the Ministry of Foreign Affairs (Prague), fonds "Teritoriální odbor-obyčejné (1945–1959)," box 20, letter from the Czechoslovak embassy in Washington to the Ministry of Foreign Affairs, dated October 5, 1957.

66 Ibid., letter from the Ministry of Culture to the Ministry of Foreign Affairs regarding planning for the 1955 Prague Spring, dated September 6, 1954.

67 Ibid., letter from the Czechoslovak embassy in Washington to the Ministry of Information and Education regarding the 1953 Prague Spring, dated October 11, 1952.

68 Ibid., draft letter from Gertruda Sekaninová-Čakrtová to Deputy Minister of Foreign Trade Kohout, undated.

character, Robeson's archive at the Schomburg Center for Research in Black Culture also includes telegraphic birthday wishes sent to Robeson in 1951 from the International Union of Students in Prague. Personal letters from Czechoslovak admirers were rather the exception, but he received official correspondence from composer Václav Dobiáš on the occasion of the fiftieth anniversary of the death of Antonín Dvořák. In his letter, Dobiáš calls Robeson "the beloved interpreter of Dvořák's songs."[69]

Robeson spoke about Dvořák on a number of occasions: in his speeches, his writings, and his autobiography *Here I Stand*. He was even supposed to appear in a biopic about the Czech composer based on a script by the author Edvard Valenta, but the project never came to fruition.[70] In preparation, Robeson even learned Psalm 137 in Czech, which he ended up recording at the Domovina recording studio in Prague-Holešovice during his 1959 visit. The recording of "Při řekách babylónských" ("By the Shore of the River Babylon") from Dvořák's song cycle *Biblical Songs*—which is available online[71]—confirms Robeson's reputation as a polyglot: According to his son, he even learned Czech.[72] None of Robeson's other planned Czechoslovak film projects were ever realized, either. These included a series of short films with Robeson in the lead role. In the end, only a short compilation documentary about Robeson was produced. It was broadcast on Czechoslovak Television in 1983.[73]

The organizational structure of cultural exchange in the Eastern Bloc, which was partially controlled by the Soviet Union, sometimes makes it difficult to get an overview of the relationships among its various participants. Robeson maintained close ties with the Soviet Union (he visited the country in 1934, 1949, 1958, and 1961), but Czechoslovakia was no random stop on the way to Moscow. Besides the above-described contacts and his relationship to Antonín Dvořák, another connection to the country was his interest in Hussite music: Supposedly, Robeson

69 *The New York Public Library Archives and Manuscripts, Schomburg Center for Research in Black Culture*, Paul Robeson Papers, Correspondence, Reel 1/6, letter from Václav Dobiáš to Paul Robeson dated September 16, 1954.

70 See Věra Žahourková, "Třináct ztracených let," *Lidová demokracie*, June 23, 1968, 5.

71 "Paul Robeson Classical," Supraphon website, https://www.supraphonline.cz/album/3270-paul-robeson-classical?trackId=52629.

72 Paul Robeson Jr., *The Undiscovered Paul Robeson: Quest for Freedom, 1939–1976* (Hoboken: Wiley, 2010), 229.

73 *Paul Robeson*, documentary film, Czechoslovakia, 1983, 10 min.

even wrote a study on the influence of Hussite chorales on international music composition. This fact received significant media attention in Czechoslovakia, and work on the study was expected to form a pretext for another visit. Nevertheless, no such text was never published.

By the time of Robeson's next visit for the Congress of Socialist Culture in 1959, he was already seriously ill. The proceedings from the congress include Robeson's presentation, in which he again speaks about Dvořák and discusses the current situation in Africa.[74] He also contributed to the cultural program. Besides singing, he performed Iago's final monologue from Shakespeare's *Othello* (Othello was one of his famous roles).[75]

Robeson's correspondence and available documents show Robeson as an equal partner to Czechoslovak officials, in which his status certainly played a part. At the same time, Robeson's role as a valued guest probably prevented him from ever being confronted by the everyday reality of state socialism in the same way as the English-speaking leftist community resident in Czechoslovakia. As Kathleen Geaney writes, for this group "it was a highly frustrating experience that did not match their original image of the functioning of communist society."[76] A similar sense of disillusionment was felt by African scholarship recipients in the 1950s and 1960s, who describe encountering expressions of racism.[77] None of the surviving records indicate whether Robeson encountered similar behavior or whether he noticed a similar disconnect between political slogans and the actual situation in Czechoslovakia.

JAZZ AND SPIRITUALS

In Josef Škvorecký's novel *Miss Silver's Past*, the narrator tries to publish a book titled *A Nutshell History of Jazz*. The editor criticizes his text, however, basing his negative assessment among other things on the fact that "Comrade Paul Robeson is nowhere mentioned, even though as a Negro he has a close connection

74 Paul Robeson, "Diskusní příspěvek," ed. Jiří Záruba et al., *Sjezd socialistické kultury: Sborník dokumentů* (Prague: Orbis, 1959), 248–249.

75 In his talk, Robeson referred to Shakespeare as an author of the people.

76 Kathleen Geaney, "Špatná strana hranice? Anglicky mluvící levicová komunita v Československu na počátku studené války," *Střed / Centre* 5, no. 1 (2013): 61.

77 For the experience of students at the FAMU film school, see, e.g., Tereza Stejskalová, ed., *Filmaři všech zemí, spojte se! Zapomenutý internacionalismus, československý film a třetí svět* (Prague: Tranzit.cz, 2017).

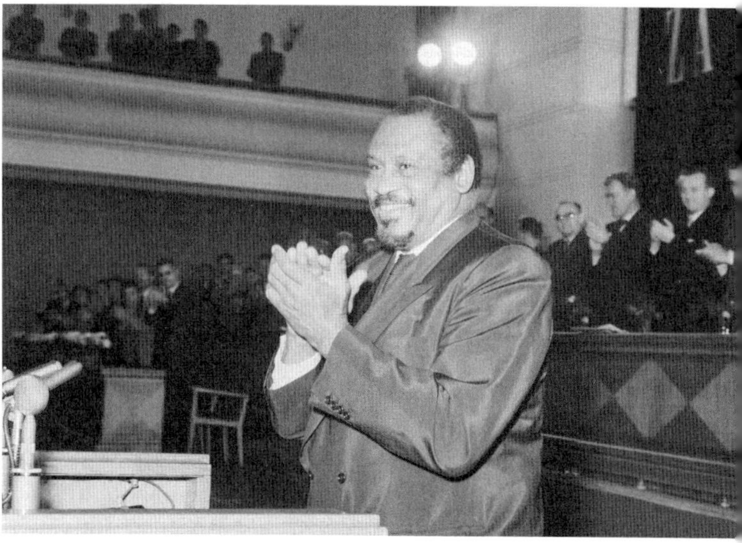

↑ Robeson at the Congress of Socialist Culture in June 1959. It was his return to Czechoslovakia after ten years. © ČTK / Mevald Karel

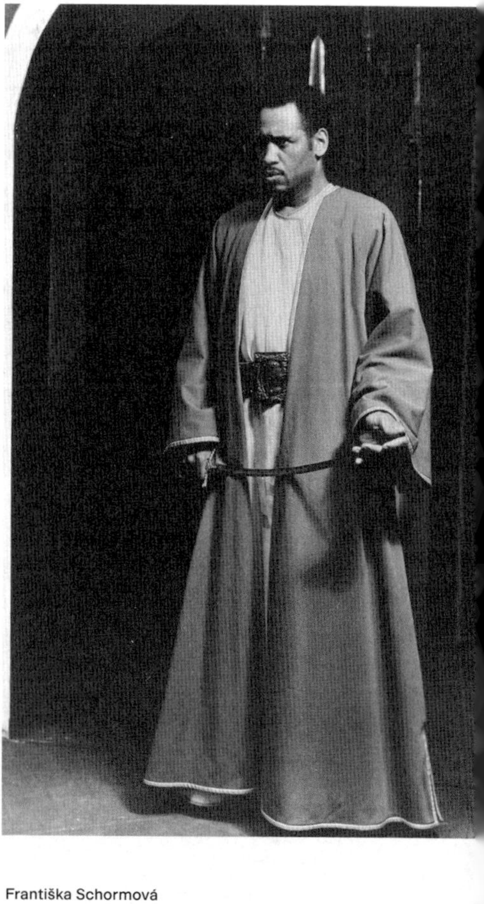

↑ Robeson as Othello. He played this role in the 1930s in London and later also with the Theatre Guild Production on Broadway in 1943–44. Despite taking a critical view of his own theatrical career, he performed one of the monologues from *Othello* at the Congress of Socialist Culture in Prague in 1959. © Library of Congress Prints & Photographs Division, FSA/OWI Collection, LC-USW331-054944-ZC with jazz. This oversight should be corrected."[78] This fictional critique is a logical outcome of a line of argumentation that Škvorecký himself had helped to shape and that used such claims to promote works that would otherwise have had little chance to pass through the system of cultural supervision. The presence of racial themes was one of the main components of this pragmatic line of argumentation. In fact, we find a great early example in Škvorecký's January 1950 correspondence with Lubomír Dorůžka: "The inspector has an understanding for my activities. Recently, he came into my classroom just as I was singing 'Joe Turner Blues' for my students (I already understand the entire song), then he silently listened to my description of how the black proletariat was oppressed in the USA that I undertook immediately afterwards, and then he praised me for the high intellectual quality of my music classes."[79]

As part of the cultural exchange described above, Robeson was a select representative of African American music. In any matter relating to this type of music, he became an obligatory reference, a way of pleasing official structures that increased one's chance of passing through the web of control. This was also true for jazz, with which Robeson had little in common. Nevertheless, with the loosening of social and cultural restrictions, jazz began to grow in popularity as well. According to the music journalist Petr Vidomus, this development was thanks to another American, the bassist Herbert Ward (1921–1994). As Vidomus points out, it is somewhat ironic that at the same time that the U.S. State Department had decided to use jazz as a part of its foreign cultural policy, it was being promoted in Czechoslovakia by an American suspected of collaborating with the Communist Party USA. In each case, however, the process was the reverse. While the State Department financed projects such as its jazz tours—or, before that, the American folk opera *Porgy and Bess*—in an attempt at using culture to promote a particular policy (while boldly ignoring the official line of American cultural criticism that "culture and politics could not fraternize"),[80] in Herbert and Jacqueline Ward's

78 Josef Škvorecký, *Miss Silver's Past* (London: The Bodley Head, 1976), 99. The original title translates as "The Lion Cub"—see *Lvíče* (Prague: Československý spisovatel, 1969).

79 Michal Přibáň, ed., *Psaní, jazz a bláto v pásech: Dopisy Josefa Škvoreckého a Lubomíra Dorůžky z doby kultů (1950–1960)* (Prague: Literární akademie, 2007), 14.

80 Baldwin, *Beyond the Color Line and the Iron Curtain*, 203.

case the propagandistic use of their fate as left-wing American artists contributed to the spread of jazz in Czechoslovakia. In the meantime, Paul Robeson was used to promote Czechoslovak jazz via comments or references in favor of this type of music. But Robeson himself had a greater influence on another musical tradition that set down roots in Czechoslovakia and that exceeded jazz in terms of political significance: spirituals.

Of course, credit for establishing the Czech tradition of spirituals does not go to Robeson alone. He may have been the first to build an entire repertoire on them, but other African American singers performed spirituals in Europe as well. (One of them, Aubrey Pankey, even asked for asylum in Czechoslovakia in 1955, although he eventually opted for East Germany.)[81] Spirituals were also performed by the musicians who appeared as part of the jazz tours.[82] But it was Robeson's symbolic position that helped spirituals become protest songs against an entirely different system than he had intended. One example can be found in the later trials against the Czech underground, during which the Czech singer Svatopluk Karásek based his arguments on his use of African American spirituals. During the main hearing in the trial against the underground rock band The Plastic People of the Universe in September 1976, "when asked by the defense whether he felt himself to have been inspired by the kind of spirituals sung by Paul Robeson, he [Karásek] answered in the postive."[83] Not only was the government-promoted Robeson a source of inspiration for Karásek's nonconformist songs, but above all he served as a useful artistic shield to hide behind.

Perhaps the best-known Czech band to include spirituals in its repertoire was Spirituál kvintet, whose songs perfectly reflect the layering of meanings that

81 The classically trained singer Aubrey Pankey (1905–1971) performed in Prague in 1947 and 1955. He first visited Europe in 1930 and later lived with his wife in Paris, from where he was deported for his leftist activities. After 1955, he worked in East Germany as a teacher at the German College of Music (Deutsche Hochschule für Musik). He earned the interest of music historians thanks to a 1959 letter for East German radio in which he protested that he had been hired only as a token black and not because of his talent. Pankey's complaint found a friendly ear with the author and cultural functionary Alfred Kurella, who wrote Pankey a response that among other things criticized the cult of spirituals. Kurella also issued instructions to investigate similar cases. See Michael Rauhut, *Ein Klang – zwei Welten: Blues im geteilten Deutschland, 1945 bis 1990* (Bielefeld: Transcript, 2016), 180.

82 See Monson, *Freedom Sounds*, 215.

83 Martin Machovec et al., eds., *"Hnědá kniha" o procesech s českým undergroundem* (Prague: Ústav pro studium totalitních režimů, 2012), 167–180. For a description of the main hearing on September 21–23, 1976, see page 169.

occur when translating songs about slaves in America, many of which had been based on Old Testament stories, among other things about slavery in Egypt. The Czech translations of spirituals—whether those by Spirituál kvintet or those used in the "rhythmic church services" that emerged in the late 1960s—resulted in ironic situations and shifts in meaning. For instance, Spirituál kvintet, which performed these songs at official venues and thus had to pay attention to their meaning, sang "Little More Faith in Jesus," which had been translated as "When Justice Is Returned to Us." Jiří Tichota later recalled in an interview that the new text struck the censors as too political: "It was usually enough to say that it was a translation of a Black spiritual. In this case, however, they felt something was off and demanded to see the original." Tichota thus turned to a colleague at the English department, who produced a fake original. The translation received official approval.[84]

As translated, however, the spirituals lost one of their fundamental aspects: the fact that they addressed the specific situation of slaves in America, including its racial context. The fate of African Americans was still there, at least on the surface, as the theme of the song, but in Czechoslovakia in the 1970s and 1980s it was used mainly as an allegory for life in an unfree state. Such shifts (including the suppression of the original songs' religious meaning even though they functioned according to a different cultural mechanism) are part of any cultural exchange. Within the context of the current debate regarding cultural appropriation, this process nevertheless deserves to be reassessed. What is more, during this period in Czechoslovakia, interest in African Americans almost completely disappears from public discourse. Although references to anti-racism continue to be a part of official policy, publishing in particular, future events in the civil rights struggle in the United States receive only marginal coverage. With some exceptions such as an interview with Martin Luther King Jr. on Czechoslovak Radio or a visit by the African American communist activist Angela Davis, it would appear that Czechoslovak interest in civil rights on the other side of the Atlantic—and support thereof—was limited to Paul Robeson.

84 Jan Dědek, "Ježíše vystřídalo právo na právo," *Lidovky.cz*, January 23, 2012, https://www.lidovky.cz/kultura/nej-hity-jezise-vystridalo-pravo-na-pravo.A120118_144544_ln_kultura_wok.

On a visit to Moscow two years after his last visit to Czechoslovakia, Robeson tried to commit suicide. Several theories exist in relation to this event, ranging from Paul Robeson Jr.'s assertions of CIA involvement to speculations that Robeson was suffering from mental illness or other health problems or that he was being blackmailed by the Soviets. After this incident, Paul Robeson withdrew from public life. He died at his home in Philadelphia on January 23, 1976. Unlike many other Western leftist intellectuals such as the previously mentioned writer Howard Fast, he never backed down from his pro-Soviet viewpoints, not even after 1956. In fact, the Czechoslovak media printed Robeson's statements in favor of the suppression of the Hungarian revolution in which he claimed that "the Hungarian putsch was the work of the same elements that buried the Spanish republic in 1936."[85]

Besides receiving numerous awards both during his life and after his death, Paul Robeson was also repeatedly honored in poetry. In addition to favorite poets of the radical left such as Turkey's Nazim Hikmet or his Chilean colleague Pablo Neruda, others who paid homage to Robeson in verse include legendary representatives of the Black Arts Movement of the late 1960s and 1970s such as Nikki Giovanni and contemporary poets Terrance Hayes and Elizabeth Alexander.

Following a long period during which Robeson's name had disappeared from public space, since the early 1990s Robeson has become a more frequent subject of discussion in the United States. Many of these texts, however, including several new biographies, focus on his early career as an actor and athlete while somewhat awkwardly skirting the subject of his political convictions—including his international activities.[86]

This glorified and depoliticized portrait of Paul Robeson is just as simplistic as Josef Škvorecký's Czechoslovak perspective. Engaging in a discussion of Robeson from a number of different angles and within various linguistic contexts thus means disrupting both these narratives. Besides providing insight into radical leftist cultural networks and how they

85 "Paul Robeson k situaci v Maďarsku," *Mladá fronta*, November 15, 1956, 2.
86 This changed in 2020, when Robeson's visions and legacy began to be mentioned in relation to the Black Lives Matter movement.

operated, Robeson also embodies a lost internationalist vision of civil rights and shows us the role, however small, that Czechoslovakia played in this vision, thanks in part to Paul Robeson.

This text is an abridged version of a paper published in *Soudobé dějiny*: Františka Schormová, "Stalinův černý apoštol. Afroamerický zpěvák Paul Robeson v Československu," *Soudobé dějiny* 28, no. 1 (2021): 183–213.

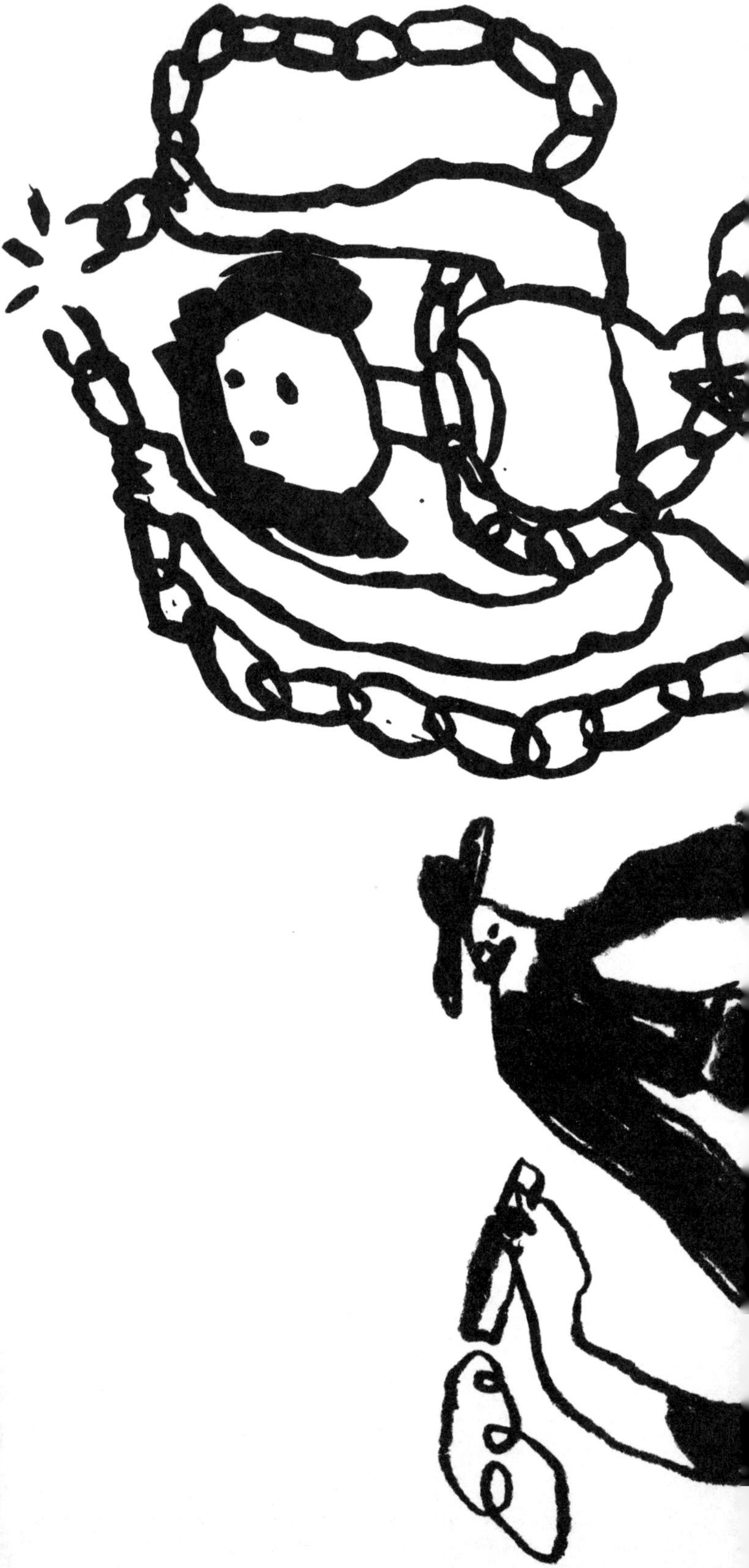

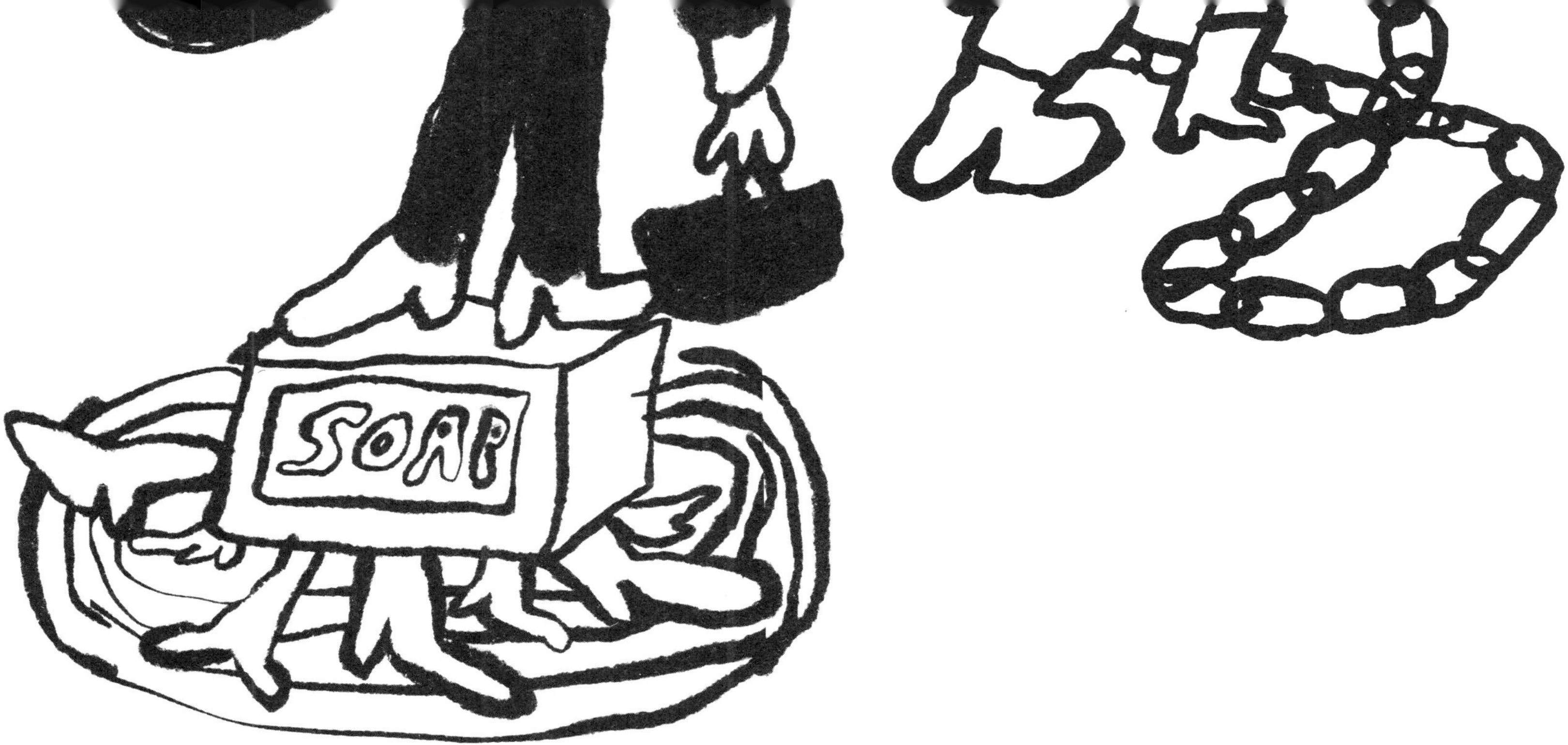
SOAP

2

ou see, an ingredient for soap often comes n a great distance. But not only that; a very fine ingredient, for besides soap it is used to produce comestibles—artificial etable oil.

And as we have seen, these fruits are often hanged for trinkets of little value, but that ow it works in the world—certainly, few people w that a thing as ordinary as soap has such mplicated origin...

"A Saved Tribe of Negroes," advertising tale n the Saponia soap factory, 1930s.

ginning, there was a washing machine, rd mechanical clothes washer that Vojtěch k brought back from the Great London Exhibi-362. The crank-driven machine measuring a meter in height was meant to liberate Czech from the burden of housework and the ation from the yoke of German domination e Austro-Hungarian monarchy.

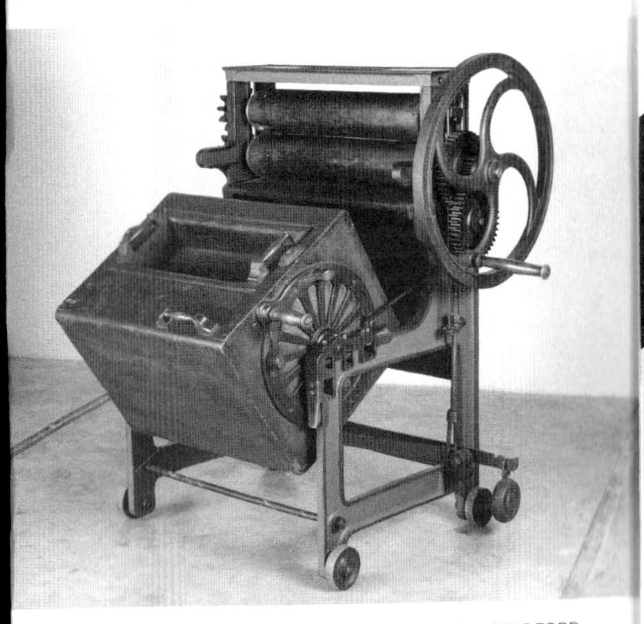

onal Technical Museum, Household Appliances Collection, BRADFORD washing machine, inventory number 61253. © National Technical Museum, ina Uksová

purposes of this text, this washing machine e as a symbol, along with soap, of the industrial ment that helped draw the line separating bal North from the South. For us, the machine mportant because it stood at the establish-f the Náprstek Museum of Asian, African and

A Washing N
ar

As y
fron
it is
als
veg

exc
is h
kno
a c

fro
In the be
a Bradfo
Náprste
tion of 1
less tha
women
Czech r
within t

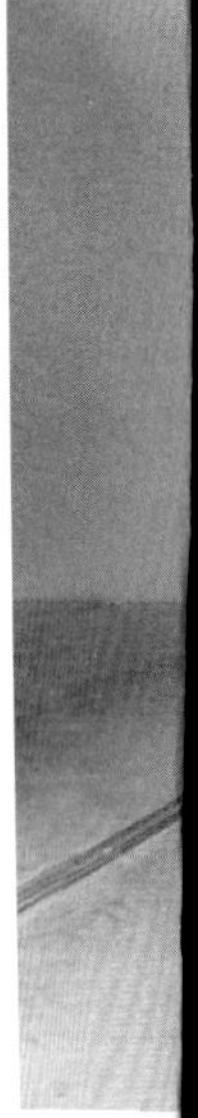

↑ Nat
mechanica
photo: Kate

For the
will ser
develo
the glo
is also
ment o

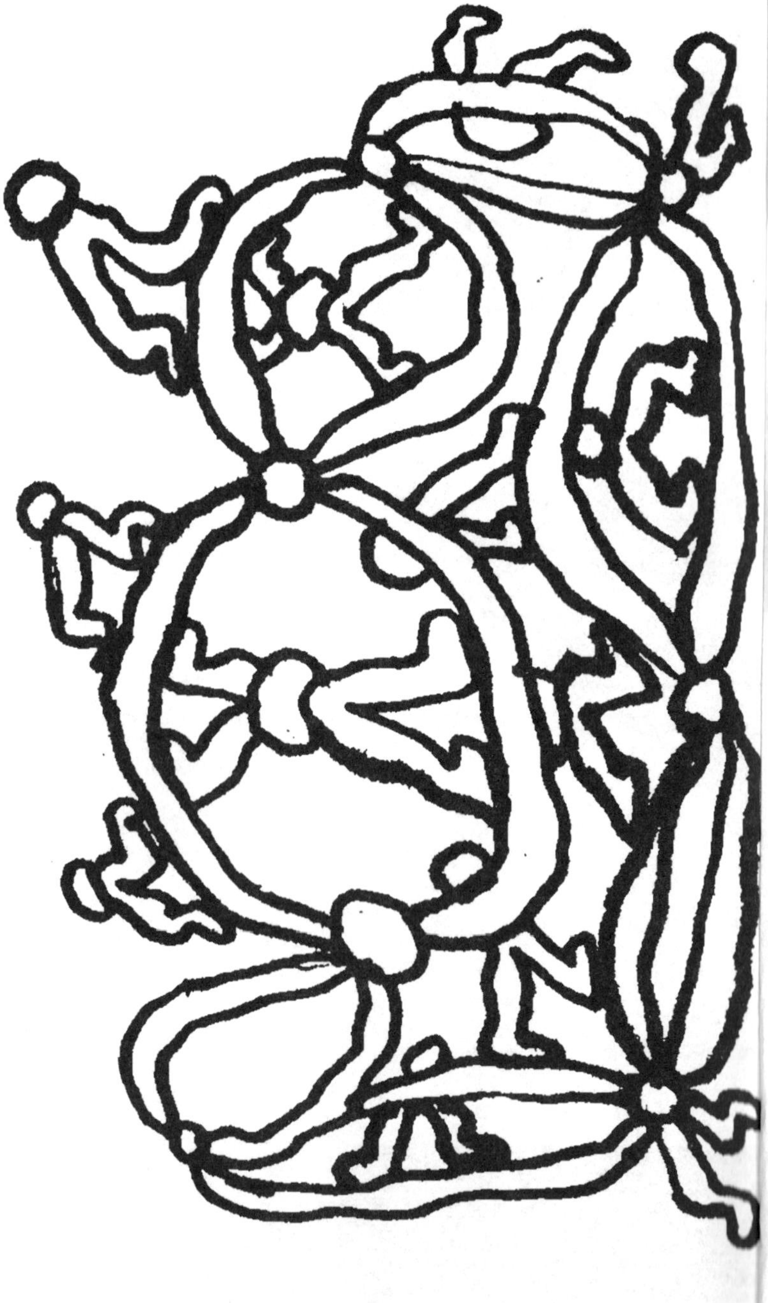

Anna Re

American Cultures, a museum in Prague with a focus on exhibiting ethnographic collections. At the same time, the washing machine helps us to look at the specifics of Czech colonial complicity, meaning the manner in which Czech society was involved in the colonization of non-European territories. It is no coincidence that both these products (washing machines and soap) serve to preserve cleanliness and hygiene—a fundamental theme of the new and modern society of the 19th and 20th centuries.

TEACHING THE CZECHS INDUSTRY

In the late 1850s, industry in Bohemia is in full swing. The first business and trade chambers and joint stock companies are being formed, and glassworks, textile factories, breweries, and heavy industry are all blossoming. But when the explorer and Czech patriot Vojtěch Náprstek returns home from his American exile, his first observations relate to the technological backwardness of Czech industrial production.
And so he decides to renovate the upper floor of the "U Halánků" building, where his mother Anna Fingerhutová runs a successful brewery and distillery, into a library. He becomes a member of the Royal Czech Museum Society and in 1862 joins the Industrial Union (full name: Union for Promoting Industry in Bohemia).[1] His membership in the latter organization will be of central importance for the future development of the museum today known as the Náprstek Museum of Asian, African and American Cultures. When Náprstek renews his membership at the Industrial Union, he begins to more clearly formulate his ideas for establishing a Czech museum of industry. The Union's members find inspiration from the South Kensington Museum in London (today's Victoria and Albert Museum),[2] whose founding was directly related to the Great Exhibition held in Kensington in 1851. Another world's fair was organized eleven years later (1862) with the aim of, like the first, showing the industrial development of England (and other European countries) during the period preceding the greatest imperial flowering. London's Great

1 Jiří Majer, *Počátky musea Vojty Náprstka* (Prague: Národní museum v Praze, 1956), 111.
2 Lada Hubatová-Vacková, "Krása věcí, průmysl a moderní společnost (1870–1918)," *Věci a slova. Umělecký průmysl, užité umění a design v české teorii a kritice 1870–1970*, ed. Lada Hubatová-Vacková et al. (Prague: Vysoká škola uměleckoprůmyslová v Praze, 2014), 37.

Exhibitions are often presented as bombastic events that served to show off technological progress and the "great genius of mankind." To a certain degree, they set the pace for the rest of the world. Above all, however, they shaped the discourse that would retroactively confirm England's leading role vis-à-vis other countries. This discourse of economic liberalism and international relations was founded on trade, and it had been decided in advance who would gain the most from these relations, as evidenced by the growing wealth of the English capital and the declining state of culture in non-European countries controlled by English trade companies—for this military-economic hegemony included the export of cultural heritage from the lands in question and the destruction of the preconditions necessary for continued cultural production. Artifacts produced outside Europe were put on display at world's fairs, where they were meant to contrast with progressive and technologically advanced European civilization, whose worth grew out of the notion of the "Orient" and its backwards otherness.[3] Such a constructed otherness measures for a culture's value had a clear goal: If industry was going to expand, it required cheap raw materials from territories whose inhabitants did not have the same rights as the colonial power. Otherwise, their demands regarding the price of raw materials would rise, significantly increasing the cost of production.

But back to Prague in 1862. A Czech delegation to the Great London Exhibition was assembled with the participation of, among others, Náprstek and Antonín Frič, head of the natural history collection of the Museum of the Kingdom of Bohemia, who had visited London in the preceding years to purchase various products and teaching materials that were exhibited at afternoon gatherings held at the Náprstek home. The visit to the London expo had several clear objectives: to purchase materials for the collections of Bohemia's first museum of industry, to learn about industrial training and teaching materials, and to negotiate an exchange of publications with English science institutes. It is a little remembered fact that the visit led to a reunion of several participants in the Prague Uprising of June 1848. Josef Václav Frič (the brother of Antonín Frič and of the explorer

3 Louise Purbrick, ed., *The Great Exhibition of 1851: New Interdisciplinary Essays* (Manchester: Manchester University Press, 2013).

Alberto Vojtěch Frič) came from his exile in Paris to meet with Náprstek (who had also been involved in the uprising), Mikhail Bakunin, Alexander Herzen, and other leading European revolutionaries.[4] This association with the anti-Viennese resistance would apparently later complicate the founding of the Museum of Industry.

London is also where the little washing machine from the beginning of this text came from. Purchased along with several other products, it was meant to form the foundations for the newly assembled collection of the Museum of Industry, which would be tasked with promoting and educating Czech industrialists and small businessmen. But we should not imagine it as we would the museums of today. In actuality, the idea behind the exposition literally imitated that of international exhibitions and their role as trade fairs: Items would be exhibited along with their price and the manufacturer's name, and visitors would receive a catalogue that more closely resembled a sales catalogue than a museum guide.[5] Nevertheless, each existed in a different context: While the Great Exhibitions in England were designed to promote national industrial development dependent on the imperial policies of a great power and the exploitation of the colonized countries' labor and resources, in Bohemia support for industry was meant to foster the Czech nation's social emancipation, which required economic advancement. The London meeting of revolutionary forces from 1848 was therefore no coincidence—it represented the continuation of patriotic endeavors, of which the activities of the Industrial Union were a part. Ironically, ethnic Czechs' yearning for economic development was intertwined with the policies of England as a great power and its ideas of the free market and the unequal global distribution of power between North and South.

After their return, Náprstek and his compatriots from the Czech delegation discovered that no Czech museum was interested in founding a section with industrial products, and so work began that same year on drafting the statutes for the Museum of Industry Society, with František Ladislav Rieger as president and Alois Oliva as vice president. Rieger is interesting from another important aspect.

4 Milena Secká, *Vojta Náprstek. Vlastenec, sběratel, mecenáš* (Prague: Vyšehrad and Národní muzeum, 2011), 115.
5 Majer, *Počátky musea Vojty Náprstka*, 123.

Both within the Industrial Union and as a leading liberal Czech patriot, he was an active proponent of economic liberalism, which he had studied in detail while in England, where he had fled in order to avoid post-1848 political reprisals. It was initially a solitary stance among Czech national liberals,[6] and we can say almost without exaggeration that Rieger was one of the first important supporters of capitalism in Bohemia. In fact, despite the negative social impacts of economic liberalism that he observed in England and that he described in his later writings, Rieger felt that it "should become a lasting component of the program for Czech national emancipation. [...] He returned from England firmly convinced that the spirit of free industrial activity and trade [...] would lead to the development of financing, reduced prices for products, increased employment, and thus also to an increase in the overall level of living, civilization, and in the end effect culture of the so-called industrial nations."[7]

While the society's statutes were awaiting approval by Vienna, several well-attended exhibitions of products were held on Shooter's Island (Střelecký ostrov) in Prague, further acquisitions were made, and more donations came in from Czechs living abroad. As the collections continued to grow, however, the statutes' approval kept getting delayed (one reason may have been that the Austrian authorities were concerned about potentially supporting the emancipation of the Czechs and their industries; another possible concern was the involvement of leading Czech patriots) and chances for the construction of a new building especially for the museum began to fade. The situation remained unchanged until 1873 and the death of Náprstek's mother Anna Fingerhutová, who bequeathed the brewery building on Bethlehem Square (Betlémské náměstí) to the Museum of Industry. By now, it was clear that if the museum was going to be established it would have to be a private undertaking. In addition, the original exhibition plan was quickly becoming dated. Nevertheless, in 1878 Náprstek published an *Outline of the Collections*

6 One example is Karel Havlíček Borovský, who in his journalistic writings was a prominent critic of early manifestations of industrial capitalism. See Jakub Raška and Matěj Měřička, "Síla země založena na rolnictví vždy spočívá pevněji než na fabrikách, skrze které se, když neslušně rozmnoženy budou, jenom velký počet nastávajících žebráků v zemi zahnízdí," *Sborník Národního muzea v Praze, řada C – Literární historie* 61, no. 3–4 (2016): 9–26.

7 Milan Hlavačka, Pavel Cibulka, et al., *Sociální myšlení a sociální praxe v českých zemích 1781–1939. Ideje, legislativa, instituce* (Prague: Historický ústav AV ČR, 2015), 66.

of the Museum of Industry in which he proposed an exhibition organized by type of industry or craft, with the exhibit items divided into tools and machines, metals in industry, minerals in industry, clay products, glass products, domestic and national industry, construction, the graphic arts, education, and artistic industry—to name a few. Industrial products were continuously complemented by gifts from Czech explorers, and although the original outline does not say so, the 1880s saw the creation of the first exhibitions of "famous explorers" and non-European cultures. By 1898, the *Guide to the Collections of Náprstek's Czech Museum of Industry in Prague* clearly shows that artifacts from non-European countries made up a large part of the museum. These were exhibited in cabinets according to country of origin, although their presentation was somewhat random and offered not so much a comprehensive picture of the various cultures as a cursory overview, a "flight around the world" defined by what items collectors or explorers managed to purchase or plunder.

In the *Guide to the Collections of the Museum of Industry*, which today is held in the archives of the Náprstek Museum, Náprstek writes that the main aim of the museum's collections was to raise the work of Czech producers to an artistic level.

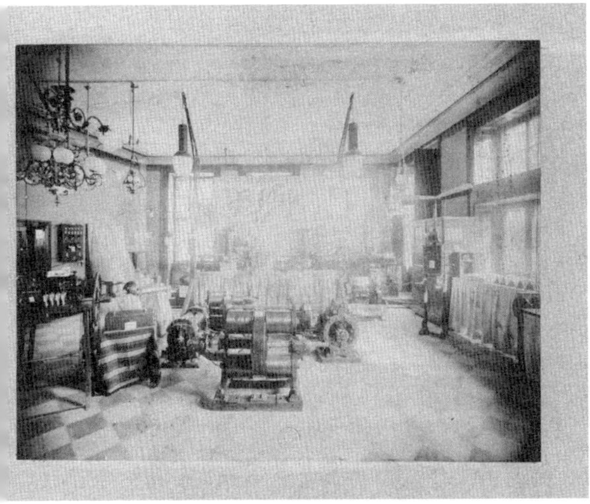

↑ Technical exhibition at the Náprstek Czech Museum of Industry, exhibition hall interior, 1888, 24.8 × 32.8 cm, Collection of historical photos, signature F.53 © Náprstek Museum of Asian, African and American Cultures, signature F.53

Little was written about foreign items, whose position thus becomes highly ambivalent. Were they supposed to play a similar role as at the Great London

Exhibitions—to show the advanced nature of the Czech nation as it gradually emancipated itself? Or were they equal sources of inspiration for industrial work in the Czech lands? Unfortunately, this interesting and ambiguous situation was never completely resolved, for in 1928 it was decided that the museum's collections would be administered by the Czechoslovak state and in 1943 its industrial products were moved to the National Technical Museum, while its European ethnographic items were given to the ethnography department at the National Museum.[8] The Náprstek Museum became an ethnographic museum that, like other museums in Europe, is today awaiting its transformation in response to discussions related to the decolonization of our cultural and educational institutions. A closer look, however, shows that the history of the Náprstek Museum requires that institutional self-reflection consider not only the presentation of otherness in its displays but also the discourse associated with the idea of Europe's industrial advancement, which was fundamentally linked with European imperialism and economic liberalism and which helped give birth to the modern Czech state, later realized in the form of an independent Czechoslovakia. For this reason, the second part of this essay will look at the period of industrial growth during the First Republic.

TEACHING THE CZECHS HYGIENE

As promised at the outset, the washing machine will be joined by one more product, the famous Schicht brand soap—a symbol of Czechoslovakia's economic development. It is no coincidence that these two products are designed to fight dirt, because a central part of this story involves the promotion of cleanliness as a fundamental theme of civilization and modernization. Although the greatest flourishing of the Schicht company, an international producer for the food and drugstore sectors, was during the First Republic, its early beginnings coincide with Náprstek's patriotic activities: In 1848, the Bohemian-German butcher Georg Schicht founded a small soap factory in his native village of Rynoltice

8 Secká, *Vojta Náprstek. Vlastenec, sběratel, mecenáš*, 270.

near Liberec.[9] The factory did well, and so in 1882 the company built a large and modern factory in Ústí nad Labem for the production of household fats and oils (for use in food products and drugstore supplies). Thus began the history of this north Bohemian town (and its air quality), which ever since has been shaped by the Schicht company and its successor, Setuza (Severočeské tukové závody—North Bohemian Fat Works).

In 1907, the company is taken over by the grandsons of the original founder Heinrich and Georg Schicht, who manage to grow the company's renown in Bohemia and abroad. Their success is based primarily on two things: cheap raw materials (and the processing of these materials in Ústí, where the Schichts built the first fat hydrogenation plant in Europe) and a sophisticated advertising strategy. The company's operations are thus an excellent illustration of capitalism's development in Europe and North American in the second half of the 19th century and the first half of the 20th century, which was founded on the sophisticated construction of demand (in this case, promoting the supposed necessity for personal hygiene and fragrancy) while reducing production costs as much as possible. Factory owners thus begin to look beyond Europe, and the Schichts are no exception. In the early 20th century, the company begins to import raw materials such as palm kernels, peanuts, and coconuts from the era's European colonies. According to historian Martin Krsek of the Municipal Museum of Ústí nad Labem, raw materials came from eastern and western India and northern and western Africa, where the Schichts even owned coconut plantations.

Let's be honest: Soap isn't really such a necessity, but we still cannot do without it. In *Svět a jelen od Schichta* (The world and Schicht's stag), Marie Macková describes how soap products show that a society has the luxury to make such goods, because they are made of animal and vegetable fats that, in times of crisis, are necessary for their nutritional rather than their hygienic value.[10] Thanks to industrialization, progress in the chemical industry, and sophisticated advertising strategies, the early 19th

9 Martin Krsek, "Schichtova epopej a její nacionální a hospodářský význam," *Svět a jelen od Schichta*, ed. Marcela Zemanová et al. (Ústí nad Labem: Muzeum města Ústí nad Labem and Univerzita J. E. Purkyně v Ústí nad Labem, 2021), 37.

10 Marie Macková, "Mýdlovarník a hardnice," *Svět a jelen od Schichta*, ed. Zemanová et al. 9.

century thus sees the birth of an entire new cultural system of social values defined by commodity fetishism.[11] A previously somewhat rare good such as soap slowly becomes a regular commodity available to all. According to the historian Thomas Richards, this new system of representation included large world's fairs such as the 1851 exhibition in London, which transformed the private consumer sphere into a spectacle that became an essential part of the products themselves.[12]

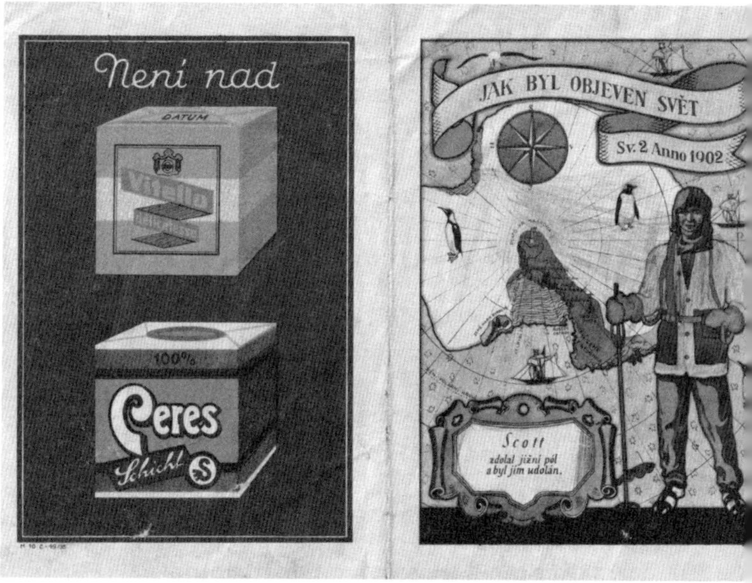

↑ "Jak byl objeven svět," ca. 1930s, promotional fairy tale for Saponia laundry detergent. Photo: property of the author

Such a spectacle was only possible through massive advertising, something that the Schichts—who in the period before the First World War became the first in Bohemia to engage in large-scale advertising—were well aware of. In 1924, Georg Schicht even contacted a consultancy agency run by the famous American public relations Edward L. Bernays, the founder of the modern approach to advertising and PR.[13] Bernays, a nephew of Sigmund Freud and a master of propaganda, worked with a strategy that included not only the presentation of the product itself but that above all focused on the entire lifestyle associated with it.

11 Anne McClintock, *Imperial Leather: Race, Gender and Sexuality in the Colonial Contest* (New York/London: Routledge, 1995), 208.
12 Thomas Richards, *The Commodity Culture of Victorian England: Advertising and Spectacle, 1851–1914* (New York/London: Verso, 1991).
13 Bernays describes his dealings with the Schicht company in his memoirs: Edward L. Bernays, *Biography of an Idea. The Founding Principle of Public Relations* (New York: Simon & Schuster, 1965).

In the case of soap, this meant a status of cleanliness and fragrancy associated with health and "civilization." But first one had to convince the consumer of this association. The success of the Schicht brand was built largely on this approach and on the creation of new consumer needs, including ideas of general hygiene (of home and body).

In her book *Imperial Leather*, Anne McClintock not only shows how the well-known Pears brand of soap used advertising to achieve fame in the second half of the 19th century, but also describes its contribution to Victorian-era imperial policy through its presentation of European hygienic habits as an example of civilizational progress—in contrast with the "backwardness" of non-European countries. For instance, in 1884 the company printed Christmas cards depicting two images in which a white child uses soap to wash its black peer until its skin turns white. Racism in advertising is hardly an exception in the 19th and 20th centuries, but it takes on an entirely new dimension when it comes to promoting hygiene and products such as soap: Cleanliness is associated with whiteness, and backwardness and dirt with non-white skin. "Soap is Civilization," proclaims the slogan of the Unilever company, which was founded in 1929 by a merger of several large European producers such as the Netherlands' Margarine Union, Britain's Lever Brothers, and Ústí's Schicht company.

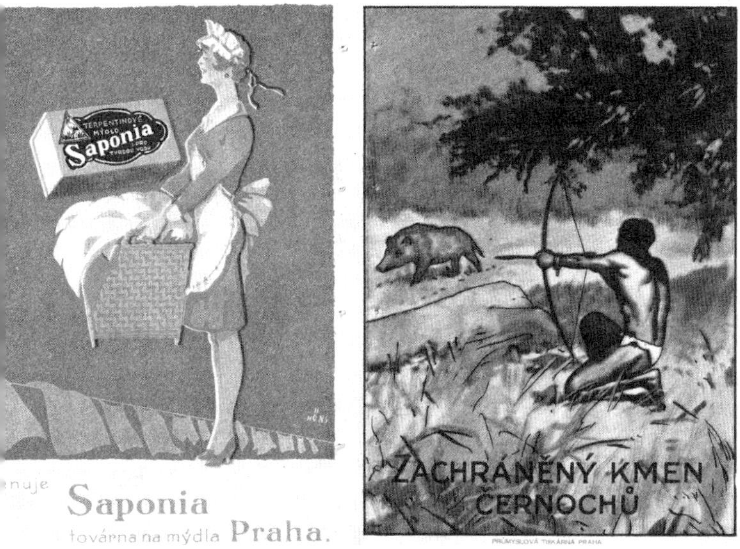

↑ "Zachráněný kmen černochů," ca. 1930s, promotional fairy tale for Saponia laundry detergent. Photo: property of the author

Georg Schicht even served as this giant transnational corporation's president from 1930 to 1937. To this day, Unilever controls the food and cosmetics industry throughout the world (its brands include Dove, Rexona, Cif, Hellmann's, Knorr, and many others) and contributes to the continued exploitation of natural and human resources in the former colonial world. The Schicht company used racial advertising as well. For instance, a calendar from 1911 includes a placard for "Ceres" coconut oil shortening being held by a dark-skinned figure wearing a suit and white gloves. Besides this image of the "civilized African," the Schichts also produced far more sophisticated advertising products aimed at convincing consumers that they were contributing to something far grander than mere personal hygiene. These included advertising "tales"—little booklets featuring a story, with an advertisement for a specific product on the rear page. These booklets were regularly produced by cosmetics companies in interwar Czechoslovakia and were given to customers along with their purchase. In the 1930s, the Schichts printed stories about famous explorers and "discoverers" such as Robert Scott and Sven Hedin. By using Schicht's soap (or also Saponia brand products) consumers became heirs to European civilization. Soap was no longer Marx's *trivial thing*, meaning an ordinary product required for a specific activity, but a Baudrillardian symbol.[14] Products such as soap gave rise to not just a need for cleanliness but also the desire to join the grand civilizing project.

INDUSTRY AND FREEDOM

If we are going to apply western European discussions of decolonization to the Czech lands in the second half of the 19th century, we must take into account the complicated paths of Czech colonial complicity in relation to Austria-Hungary. Industry and its dependence on the discourse of economic (and imperial) progress, on raw materials from non-European territories, and on the idea of the free market played an important role in modernization and emancipated Czech craftsmen, small business owners,

14 Jean Baudrillard described the theory of symbolic exchange, which arises not from production but from the process of consumption (supported by communications strategies such as advertising) in his 1972 book *Pour une critique de l'économie politique du signe* (For a Critique of the Political Economy of the Sign).

and—through domestic technological products—women. Additionally, in the second half of the 19th century, Czech national liberals saw industrial development as a way of breaking free from German domination in the Austro-Hungarian state. According to the discourse shaped by influential personalities such František Ladislav Rieger, this industrial development would take place within the context of a capitalist economy. The freedom of one class was presented as freedom for all, except that it was literally conditioned upon a lack of freedom for others: other social classes that did not own the means of production and other non-European nations and ethnic groups.

Similarly, the First Republic was faced with the need to fortify its position as a new European state by building a strong and independent economy, among other things by seeking its own Czechoslovak colony in Africa. Although most people in the Czech Republic today believe that this idea was mere wishful thinking by the First Republic's dreamers,[15] the example of the Schicht family's oil and fat company shows how non-European resources could be exploited even without the existence of the country's "own" colony, and how this approach was strategically framed as a European civilizing project. Both ordinary items—the washing machine and soap—thus bring together two important institutions that played a fundamental role in shaping (the globally connected) modern state: the museum and the factory.

The history of the Náprstek Museum of Asian, African and American Cultures is part of my doctoral research at the Academy of Fine Arts in Prague. I would like to thank my advisor Vjera Borozan, and Vojtěch Märc and Jakub Rašek for discussing the text with me and offering their commentary on it.

15 The theme of dreams or dreaming frequently comes up in relation to Czech patriots' ambitions of setting up their own colony. See, e.g., Markéta Křížová, "Koloniální sny českých vlastenců," *Vesmír*, no. 10 (2020), https://vesmir.cz/cz/casopis/archiv-casopisu/2020/cislo-10/kolonialni-sny-ceskych-vlastencu.html; "Civilizace: Sen o české kolonii v Americe," Czech Radio Plus, https://plus.rozhlas.cz/civilizace-sen-o-ceske-kolonii-v-americe-6610104; or "Československo po svém vzniku snilo o koloniích, řešilo se africké Togo," Idnes.cz, November 3, 2018, https://www.idnes.cz/zpravy/domaci/togo-ceskoslovensko-vyroci-kolonie-100-let-jaroslav-olsa.A181022_112536_domaci_lesa.

Decolonization Through People's Art

Brenda V. Fajardo
Professor Emeritus
Department of
Art Studies
University of the
Philippines, Diliman

The recognition of traditional and current people's art, the study of its form, function and content, an analysis of its relation to our life and culture at this point in our history will provide us the direction towards a culture that is authentically ours.

To focus on the art of the people as a point of departure is to acknowledge the important role it has in our effort to reeducate ourselves and counter the colonial consciousness that we have. This requires a restudy of approaches and methods of providing points of unity for the people with their own activities as its base.

The forms we see around us create a cultural environment that may be natural or incidental. For whatever intent it was made, these forms are perceived and are clearly the manifestations of the life of the people who made them.

In these times of depravity and depression, these forms assert themselves culturally and contribute to the continuity of our life thread as a people.

Art reflects, interprets, and supports man's concept of himself and the significance of his role in the world. It is an integral part of the mechanism of social existence just as it is concerned with personal expression and aesthetic exploration.

The nature of art is such that it has a life of its own, a quality of "separateness" which makes it not only a description of reality but a parallel reality of its own. This does not mean that art is unconcerned with other things, because art has no meaning without a social context.

Art and human perception is a creation. The individuals who create and perceive art are part of society therefore people, art, and society are interrelated.

The intent of this paper is:
First, to focus on the art of ordinary people so that we may begin to recognize that there is a way of doing that is a result of a way of life, therefore, form carries both function and meaning;

Second, to discover aesthetic values in people's art so that we may appreciate a sensibility that evolved from local history and local conditions, helping us to become aware of our identity as a people;

And third, to propose possibilities by way of concrete suggestions on a process of decolonization through people's art.

THE PROBLEM OF IDENTITY AND CONSCIOUSNESS

One of the fundamental causes of the corruption of our national character is the infiltration of our psyche by colonial cultures. Renato Constantino[1] says: "the crisis of identity is so serious and difficult to resolve precisely because westernization has been so pervasive that by and large the Filipinos are unaware of their own lack of a national consciousness."

Pre-colonial Philippine society was not sufficiently developed as a nation when the Spanish colonizers came, conquered, and eroded whatever culture there was.

Using religion as a ploy, the Spaniards modified and changed the authentic historical development of a people when they Christianized them.

This process of westernization continued with the Americanization of the Filipino, and this time, through education, the Indio was taught how to think, feel, and appreciate what was American, a phenomenon that we still witness to date.

As a result of colonization, we have an impoverished culture, deprived of natural growth, a culture much abused and bastardized.

Culture is a production of the interaction and interrelations within a society. It differs from one society to another as a result of the dynamic forces within it, including factors such as ecology, geography, systems of thought, politics, beliefs, education, and so on.

Concretely, we can think of a culture in terms of modes of activities that express a collective competence or capability of what the society has learned to do or make, such as ways of building, dancing, settling disputes; or in terms of entities such as institutions, customs, languages, tools and art works, embracing social systems and settled practices.

Culture competence is dependent on skills and talents of the members of a society but this competence is possessed by a society, thus it is a collective entity.

There are two types of cultural competence:[2] Causal competence, referring to technology such as irrigating land, making weapons or weaving fabric, bringing about results by applying means-ends rules;

1 Renato Constantino, *Insight and Foresight,* (Quezon City: Foundation for Nationalist Studies, 1977, 3rd printing 1983), 103.

2 Monroe C. Beardsley, "Art and Its Cultural Context," *The Aesthetic Point of View,* ed. Michael J. Wreen and Donald M. Callen (Ithaca: Cornell University Press, 1982), 352-70.

and Conventional competence, which gives added character or meaning to actions through the estalishment of conventions, such as instituting marriage or devising systems of visual symbols.

Artistic activity is one of the components of culture and part of the life process that carries the seed of creative change. The meaning of a people's life is manifested in the products of artistic activities. The works of art created by people describe their past and present conditions and express their needs, values, thoughts, and emotions.

It would be easier if we were, as a people, homogenous in culture but our history attests to he fact, like it or not, that as a people, we have been exposed to diverse cultures. We see this in the number of languages that we speak, the different ways by which we cook and flavor our foods, the way we clothe ourselves, our manners, idiosyncrasies and differences in behavior.

Before our country was colonized, our people are said to have had a diverse nature and differed somewhat in their ways of life. With colonization, the people were forced to conform with the culture of the invaders.

People assimilate experiences, so naturally, the foreign culture brought by the colonizers became models of our people who, exposed to new forms and systems, incorporated these in their lifestyle.

Consequently, we have become a people of conglomerate cultures and much confused so far as a national identity is concerned.

PEOPLE'S ART

"People's art," in the context of this paper, refers to the art created by ordinary people. Art created by ordinary people has also been referred to as folk art, to mean the artistic production of the peasantry, of rural people. This is a narrow definition in the Philippine context, since a great number of rural people have migrated to urban areas.

Rural folk who migrate to the cities in search of better life conditions, carry with them their traditional values but are shocked culturally by an alien and alienating city culture. They nevertheless assimilate this confused and polluted culture, increasing the number of the population who have been displaced culturally. In a broad sense then, we shall refer to people's art as the art of the greater majority of the people. In our society, it is unfortunate that the greater majority of the population belong to the lower rather than the middle or higher strata. Thus, the word "people" also implies a social class which is lower in economic rank in comparison with the rest of society.

A low economic status, however, limits the greater majority's chances for thorough cultural pollution since exposure to foreign culture is limited by a deprived opportunity for education, travel, or the luxury of going to the movies, viewing video tapes and so forth. Somehow, values remain authentic and most of the art they influence transmits value-images that their culture has of itself. Even as they are prone to imitate models of alien cultures, whatever unfolds from them are still more natural and naive, more authentic as the expression of a people.

There is a need to recognize people's art as an authentic manifestation of identity. Art is one of the systems of culture having its own dynamic, capable of transforming the status quo of colonialism in culture through the development of forms of expression and action that will crystallize into a people's culture, a culture linked to the people's needs and aspirations.

THE NATURE OF PEOPLE'S ART

Before the age of modernization, crafts used to spring out of the hearts and hands of man because he needed them. These products were made for use without any thought of creating works of art.

A people's art arises from cultural needs even if it is subject to natural conditions. It maintains traces of a primitive communal practice of art where we can hardly distinguish producer from consumer.

This art can become so popular that finally no one can say who invented them and as a result of continuous repetition and constant adaptation, take on such a conventional appearance that their unique, individually conditioned features disappear. The work comes into being as the constantly changing result of gradual adaptation. The creation of individuals and the property of many, this art assumes many versions and all versions are relevant and reliable.

People's art is created for its function and the maker is usually not conscious of producing art. As an art, it is considered stylistically behind the art of the "fine artist." However, the people who create the art are not conscious that they are producing something which goes beyond the boundaries of their daily forms of life and needs. The people are aesthetically innocent in their lack of the concept of art for its own sake but it does not mean that what they produce is artistically inferior.

In people's art:

(1) The producer is an unknown craftsman, not an artist-craftsman (the artist-craftsman being an individual artist who is conscious of himself as a "signature" artist);
(2) There is a close connection between technology, the development of skill in an industry, and artistic activity;
(3) Culture is a major consideration being the result of historical happenings, and therefore, patterns of culture carry with them particular points of view.

Let me discuss these points one by one, for in considering the art of a great number of unknown craftsmen, we hope to discover a directness of vision and honesty of purpose that will help us in our effort to define ourselves in history.

(1) THE PRODUCER IS AN UNKNOWN CRAFTSMAN

People's art is the art of anonymous craftsmen who produce crafts in quantities used by the masses in their daily lives. Initially, the art work is the creation of an individual but this is taken up by a social group, and by adoption, reproduction, or variation, become "folk art," i.e., people's art.

Many individuals work on the craft and as this happens, technology is transferred from one to another and the process becomes a tradition, learned over generations.

The repetition of the same process and constant adaptation takes on a collective character and a conventional appearance so that the individually-conditioned features disappear.

(2) THERE IS A CLOSE CONNECTION BETWEEN TECHNOLOGY, THE DEVELOPMENT OF SKILL IN INDUSTRY, AND ARTISTIC ACTIVITY

The process by which an object is created affects the resulting product. There is a close relation between technical virtuosity and the development of artistry.

When the craftsman has become technically proficient, he is able to explore various possibilities in design.

Basically, people's art is a product of an industry in which feeling for form is inextricably bound with technical experience. Form and style depend on the development of technique. People's art could be anything from basketry, carving, weaving, metalwork, pottery and so on.

The initial motivation for production is its use and the form results from this functional need. Limitations of technology affect the nature of the forms that come out technomorphic.

Different crafts have technical limitations and possibilities which affect the resultant product, but the proficiency of the craftsman and the development of technique makes for artistry.

Franz Boas[3], in his work on Primitive Art, pointed out that certain elements are apparent in all forms. One of these is SYMMETRY. By symmetry there is reference to balance, the most common being bilateral symmetry which is physiologically determined.

Craftsmen work with their arms and hands and the right and left motions lead to the feeling of symmetry, which may be arranged vertically, horizontally, or radially. It may also be inverted where we experience two symmetrical halves facing each other, in rotation.

RHYTHM is another important element evident in people's art. Technical activities with regularly repeated movements lead to rhythmic repetition which leads to pattern. The craftsman who has the ability to perform a more complex action, produce a more complex rhythm.

Both symmetry and rhythmic repetition generally run on horizontal levels. This is why we commonly see repetitions in horizontal bands.

Treatment of surface leads to the development of patterns. While patterns are usually decorative, they are also visual symbols that are, in effect, the viewpoint of the producer.

3 Franz Boas, *Primitive Art* (New York: Dover, 1955).

(3) CULTURE IS A MAJOR CONSIDERATION; ART WORKS TRANSMIT VALUE-IMAGES

A look into the relationship between art and religion is one way of looking at art as an integral part of the mechanism of social existence and its being interdependent with personal expression and aesthetic exploration.

The relationship of art and religion as manifested in the art of people tell much about their life.

Art and religion have existed together in some form since the beginnings of organized communities. In interpreting the universe, all aspects of life were bound together in image-making. For the indigenous Filipino, *Bathala* was the "all-powerful god" represented by the sun, the moon, and the stars. They believed that there was a divine energy that animated the universe and this was manifested in every aspect of the natural world such as in stones, trees, clouds, fire. These symbols are represented in people's art: in baskets, blankets, tools, and implements. Early Filipinos must have incorporated them to ensure a good life.

The indigenous form of worship was done through the mediation of the *anito* or spirit of dead relatives represented by idols that were carved from stone, wood, and ivory. The carved idols were the conceptual representations of the divine power of *Bathalang May-kapal* and the other spirits in the universe.

Sacrificial offerings were given to the idols for the recovery of a sick person; for a good harvest; for a prosperous voyage; victory at war; or successful delivery in childbirth and other such favors.

The *anito* was carved by anyone and regarded as a household guardian. Every family had such an image and carved one whenever a relative died, so that a household could have as many as 200 *anitos* passed from generation to generation. These figurative forms were carved rather vaguely sinceanimism did not clearly delineate the appearance of supernatural beings.

When the Spaniards came, these carved figures were destroyed and in their stead religious images, called *santos*, were carved in the likeness of Christian saints and were venerated.

If we were to examine the sculpture produced in pre-Hispanic times, crude as it may be, we can still say that the art of carving the *santos* had a primitive tradition, although in the *santos*, Christian iconogrphy and Chinese elements were incorporated. The pre-Hispanic form may have been Christianized and given a new face but it remained very much the indigenous carved figure that represented the *anito*. Basic values and practices persisted with external concepts modified to suit local patterns of doing, believing, and thinking. For areas converted to Spanish Catholicism, the Filipinos creatively evolve a folk Catholicism where traditional elements of worship fused with the new religion, and the traditional system of values overlapped with Christian practices. This folk Catholicism gave rise to forms that show its syncretic nature.

Medallions made of copper or bronze, engraved with images of the Holy Family; the Blessed Virgin Mary, or of the saints, together with Latin scriptures, are examples of syncretic Catholicism. The early Filipino believed in the *anting-anting* or amulets, objects—natural or man-made, believed to have special powers, like giving protection (*panagang*) or of bringing good fortune to the believer. Amulets carried or worn by a person are kept in a place which is the desired sphere of influence, as on a roof or in the field.

When the Spanish missionaries brought medals to replace the *animistic idols*, the people developed a new system of faith and prayers; animistic beliefs and practices, however, continued and fused with Catholicism resulting in the metal *anting-anting*, an adaptation of the medals brought by the friars.

Because the *anting-anting* protected the wearer against witchcraft, sickness, or accidents, and made them invisible in the eyes of evil, it played a significant role in the thinking and motivation of peasant rebels, bandits, soldiers and generals.

There were many methods and variations of obtaining *anting-anting* but the most common way was to get hold of objects used or associated with Holy Week rituals. However, it was not merely a matter of obtaining objects that magically protect their wearer, it also points to a complex system of beliefs and practices which is half-Christian and half-indigenous.

The fusion of beliefs, both colonial and indigenous is also evident in the syncretic form of wax effigies called "*katawan*," similar to *ex votos*.

These votive figures are set alongside votive candles as offerings to God or the saints, requesting various favors such as the healing of some illness, protection of property and possessions, or as thanksgiving for requests granted.

As a votive figure, it functions much like the carved figures of animistic worship. The *katawan* is a supplement to prayer and through it, the faithful believe it will help solve problems such as marital infidelity, sickness, or even difficult examinations. It may be an offering to the departed or an expression of gratitude for favors granted such as the healing of a disease.

Most of the people who believe in the viability of the *katawan* rely on faith for most everything. For those who cannot afford a doctor or a counsellor, there is faith, the *katawan*, the *anting-anting* and "bahala na ang Diyos." The poor have nothing else but faith to see them through life's problems. And the *katawan* is an inexpensive remedy at 35 to 50 centavos each, much cheaper than a visit to the doctor.

When problems are chronic, a sustained prayer in the form of a nine-day novena is usually practiced. The votive figure vendor becomes the "suki" of the person who has a problem and often becomes some kind of a shock absorber as she asks the other how she is getting along.

Both the *anting-anting* and *katawan* are people's art. The craftsmen who create these objects are anonymous; the processes used are simple and economical.

The *anting-anting* is done through a lost-wax process in small workshops using very simple and crude equipment. Because of constant use, the negative molds have eroded so that the linear quality of the images and inscriptions are no longer legible.

The process used in making the *katawan* is also economical. In fact, the melted wax (*pagkit*) from the burnt wax sold earlier, is recycled. Negative molds are carved out of wood and constant use has also partially erased the features of the images.

Those who make the *anting-anting* and the *katawan* are not conscious of technical refinement or its aesthetic qualities. It has taken on a commercial purpose for the maker and the objective is to finish as many figures to sell, a means of economic production. Meanwhile, those who acquire either or both still believe in its magic.

Both forms are manifestations of faith and beliefs that go back to indigenous beliefs and practices, a fusion of two systems which adhere to the ideas of the colonizer and the viewpoint of the indigenous.

There is a social perspective, a creative perspective and a perspective which has to do with the medium itself. People's art is affected by social, economic, and aesthetic differences as much as underlying continuities of belief, imagery, and subject matter.

A conscious effort is necessary for decolonization. After all, the penetration of our hearts and minds by colonial cultures have all but anesthetized us. The people should be encouraged to think, question, reason, and create from their life experience. As a counter consciousness movement, it necessitates an awareness of issues and the need to destroy the colonial frame of mind.

It was through education that our consciousness became alien to our own culture. The American pattern of life became our model, which encouraged imitativeness rather than originality, geared to a culture that we have psychologically accepted as our own, justifying it as being contemporary and international enjoying all the gloss of a canned culture that is nonetheless artificial.

Our sensibilities have become confused. We are more familiar and comfortable with western modes rather than Asian or eastern modes. A Philippine aesthetic cannot develop naturally because of the constant bombardment and continued intrusion of ideas and forms from without. Our concepts and standards of beauty are learned and acquired rather than lived and felt.

Decolonization will need some kind of internal revolution, a soul-searching that promises to be painful but inevitable if we want to survive as a people. An awareness and acceptance of the need to decolonize is the first step to authentic consciousness.

Art, being a total experience, is one medium which may be used for this purpose; the more authentic and powerful experience would be that which starts at the base.

Decolonization is possible through people's art:

1) Through documentation, preservation, revival, adaptation and popularization;

2) Through a program of conscientization of the craftsmen;
3) Through an art program that focuses on the people's art, life, and culture in its curriculum.

Documentation, preservation, revival and adaptation of people's art is the initial stage of the process. A systematic collection and classification—a thorough study of people's art—is necessary for us to take stock of our strength as a people. It is possible to conceptualize various programs after this initial phase, and to popularize it so that a great majority of the population will recognize the aesthetic of the people.

A second course of action is the program of conscientization of the craftsmen themselves; so that they may realize the power that they have in their hands as a people, shifting their goal from material profit to the higher goal of identity and consciousness.

Many craft communities have all but lost their tradition to meet the urgent problems and needs of a society in crisis. Such a community as Paete, for example, is rapidly being consumed by commercialism and the industrialization of handcrafts.

Paete is a town of creative people. Each household seems to be involved in one craft or the other such as wood carving, *bakya*-making or papier-mâché toys (*taka*).

National consciousness does not at all come into the production of miniature wooden toys and dolls copied from printed catalogues as commissioned by wholesale purchasers from as far away as Europe. Wood carvings of duck decoys, elephants, and figurative forms are done by reproduction, using machines to make the basic shape with the craftsman hand-finishing it at the end of the assembly line. Even the inexpensive *taka* sold outside church doors at fiesta time are no longer just the horse and the carabao. The giraffe and the elephant have joined the menagerie.

Economic need coupled with a disintegrated consciousness has contributed to the pollution and erosion of the authentic expression of people.

It is necessary then to raise the level of consciousness of the craftsmen themselves to counter the continued production of mindless crafts intended for the outsider but provide the insider with the outsider's images, thereby changing his own system of doing.

To further explain how a craft can evolve from its traditional form to a commercial form and then possibly to a conscious form, we will take mat-weaving as an example.

MAT-WEAVING: A STUDY OF CONTRAST IN FORM AND CONTENT

Traditionally, the mat (*banig*) is used to sleep on, especially in many areas where raised beds are not used. The *banig* is also used like a carpet, for praying; to dry *palay* on, and more recently, as a piece of art collected for display. It varies in size and quality, it can be coarse and rough but it can also be fine and soft.

Two areas are especially known for the *banig* that they produce. Those woven in Sulu and in Samar. Both have achieved recognition for their craftsmanship but they differ somewhat in technology and in content. Mat-weaving, because of the very nature of its process, contributes to the geometrization of forms found in its design patterns. Local culture also affects the nature and quality of the expression and the visual symbols incorporated as designs.

THE MATS OF SULU AND TAWI-TAWI

Mat-weaving is a woman's craft in Sulu and Tawi-Tawi. It is found in different parts of Sulu but Laminusa, Siasi and Ungus Matata, Tandubas are considered the best centers of mat-weaving in the area.

The mats of Sulu and Tawl-Tawi are double in thickness on account of a lower mat (*lapis*) which is plain and coarse, and an upper mat which is of finer weave and has a patterned design (*diam*). The size of a mat varies from three by six feet to ten by fifteen feet.

It takes about a week to prepare the fiber for weaving. First, *pandan* leaves are cut and the spines (*legget*) and center rib are removed. Then the halves are separated and rolled (*angalikid*) in a coil (*pinatoho*), tied, and placed in a pot, held down by a rock, and softened in boiling water (*billa*). Later it is dried in the sun, uncoiled and flattened with a stick (*ambuhut*). The leaves are drawn through a small metal-bladed gauge (*jangatan*) which cuts each leaf into four to five narrow strips. These are loosely bundled and left in the sun before it is again soaked for twelve hours in cold water. When the fiber is dry, it is again softened with the *ambuhut*. By this time, the natural color has almost completely faded and the fiber is dyed (*angangibi*). Commercial dyes (*angibi*) of green (*gadung*), orange (*kulit*), red (*kapot*), violet (*taluk*), and blue (*bilu*) are used. After dyeing, the strips are dried in the shade to prevent fading and gently beaten to ensure softness. The actual weaving takes from two to four weeks. Weaving begins at the middle with a special simple pattern (*amatal*). The strips are usually not long enough to reach the edge and a technique called *anugpat* is used where strips are added as continuators (*sugpat*). At the edge, the strips are knotted (*lipi*) to prevent unraveling.

All designs are directly woven into the mat. Patterns of design are never planned in advance. Because design motifs are traditional and small in number, there is a high degree of uniformity in design. There are four patterns (*sasa*):

1) stripes (jail)
2) multi-colored squares (tabanas)
3) checkered pattern in white and any other color (kusta)
4) zig-zag (seko), also known as sasa kalis because it is reminiscent of the wavy blade of the kalis (kris).

When a special design is made, a more difficult technique of weaving in the design is used (*sasapanapana*). A special border pattern (*sasadandan* or *sasaibud*) usually surrounds the inscription.

Generally, the quality of the mats is not based on the design but on the texture and softness of the weave.

In Ungus Matata, the weaver's pride is in his ability to produce more complex rhythms. Variations include long rectangles in different colors (*palang borus*); large squares in alternating colors (*kabang*), a complex zig-zag design (*binaliku*), a combination of stripes and diamonds (*balintung*); a pattern of small hexagons, and a popular pattern called *Tinabi*.

THE MATS OF SAMAR AND LEYTE

The Samar-Leyte mat is slightly different in technology and design from those in Sulu and Tawi-Tawi. The actual weaving center of the area is Basey, a small coastal town in Samar, 27 kilometers from Tacloban City. It is not known when mat-weaving began but it is also a woman's craft in Samar.

The basic material used is the *tikug* plant. It is usually grown after rice harvest but *tikug* grows as weed with the rice in the fields. After harvest (*pagpili*), the *tikug* weeds are dried under the sun (*pagpamara*), then dyed (*pagtina*). Originally, vegetable dyes such as yellow from the *dulaw* plant and red from the *barok* tree were used, but now, synthetic dyes are used. Flattening of the fiber is done with a piece of wood before actual weaving (*paglara*) begins.

In contrast to the Sulu process, the design is pre-sketched on the mat, after it has been woven (*pagbadlis*). A piece of chalk is used to sketch motifs such as flowers, peacocks, fruits, landscapes or a map of the Philippines. While the design motif is directly woven in Sulu, the designs in the Samar mat are embroidered (*pagpahut*). The designer suggests colors but the weaver and the one who embroiders may change the colors as they prefer. Buri is used as the embroidery material because it is softer than *tikug*.

Earlier design motifs were the hibiscus flower (*gumamela*) and landscapes of a farm, mountain and a nipa hut. Recently, other motifs have been added such as roses, dahlias, and orchids, the peacock, a map of the Philippines, and the San Juanico bridge.

Representational motifs require a sketch but checkered patterns are also made without previous plan. Recent mats also carry designs that have been influenced by mats from Sulu but while the mats from Sulu are lighter in hue, the Samar checkered mats are heavier, and colors are brighter. Border outlines are also used to frame central motifs.

Although bright and vivid colors are preferred, economic conditions have affected design trends. Design motifs have been embroidered using only natural and undyed fiber, creating a monochromatic scheme which is less costly and can be completed in a shorter time.

The mats of Basey are considered special. Many buy these as gifts for weddings, birthdays and special occasions. Monograms of the recipients, "His & Hers," or "Recuerdo" have been made to order. It has become such a special craft that the designs conceived cater to the demands of the buyer or of souvenir hunters, tourists, and collectors.

And while it remains a people's art as a craft, most of the consumers are those who can afford the price.

There is a slight difference in the processes used by the two areas in the weaving of mats but the greatest difference is in the design motifs used. The difference is basically cultural. With the difference in material and process came the difference in quality. Culturally, the mat-weavers of Sulu are Muslims and traditionally use geometric rather than representational motifs. In contrast, the weavers of the Samar Leyte region come from a Hispanized area and use motifs that are representational.

COMMERCIALIZATION OF TRADITION

Whereas the *banig* was originally intended for home use, it has also become "art" bought by local and foreign connoisseurs for display in their homes. This has contributed to the commercialization of the craft which has in turn changed the attitude of the craftsman towards the craft. When the craftsman wove mats for home use, he made sure they were durable and colorful. As the product became popular and in demand among consumers from the craftsman's own social group, the product assumed a new function, that of community, so that the quality diminished to meet the demand and keep the supply going.

Both Sulu and Samar mat-weavers have now been affected by the open-ended nature of our culture. While motifs used to be traditionally geometric in Sulu, it now produces mats as well as woven wall hangings with motifs that are representational. Both areas still weave traditionally where technique is concerned, but both areas have adapted motifs more likely to be sold on the contemporary market.

In Sulu, a contemporary rendering of a landscape, almost descriptive of the area and its life and people, is used. The design is interesting but one doubts the authenticity of the motif as a natural expression of a people. It could very well be the design concept of one who studied design. In Samar, themes for the *banig* are made to order and lately, motifs such as the San Juanico bridge have become popular, as evidence of the adaptation to contemporary life.

We see the people creating an art that is not entirely theirs because content no longer comes from within but is made to order from without, to meet economic demands.

The original function and motivation for creation is lost in meeting the demands for products which have taken on a commercial nature so that motifs and images may not even be significant to the person creating the piece.

DECOLONIZATION: A CONSCIOUS FORM

As tradition continues in people's art, the content evolves in process and tradition becomes dynamic and can rightfully be referred to as a living tradition.

A living tradition implies a dynamic energy of a continuing tradition, changing in process yet retaining its tradition without being fossilized. As a living tradition, people's art, by way of technology, form, and content continues to provide meaning for both the producer and the consumer.

It is with this in mind that the process of decolonization is possible. The craftsman, if decolonized, will help hasten social transformation and provide the impetus for the decolonization of other minds.

First, it is important to recognize and become aware of our colonial consciousness so that we can provide concrete steps for social change. It will require great effort from those who will take on this proposed course of action, putting industry and energy together to liberate our consciousness from colonial hang-ups and work together in capturing the spirit of the people, concretizing and objectifying it in different forms of expression. If it is possible to have contemporary motifs using the age-old tradition of mat-weaving, then it is possible to weave mats that will document and express insights from life perceived by the people themselves. The recording of these perceptions in the weaving of mats will actually document our history visually. It will provide future generations with important visual evidence of our history as recorded by unknown artists who, in effect, will be the recorders of our history. Motifs, subject matter, or themes to be produced should not be dictated to the craftsman. It is necessary for the craftsmen themselves to become conscious of the situation, to critically think of their socio-economic and historical processes so that they may express their own thoughts, ideas, and feelings about lived experiences, and for them to use their own symbols and images in the depiction of these experiences.

Motifs that depict local history, graphic analysis of society, contemporary news events and actual village experiences should be used more than those motifs which are stale, obsolete and empty. This is true not only for mat-weaving but for other crafts as well.

The potential of such a movement cannot be underestimated because it will draw from the power of the people's spirit and provide a dynamic force in the formation of a national consciousness. But before this can happen, there has to be a group of dedicated persons who will work with people. Their approach should be different from the middleman who imposes specific designs on craftsmen for profit. The group who will implement such a program should consider the people and their culture even in the conceptual framework of the program itself. They should be people who can appreciate the aesthetics and technology of people's art even if the standards are different from those they have learned before. This dialectic manner of working with people will allow both of these groups to learn from each other and hopefully evolve a people-based aesthetic.

THE BOTSWANA EXPERIENCE

A similar movement has been initiated in Botswana. Stories about the life of the people are woven into tapestries or wall hangings as part of a program of conscientization.

1) *On Drought*: If rain doesn't come, there will be drought and the life of the people becomes grim because of too much heat and little water.
2) *On Women*: A woman is on her feet the whole day. She does different tasks. In a poem on women, she is asked: "You're doing everything—what don't you do?"
3) *On Woman*: The meaning of woman is often underestimated and because she is ordinary, she is not noticed. The woman provides light in the home and a lot of her tasks cannot be paid with corals or gold. She has a central role in society.
4) *Exodus of children*: This particular visual example shows how Botswana has been the refugee center for neighboring countries (South Africa, Namibia, Angola, and Zimbabwe). The theme shows the escape of 300 schoolchildren altogether in buses as they went over the borde. This particular exodus has not yet been surpassed.

5) *On Mine workers*: The employment rate in a mining area in Botswana grows as production grows. Thousands are sent to the mining areas in South Africa, which is a bitter necessity. For months, the mine workers' families are fatherless as they work in the mines. They are not allowed to go home after working hours. The daily wage earnings do not last from morning to evening but the workers continue to work.
6) *About tradition*: What is the value of a marriage if it is not talked about? My husband will never be home anyway because he can find work only outside the country. Our marriage will become very expensive because of wedding traditions: the bride's dowry, the wedding gown, the reception.

The example of Botswana is an inspiration for all people who have been colonized and who suffer on account of their colonial history, notwithstanding present conditions of neo-colonialism. There are many ways and means of fighting the problem of identity and consciousness; the best place to start is at home, and from the people themselves—with the language of their hands, hearts and minds, and their art.

In effect, the encouragement of the production of conscious forms implies a micro-media countercultural movement of educating the craftsman in terms of perceiving the actual realities of their socio-cultural environment. All aspects of production need to be studied so that the craftsman, while conscious of his form and content, will also be able to think of the economic aspect of production.

As technology and the skill of the craftsman is developed, raising the artistic level of the works, it likewise becomes a document of the life of the people with their own perceptions and insights inextricably woven into the form.

A third program of action for decolonization through people is to consciously Philippinize the art programs in schools, on all levels: primary, secondary, and tertiary. This does not limit itself to mean the mere use of Philippine materials as subject, nor the use of indigenous, natural, and economical materials available in the local market but a conscious effort to change attitudes and expectations with regard to education through the arts.

Instead of imposing the standards of other cultures with the teachers providing the criteria, the learners need to be allowed to articulate and verbalize the visual expressions they themselves created or the visual perceptions that they have of their environment.

The general concern of art programs in most of our schools has been materials and techniques, the production of works which are brilliantly colored with focus on skill for those schools which have a budget. In the meantime, pallid and timid works come from schools which have no budget. Art is not a matter of materials alone but the power of the expression. If the one who creates has something to say, then the work will be powerful even if they were to use a piece of charcoal.

An overemphasis on the learning of skill and technique limits the learner's capacity for expressing ideas, insights, and feelings or for the exploration of thought-out themes based on actual realities. Many art programs are perceived as a luxury course that develops originality, spontaneity, and creativity. Many do not see it as a serious medium of education where learning is total because the creation of art is a whole experience of both mind and senses.

To decolonize through art programs would require a training program for teachers and the making of a curriculum that will have at its core the history and conditions of Philippine life and culture from the point of view of the people. This proposed program will study the art of the people in their community and the community at large. It will include the learning of crafts which are traditional and all creative work and exercises on sensory perception will be based on the specific culture of the learner. Such a curriculum will help learners recognize the worth, potential, limitations, and problems of culture.

Decolonization through people's art implies a campaign against a culture of ignorance. Focusing on the art of the people hopes to surface the needs, aspirations, and frustrations of the people. And by revitalizing and popularizing people's art, it may yet be a potent and dynamic force in the remaking of our history.

This text was originally published in *Asian Studies: Journal of Critical Perspectives on Asia* 28, (Quezon City: University of the Philippines Diliman, 1990): 92–111.

Violently Peaceful: Art, Decoloniality and Institutional Inclusion

Amanda Carneiro

"like a heart attack in verse
violently peaceful veridic
I'm here to sabotage your reason
to shatter your nervous, circulatory system"
Cap. 4, vers. 3 —Racionais MC's

Much has been said and debated about the colonial origins of museums, and how these institutions are linked to the political and economic elites, which are some of the reasons behind the demands to decolonize them. What this means in both theoretical and practical terms is up for discussion, an ongoing dispute.[1] For instance, it might entail revisiting the discussions around the colonial pillaging of artefacts and objects of material culture and their repatriation, focusing on ethnographic museums.[2] It has also been highlighted that modern and contemporary art museums are not alien to the rationale of accumulation, conservation and display that, despite their singularity, can play an analogous function.[3] In general, the denunciation of these links draws on the need to break with the permanence of colonial structures. Some parties associate decolonization with inclusion and diversity, that is, with the incorporation of historically subjugated groups into institutional hierarchies. Others contend that it is necessary to be radically anti-colonial and anti-racist, positioning themselves in favor of a radical break from the fundamental

1 This essay is the result of my participation in the long-term research carried out in the context of the Art and Decolonization Project jointly by the Museu de Arte de São Paulo and Afterall – the research and publication center of the University of the Arts. The project investigates the colonial roots of museums, art institutions, and universities as well as the emergence of new artistic and curatorial practices that explicitly question and criticize colonial legacies in art production, curation and criticism, through seminars and publications. The research generated in this context subsidizes the reflections presented here. There are a number of lectures and texts online. See: https://masp.org.br/en/arte-e-descolonizacao

2 The bibliography on the subject is quite extensive—good entries on the subject can be found at "The Dakar Festival Colloquium on Negro Arts, April 1966," *Africa 36,* no. 4, (1966): 439–41; Dipesh Chakrabarty, *Provincializing Europe: Postcolonial Thought and Historical Difference,* (Princeton: Princeton University Press, 2009); Douglas Crimp, *Sobre as ruínas do museu* (São Paulo: Martins Fonte), James Cuno, ed. *Whose Culture? The Promise of Museums and the Debate over Antiquities* (Princeton: Princeton University Press, 2012); Clémentine Deliss, *The Metabolic Museum* (Berlin: Hatje Cantz Verlag GmbH, 2020); Ailton Krenak, *Ideias para adiar o fim do mundo* (São Paulo: Companhia das Letras, 2019); Achille Mbembe, *Out of the Dark Night: Essays on Decolonization* (New York: Columbia University Press, 2021); Walter Mignolo and Catherine Walsh, *On Decoloniality: Concepts, Analytics, Praxis* (Durham: Duke University Press Books, 2018); Anibal Quijano, *Ensaios en torno a la colonialidad del poder* (Buenos Aires: Ediciones del signo, 2019); Sally Price, *Primitive Art in Civilized Places* (Chicago: University of Chicago Press, 1991); H, Glenn Penny, *Objects of Culture: Ethnology and Ethnographic Museums in Imperial Germany* North Carolina: University of (North Carolina Press, 2002); Suely Rolnik, *Esferas da insurreição: notas para uma vida não cafetinada* (São Paulo: n-1 edições, 2019); Beatriz Sarlo, *Tiempo Pasado: Cultura de la memoria y giro subjetivo: una discusión* (Buenos Aires: Siglo XXI, 2012); Michel-Rolph Trouillot, *Silencing the Past: Power and the Production of History* (Boston: Beacon Press, 2015).

3 It is worth noting that museums operate in different ways related to time, space, historical contexts and the different interest groups associated with them. The generalization pointed out here serves only as a signal for the breadth of practices, also multiple, of the perpetuation of logics linked to colonialism in the field of the arts.

pillars of the art world, which have often been anchored in the colonial extraction of resources and knowledge. Others also denounce the co-opting of the term itself.

For art museums and institutional spaces, the beginning of the 21st century was marked by the introduction of notions around decolonization and decolonial theory. Artistic and curatorial practices that shine light around the canon, as well as the cracks and continuities of hierarchical power structures, have gained momentum to express long-standing dissatisfactions, such as the insufficient representation of socially subordinated groups in collections, exhibitions and public programs in museums and art galleries. More lately, these demands have been supplemented by a radical understanding that the regime of visibility and representation is "violently peaceful" and a desire to effectively "shatter [the] nervous, circulatory system" of museums, universities and art history books.[4]

Museums are conservative institutions, at their core it is the conservation nucleus, often defined under notions of protection, restoration, and documentation.[5] The interest to collect and exhibit is frequently linked either to national projects or associative groups, be private or public. Until very recently (prior to the emergence of critical museology and community museums) museums have almost always reflected the tastes and symbolic capital of the ruling political and economic minorities. Associated organizations, such as art galleries and cultural spaces, have often reproduced the same hegemonic interests. This undeniable observation must not, nonetheless, ignore the initiatives that operate outside this landscape and that exist with more or less independence.

Running the risk of sounding redundant, it is important to highlight that museums and other institutional art spaces are not organizations outside society, unsusceptible to the problems arising from broader political disputes that take place beyond its walls. Museums are enveloped in a noble aura and prestige—

4 As an example, among countless others, the movement Decolonize This Place, in the US, has acted with significant visibility between art and activism with the objective of demonstrating responsibility as well as formulating policies for the reparation acts of museums and art institutions, organizing communities and actions around the denouncement of "colonial tendencies in the art world". See: https://decolonizethisplace.org/

5 Definitions about the role of the conservation sector at museums can be found in general museology manuals and are quite revealing. See: André Desvallées, François Mairesse, *Dictionnaire encyclopédique de muséologie* (Paris: Armand Colin. 2011).

to which not even its own intellectuals are immune—that grants them validation through specific quality and value criteria. The selection of works, practices and artists included in museum collections is generally not transparent, in unfolding the relation of its different agents there are identifiable criteria, but few institutions publish guidelines that mobilize such choices and insertions. It is worth pointing out, however, that criteria engendered by galleries, collectors, curators and artists are mobilized by issues beyond notions of "quality," in itself subject to criticism and always relational. These are often made up of fixed points of reference that focus on a particular set of artists and themes. Programs aimed at expanding access to broader audiences have proven effective, and the profile of visitors has indeed changed, most of all through partnerships with programs for the young and for schools. However, visiting a museum is still an activity of distinction. Certainly, different according to contexts, it is possible to dare to say that museums are not primarily visited by persons from the peripheries and the working classes. Furthermore, when looking at museums' boards of managers and directors (including both artistic and executive functions, as well as advisers and patrons), the representation gulf and the disparity between the different social groups becomes even more apparent.

Despite typically reflecting the tastes of elites, museums have at times been open to practices outside the hegemonic domain. By playing the role of a social institution they have addressed political issues and the impact of social movements. It is not a coincidence that we have witnessed paradigmatic changes in their collections and programs, and this is not something new.

Less contradictory, but still highly elucidative, community museums responded to the demands of marginalized social groups and their need for memorialization, collection and dissemination of practices that had frequently been denied access to the artistic spaces of the ruling minority. However, it is important to remind ourselves that these paradigmatic changes, both diverse and ambiguous, have also produced exclusionary patterns, either in charitable or authoritarian ways, particularly in terms of gender and race discrimination and oppression. This is markedly more evident when we look at the hierarchical structures and representation in positions of power, and less so in terms of collections, even though the former is part of the latter. Given the complexity of the theme, what does decolonizing a museum really mean? Very few people call into question the importance of, at the minimum, pluralizing museums. The more radical stances endorse removing any trace of colonialism. In fact, it is not unusual for diversity, plurality, decoloniality and decolonization to be treated as synonyms. In general, this level of confusion has played into the hands of neoliberal policies, reproducing, on the one hand, its directives and, on the other hand, appearing to respond to social demands. One of these notions, which is rather obvious yet causes serious misunderstanding, is that if museums are diverse they are automatically decolonial.

Does the inclusion of Black, women, trans, and Indigenous artists in exhibition programs and, more incisively, in collections, mean that the museum is aligned with decoloniality? It is clear that this is a key step, particularly when we consider that this push has not been the result of the good will of institutional directors, but rather a response to social claims. It is fair to question how the inclusion of these subaltern groups can, for instance, change the standards that validate and qualify the canon. Does "plurality" mean inclusion into or expansion of the canon? Or does it mean a radical rupture from current ways of implementing, thinking, and acting politically within museums?

These issues have played a key role in our understanding of the complex parameters that turn art into Art, which have been well examined in the celebrated essay by the American art historian Linda Nochlin, *Why Have There Been No Great Women Artists?*[6] and in the excellent follow-up by the African American author and cultural critic Michelle Wallace, *Why Are There No Great Black Artists?*,[7] both written before the introduction of the decolonial discourse as the most prominent theme impacting museums. Therefore, it is relevant to question where decoloniality and the need to decolonize began.

At the end of the 1990s, the Peruvian sociologist and humanist thinker Aníbal Quijano described coloniality as a matrix of power that produces racial and gender hierarchies on global and local levels,

6 Linda Nochlin, *Por que não existiram grandes mulheres artistas. Histórias da sexualidade: antologia* (São Paulo: MASP) 16–37.
7 Michelle Wallace, *Por que não existiram grandes artistas negrxs. Histórias das mulheres, histórias feministas: antologia* (São Paulo: MASP).

functioning alongside capital to maintain a modern regime of exploitation and domination.[8] It means, if knowledge is colonized, then one of the keys is to decolonize knowledge. Coloniality remains present despite the end of colonial regimes in the so-called "Global South" persisting in different forms in space and time. As such, coloniality is also manifest in the field of culture. According to Quijano, the coloniality of knowledge is the most difficult mechanism to discern and yet the most crucial to overcome.[9]

In this sense, the compreenhsion of coloniality is based on the configuration of what the Colombian American anthropologist Arturo Escobar systematized around the analytical categories Modernity, Coloniality and Decoloniality.[10] Frequently, this notion of coloniality includes other critical traditions with different genealogies and interests, such as subaltern and postcolonial studies.

Coloniality has also been called by Quijano the *colonial matrix of power*, a long duration mechanism that controls and impacts all aspects and trajectories of human life as far as the oppressed are concerned—to whom the effects are treacherous—and secures the maintenance of the oppressor's privileges. Since the inception of the notion of *coloniality* to discuss the 16th century, transformations in Western discourses and narratives of modernity and civilization have shifted. Some intellectuals point to the first decades of the 21st century as the beginning of the collapse of the global project of Westernization; however, it is possible to question if meant the end of the Western world, or perhaps highlighted the Westernization's ambition: neoliberal globalization.

The notions around decoloniality refer to an extremely diverse set of research and theoretical contributions on coloniality. Some theorists suggest that the genesis can be found in studies on the independence of Haiti, a watershed for the academic research and historiographical revisions that followed. There are also other examples of case studies, such as the Demerara Rebellion of 1823 in present-day Guyana, and other analyses that view marginalized populations as agents with their own autonomy.

8 Aníbal Quijano, "Colonialidad y modernidad/racionalidad," *Peru Indigena*, vol. 13, no. 29.

9 Aníbal Quijano, "Colonialidad del poder, cultura y conocimiento en América Latina," *Amauta*, vol. 9: 113–122.

10 Arturo Escobar, "Mundos y conocimientos de otro modo. El programa de investigación de modernidad/colonialidad latinoamericano," *Tabula rasa*, no. 1, 51–86.

This wide range of research was supplemented by a review of Latin American critical thought and associated conceptual and theoretical strategies. More than a project that has managed to establish itself as a political movement, reaching beyond academic spaces, decoloniality suggests other forms of political imagination, not free from contradiction and conflict. Its unity, if it exists, relies on the problematization of coloniality in its different forms.

Accordingly, modernity does not open with the Enlightenment, nor with the Industrial Revolution. Instead, the watershed is the occupation of America and the control of the Atlantic, including the trading of enslaved people in the 15th and 16th centuries. In addition to this the constitutive dynamics of colonialism, the capitalist world-system, and its specific forms of global-scale accumulation and exploitation. Coloniality is, therefore, a planetary phenomenon marked by asymmetrical power, space, and time relations.[11]

The asymmetry of these power relations between the West and the 'non-westerns' entails the subordination of the practices and subjectivities of the people affected by the hierarchies imposed by colonization. This process reinforces Eurocentrism as a specific form of production of knowledge and subjectivity in modernity, connecting museums to reflections around the decolonial, particularly post-2000s, when the decolonization of art institutions has become an urgent matter. Projects are widely varied, but we could cite here the conceptual revision of ethnological and ethnographic museums into art museums; the renovation of collections including more works by women, and indigenous and black artists; and also large-scale exhibitions and biennials curated by non-white curators and collectives.

Nonetheless, the problem still persists, as the epistemic basis and *raison d'être* of museums, as modern institutions, are rooted in the colonial rationale, regardless of whether a particular museum was conceived to assert a nation-state narrative and its associated legacy processes and memory discourses, or if it is considered an organization that can influence power structures by, for example, exercising,

11 Pablo Quintero, Patrícia Fuguera, Paz Concha Eliyalde. "Uma breve história dos estudos decoloniais." Available at: https://masp.org.br/uploads/temp/temp-QE1LhobgtE4MbKZhc8Jv.pdf

or not, a visibility mechanism—to exhibit and be exhibited.[12] If there is an epistemological rift and the museum is the product of historicity, of a colonial episteme, if decoloniality presupposes a radical displacement of this institution, wouldn't the decolonial museum be a non-museum, demanding the end of the institution?

This reflective exercise is necessary to understand whether diversity initiatives in museums really mean the overcoming of these contradictions or if the pluralization of collections and public programs is really enough to solve the problem. Even though many curators and art institutions worldwide have adopted unprecedented inclusion policies, the integration of histories that were previously made invisible inside museums has been proven insufficient, even recognizing its relevance. In fact, when these efforts are not carefully implemented, the result can be institutional tokenization, which serves to reinforce and maintain power hierarchies. Such institutional conditions, along with the use of classificatory categories such as non-Western or global art, in opposition to canonical art impact and restrict curatorial practices that could be effectively radical. It is necessary to be aware of the extent to which colonial structures keep playing an insidious discriminatory role, particularly in terms of the hierarchy of functions, wages and positions of power and decision-making within institutions, often left out of this reflection; these are not mere narratives, they are concrete policies of exclusion. In fact, we have not witnessed the creation of mechanisms that allow for an effective representation in collection and exhibition policies. Even though a diverse focus has been prioritized, points of view and attitudes have remained complacent and subordinate to the perspective of the "white specialist".

The Indigenous, the woman, the Black, the Latino—turned into a theme or fetish—have been "given a voice" through others, and rarely by themselves. Several inclusion policies have led to the extreme "racialization" or "folklorization" of artists, denying differences, power struggles and ongoing negotiation processes and conflicts. In turn, the alleged rupture of cliches has triggered the creation of new labels such as the "authentically indigenous",

12 Brenda Caro Cocotle, "Nós prometemos descolonizar o museu: uma revisão crítica da política museal contemporânea." Available at: https://masp.org.br/uploads/temp/temp-X87a1s0ahKuQghS3VJ4D.pdf

to point one example. Non-white artists and curators can act in the international scene as long as they represent their places of origin or communities, reinforcing atavisms. It is plausible to question in which ways the inclusion and visibility of artistic discourses identified as being non-hegemonic challenges museum structures and rationality or, more specifically, articulates relations of power and value. Therefore, the validation or legitimation of artistic discourses seem to result from a sort of "personification of difference," understood in many cases as a place of residence or affiliation to a social or cultural "minority". It is worth questioning how the "claim of dissent" plays into the hands of a certain way of producing value in art, perhaps adopting that same logic one is supposedly criticizing.[13]

In other words, there is frequently the expectation that a Black curator curates a Black-themed exhibition or that a Black artist works with "Black topics". In most cases, recognition has not gone beyond the realm of exhibitions, and even here, more than a first-person expression with all the complexities it might raise, these exhibitions revolve around a discourse of alterity. By claiming an inclusion too related with the expectation and acceptance of the elites, diversity can mean little conflict or historical tension. And even then, how many museum directors or chief curators are Black? How many queer intellectuals feature in your course syllabus? How many indigenous artists are in museum collections? How many working-class professionals hold positions on boards? Avoiding the rhetorical trap of inclusion prompts radical exercises of un-thinking, un-disciplining and un-learning that can at least reformulate the key issues around museums, including dealing with collection, exhibition, cataloguing, programming and access policies, as well as its framework of status quo maintenance, co-optation and power.

The progresses achieved by the opening up of new discourses and practices with the aim of expanding the platform of visibility that the museum represents is identifiable. The remaining question is if the "decolonized" museum is only concerned with not losing status and its role as the main vehicle of the legitimation of artistic discourses and art historiography while institutional management and

13 Ibid.

organization policies continue to use criteria that are closer to those of the culture industry in its neoliberal version.

Decoloniality as a practice, more than a theoretical frame, could work based on a radical shift of the mechanisms ruling art institutions. No single project or answer will solve the problem, which does not mean restricting the radical imaginative exercise that rejects this world in favor of the one we are able to aspire to in our dreams.

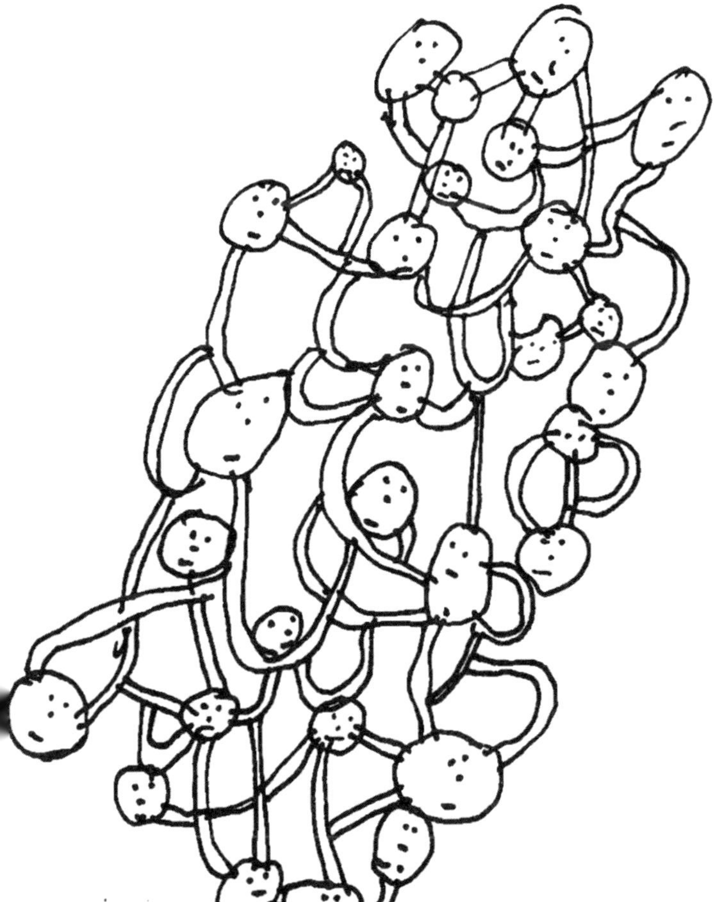

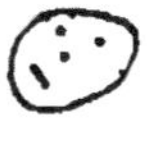

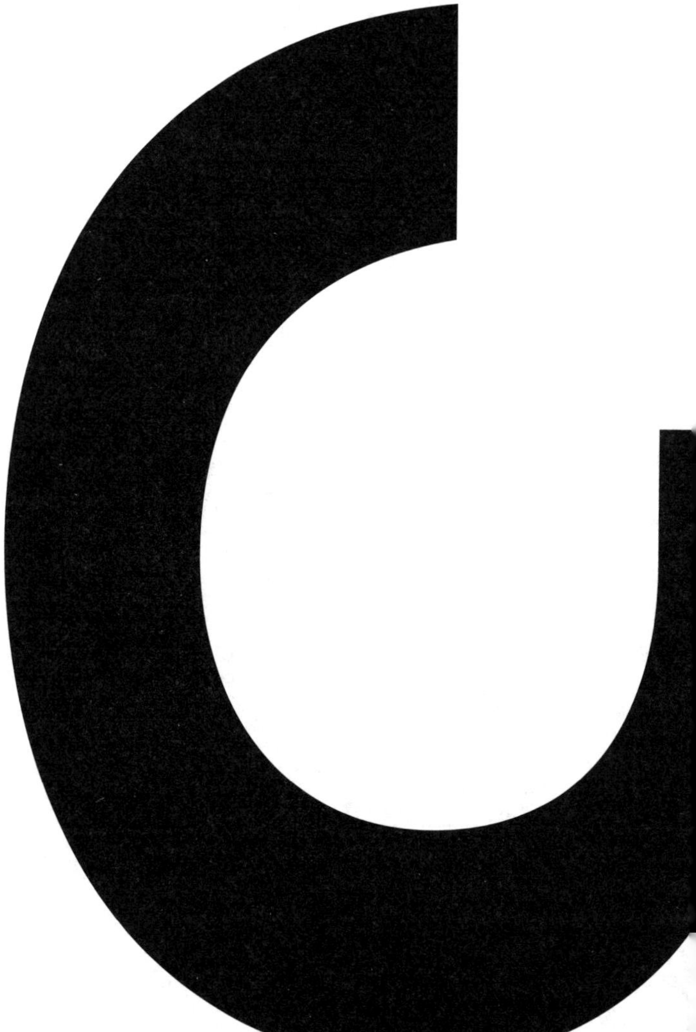

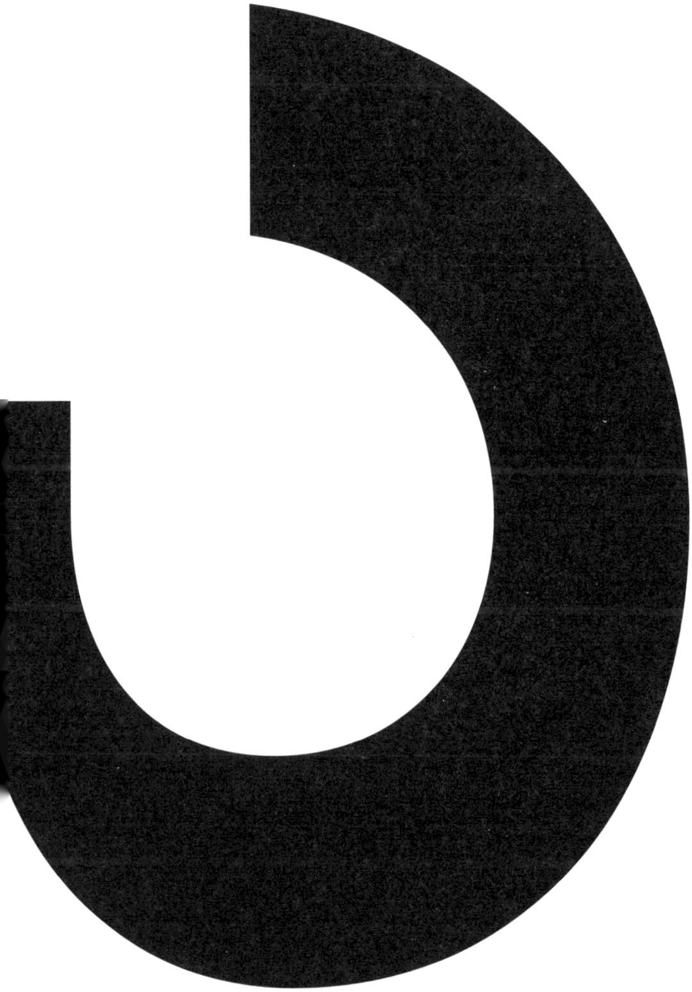

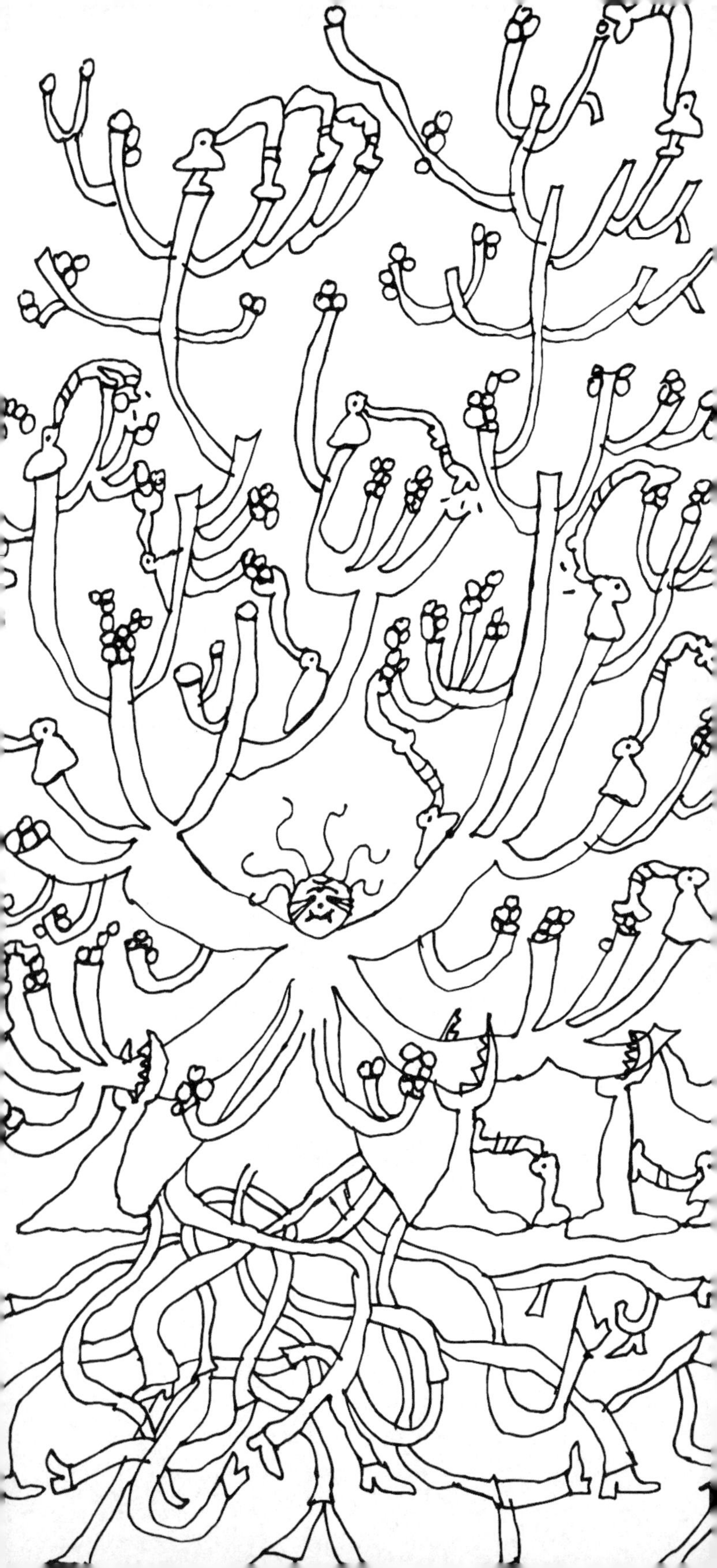

ERROR and Its Alliances

A discussion
between
Robert Gabris,
Ábel Ravasz &
Jana Horváthová

Tereza Jindrová We are here today for a follow-up discussion to Robert's project ERROR, which deals with the needs of the Romani non-binary community. The project arose during the author's residency in Košice, where Gabris met with representatives of this multiply-marginalized and disparate group. Their meetings and discussions led to the creation of a physical installation at the Moravian Gallery in Brno on the occasion of the exhibition of laureates of the Jindřich Chalupecký Award (September 9, 2021 to February 27, 2022), which was composed of collaborative photography and texts. The installation was then followed by the process-based section of the project, of which today's discussion is a part. Together, through a kind of free conversation, the participants will analyze the current situation of multiply-marginalized identities, their origins, and their position in relation to social events in Slovakia and the Czech Republic. The discussion will address one of the key questions of the ERROR project, which is how to tangibly improve the situation of groups representing queer Romani physicality.

Robert Gabris Ok, so to start with, I'd like to emphasize one thing. I'm not sure whether, when we talk about the Romani non-binary community, we are talking only about it or about the Romani community as a whole—because there's no way to actually separate them. But at the same time, I don't want anyone to think that I am pigeonholing all Roma into one group, because that is not the case. We already know that this group can't be homogenized at all—it is not homogenous—so I am always careful when I talk about them, and I try to separate them, but I don't know if we will succeed here. It often seems almost unbearable to talk about it. With this, I'm building on the discussion about how this problem that I have is so existential and so acute that it's really difficult to somehow diplomatically get over it and start using some big words to address a society that is constantly pushing me, my family, and the people I know around me out of these affairs. So, I have a very big problem with that, and that's why I thought of one such possibility. While doing ERROR, it occurred to me that what I'm talking about is actually the ultimate utopia, and I don't know whether something like that is at all viable or realistic. And the question that occurred to me was this: Let's imagine society three hundred years from now. Can you imagine no longer having this problem, these pitfalls? Or is this all completely pointless?

Jana Horváthová Oof, three hundred years from now—that's kind of impossible to imagine. But I'm more of an optimist, because I believe that the integration of the Roma will be successful. But on the other hand, the question is whether the Romani nation will be pre- served. In fact, this worries me a little bit because, as I think we all can see, integration often goes hand in hand with assimilation—a somewhat natural assimilation—and that was one of the reasons I came together with people in 1991 and wanted to found a museum—because I saw how quickly Romani values were actually disappearing. On the one hand, we want integration—for society to accept the Roma—but for now, at least here in the Czech Republic, I have a strong feeling that there's not a lot of interest in this—and zero political interest. It's more of a political issue that there's no real interest, but nevertheless, it's being discussed, and some kinds of steps are being taken, and there are certainly some options here. One of them is the Museum of Romani Culture. So, I think that in three hundred years, as long as there are no other problems related to the environment or as long as humanity's not constantly at war, then I hope that we won't see these kinds of situations again. I don't know, but if there are no such turns, I think the Roma of that time will already truly be included in society—even assimilated. And I'm afraid of assimilation because I'd like for Romani culture to retain its values. I'm repeating myself now, and I'll pass the floor, but that's the reason we founded the Museum of Romani Culture.

Ábel Ravasz Thank you too, Robert, for making it possible to create the space for this discussion. And I feel the urge to start by saying that we're dealing with very intimate issues of identity, of marginalization, but that's probably also why we're dealing with it in public like this—because it's not just about the individual, but rather these are societal issues, and I think it's very important to talk about them. Because in the case of minorities, these topics still somehow polarize us, both in the Czech Republic and Slovakia. And it's my perception that, despite the fact that many people are trying to bring these topics to a point of closure, where we would know what we want to do, how we want to treat minorities, these conflicts in some cases are only getting worse, and people who used to be certain that they were on one side are now no longer so certain. Somehow, it's completely breaking down, even among the elites who are trying to help minorities. I think it's because we have an awful lot of things we haven't said, and today we're going to talk about them, so I think that's the first step and an important step. But to answer your specific question, I'm completely convinced that not in three hundred years but rather in one hundred we will have a very different situation here in terms of social groups. And the reason I think so is because I know the history, and when we look at what it was like in our greater region a hundred years ago, what groups lived here in what numbers, compared to what is here now, we see that it has really, really, really changed a lot, and state-based identities have come to the forefront. In the case of the Czech Republic, it's the Czech identity, in the case of Slovakia, of course, the Slovak identity, and regional identities have taken a back seat. There's a certain degree of "revival," but even so, state identities and communities are very strong. And minorities are in a completely different position than they were in at the beginning of the 20th century. We don't know what will happen with the Romani communities, but I strongly agree with what Ms. Horváthová said. I would come back to this from an analytical perspective. Yes, there are various strategies, like where to shift the fate of the Romani communities in the region, and one such possible fate is actually assimilation, meaning that we manage to bring people together so "well" that the culture, the uniqueness of the Roma communities simply dissolves into one big national culture. I agree that this is not what we want. The other pole is when there is a disintegration, meaning that the Romani communities will be further segregated, the Roma culture and Roma identity will become even more marginalized, and in that case the national cultures will not come into normal contact with the minority culture. That's the other pole, which we really do not want, and which, to me, is even worse than assimilation. Assimilation is bad, but this is even worse. And in the middle is this space where we have so-called integration or inclusion. And it's very important to say that inclusion and integration are two-way processes, meaning that yes, the minority moves toward the majority, but the majority also opens up toward the minority. Without that, it won't work. This means that if we're willing to continue this two-sided process and build bridges to each other, I think the future will be quite nice and pleasant. Nowadays we are no longer dealing with some of the national issues that were still completely dominant in the 20th century, and I'm not talking about minorities that were deported or exterminated—it would be cynical for me to comment on it like that. I mean other things, for example, as regards new minorities. These are being addressed even more intensively. We'll see whether the Romani community versus the majority moves toward reconciliation, toward integration, or whether we'll see further conflicts. But as I said, I'm rather optimistic.

RG I'm really glad you brought up the concept of bridges, because there's all this vocabulary like assimilation and integration, and I always have the connotation from postcolonial studies that this is supremacist language, that we have to assimilate to others. The bridge really works from both sides, and that's very important to know, because in my opinion, or in my surroundings, society always suggests that we're the weaker ones and that we have to adapt to the others, and then we'll be assimilated. But did I understand correctly, Ms. Horváthová, that you are against the Roma assimilating into mainstream society?

JH I can't say I'm not. That's everyone's choice to make. I would be sorry if the Roma dissolved, but I think there's something every system, whether the Czech Republic or the Slovak Republic, should address, and that is the uneven playing field. Social exclusion is a big problem in the Czech Republic, even bigger in Slovakia, and that's what concerns me—that the entire complex of social exclusion makes it impossible for Roma to benefit from society. On the contrary, they are accused of abusing the system, but that's just a consequence of social exclusion, and this is already known. However, I really feel that this is a kind of political issue, because political parties have no interest in solving the Romani problem. They can't campaign on it—they'd lose voters. So, de facto, what is being said in our country—that we are trying to integrate the Roma—is more of a proclamation, and it's not systematic, because it's unacceptable for the government and the large political parties that make up the government. The government will never connect on this issue, and it's not their mutual problem. It's something that's completely in the background. Although we have a Romani council in the government, it has absolutely no power and will accomplish nothing. It's merely cosmetic, so to speak. Because, for example, it bothers me that for thirty years already certain people here have been trying to ensure that Romani children aren't segregated in Czech education. I won't talk about Slovakia. We are trying to make sure that all children—not just Romani children but simply all children in this society—learn a little bit about Romani people in school because young people, the middle generation, and even more so the older generation are awash in myths and stereotypes about the Roma. I run into it everywhere. It bothers us and impedes the museum's activities, and that's just the beginning. It's a huge, complex problem. For example, just including information about the Roma in school curricula is simply impossible. I've been running into this for the last three years, that it's impossible, because even at the Ministry of Education there's no understanding for it, you know. It's a big problem that can really snowball.

RG But you're working really hard on it, because your museum's agenda is to make sure that there really is an awareness.

JH Yes, and that's just it. At our museum, we offer excursions into history, into civics, so that schools can come and learn something. But when these schools come, it's always at the initiative of one enlightened teacher or sometimes principal, but they have to somehow frame it within the curriculum of their existing educational programs. It's usually very hard to find the time to come to the museum at all. We need it to be implemented within the system, so that there doesn't have to be a guerilla teacher, and it's simply established. If you go abroad—to America, to Los Angeles, to the Holocaust Museum—you'll see one yellow school bus after another stopping there, because it's routinely included in the curriculum. No matter the school, you simply have to visit the Holocaust Museum. It's just normal there. But it's not normal here, so I think we have room for improvement.

ÁR Well, I'm only going to respond in general terms, because I feel the need to say that as far as these institutions, or rather minority institutions, are concerned, I think that it's necessary to differentiate or separate the different stages of what the state can do for minorities. The first stage is recognition of the minority, and in the case of the Roma, this has only happened in the last few decades. For example, in Slovakia—but probably in all of Czechoslovakia—until 1991 people couldn't indicate their Romani nationality in the census. The Roma were perceived as a social group, not an ethnic group. In other words, we took this first step just thirty years ago, recognizing that being Roma isn't a lifestyle, it's not a social status—it's a nationality. I think today no one operates with the notion that Romani is not a nationality. I have to say that personally I hate it when someone says that the Roma are an ethnic group. Romani is a nationality like any other, albeit very much a special nationality in that it has no homeland—its homeland is everywhere and nowhere. I am of Hungarian nationality, and for Slovak Hungarians, the home state that supports this minority is Hungary. Roma are able to support each other either between communities or in relation to their own state, but not in relation to a motherland. So, the first stage is recognition, which is more or less complete—I say more or less. The second stage is creating institutions. This is the stage we're in now, and I don't think we're doing very well. We have some things which are functional and that-need to exist, for example, the Museum of Romani Culture and some other things, but where are our minority schools? You said you weren't going to talk about Slovakia, so I will speak to the Slovak context, as it's what I know best. We have four hundred fifty thousand Roma in Slovakia and no more than ten schools in the Romani language. That's outrageous. Of course, not every Romani speaks the Romani language at home, but about half do. Where are the schools? Where are the institutions? We have some non-profit organizations and cultural associations, but we need to strengthen the officially organized cultural establishments of the Romani national minority—to strengthen all of these institutions—which is happening now but I think not as quickly as we'd like. A lot of conflicts arise from this because a significant portion of the so-called Romani intelligentsia feels enormous frustration that these institutions are not being created or are being created in the wrong way or are being created and then abolished. But I will also say that this is only the second level, and on the third level we still need to create a third thing, which, I will repeat, is these communication bridges. Because we can see that when a country creates institutions for minorities and then lets these institutions close in on themselves, the communities around them disintegrate. This is a criticism of multiculturalism—it creates some small islands, but the islands aren't connected.

By the way, anyone who criticizes multiculturalism in the Czech or Slovak context is, from my perspective, someone who doesn't know what it is they are talking about, because we haven't even gotten there yet. But when we get there, we will have to—and we already can—lay the foundations for the bridges that will connect these communities. Because it's pointless to create all the institutions the minority needs in communities with high Romani populations if we then see that in those communities the Roma go to one area, and the non-Roma go to another area, to one cultural center, to another cultural center, one school, another school. We mustn't forget this. Yes, we more or less have the recognition now, and we're building institutions, but let's also start building the bridges that will connect the people who go to these various institutions.

RG I have to admit, Ábel, that I've thought a lot about the Romani nationality, and I only recently discovered that it exists—and I've been dealing with this for a long time. I mean, I knew it existed, but now I really accept it. And during the census—it was last year—there was this conflict in the media about who we really are, and to tell you the truth, I really didn't have an opinion. I suddenly didn't know where to put myself—on what side—whether I belonged to the Romani nationality or the Slovak one. It really stems from anger as well, that this is another consequence of oppressive politics, where we are forced to decide because we are born in bodies that just... You just have to think about this strategy that other kids at school or people at work don't have to think about.

JH I just want to ask: In the Czech Republic, you could declare as many identities as you want—you could be Czech and also Romani and whatever else—so it was presumably the same for you too, wasn't it?

RG Yes, but on the other hand, I liked that it became a topic for the Roma themselves. I didn't care all that much about society, but I did care that Roma would now start to take a position on this again, and that was interesting. What we need is awareness, so we really start to think politically, so that non-voters become voters, so that we care, and not just a few of us. But I have another question, Ábel, which I can't answer for myself. It's like a double-edged sword. Are there any strategies we ourselves can use to deal withthis? Or do we in fact need the state, because we can't get by without it, and my family won't have toilets if the state doesn't cooperate? Maybe this question stems from the fact that I myself don't know how to advise my family on what strategies to create in order to somehow make it in this society.

ÁR Okay, very briefly on the census and identity, and then I'll get to your question. So, as you indicated, Ms. Horváthová, in Slovakia we also have the option to declare more than one nationality, for the first time now. We fought for this for a long time, and yes, some people argued about what to write, because there are people who until the 1980s had no possibility at all to express that they're Roma—the older generations were used to writing down Slovak or Czech nationality, then for a while they wrote down Romani, and now they can write down more than one. It's chaotic, but I think these are the first steps toward people being able to have a normal relationship to their identity. I've always said that declaring a nationality is a completely neutral act which doesn't help anyone, because the state is for the majority nationality regardless, but if someone has a relationship to a minority, then they have to admit it. A lot of different opportunities for financing culture, education, language rights, and so forth are based on the census, so I tried to frame this situation or conflict of majority versus minority identity completely pragmatically—if you write minority, you help someone, and if you write majority, you don't help anyone, and if you can't decide, you write both. Of course, and this is just parenthetical, there are also Romani communities that have another mother tongue. In Slovakia, for example, the Hungarian-speaking Roma could write down Hungarian, Slovak, and Romani nationality, but they had to choose only two of these options. It was more difficult for them, but that's a very specific situation.

And now to your question. Again, that's how the Slovak situation is, but the Czech situation is very similar in that we have a huge diversity of Romani communities. We have rural communities, urban communities, well-integrated communities, poorly integrated communities, settlements, housing estates, all sorts of things, and there's no recipe for success so that I can just go somewhere and say, "If you tick these ten boxes, you will definitely move forward." There's a big toolbox, and you have to choose the tools that suit the situation, but what can't be missing is a kind of triptych of collaboration. You mentioned some of it, but I'll add that third level. You need the state, you need the municipality, you need the community. And none of these actors will move on their own. The state can come up with all sorts of good policies, but if it doesn't reflect the local level, it's all for nothing. We don't live in countries where the state can execute its policies by itself—it needs both local governments and people for that. Local government's good ideas are useless if the state doesn't create the tools or if they don't consult the local community. This is such a classic thing I always say, and we often see it, even with well-meaning mayors, that they sit in the municipal offices, maybe even late into the night, thinking about what the Roma in that community need. But for them to actually go there and ask someone how they see it—that'll never happen. And until that happens, any well-meaning thoughts will remain just thoughts. Which means that yes, there needs to be that level of collaboration, because there's a local community there. The state and municipality can try very hard, but if the local community doesn't reciprocate that effort, community leaders need to emerge to help put these things together. But in my experience—and I have honestly been to several hundred settlements and communities, especially in Slovakia but also in neighboring countries—there are no Romani communities where a man or woman won't eventually step up to lead. They will step up, but they need to be given the space to show themselves. And then, once we have this cooperation, the states create the tools, the municipality chooses from among them with the help of the local community, and the local community accepts the solution. Then something can be accomplished, but without that, it's very, very difficult. About us without us doesn't work, whether it's in the relationship between the state and the local government, the local government and the municipality, the municipality and the community, or the community and the state.

JH I would perhaps add—if I may, because it's quite a broad topic now—but I'd still like to go back to social exclusion. The socially excluded, of course, are not a partner of the state or even of the local government. I see a problem in the fact that we really need the state and the local government to acknowledge Romani leaders and Romani representatives, because without them, integration really isn't possible. But the state doesn't yet realize this, or it has the luxury of not needing to realize it. It doesn't really want to. This is why there isn't a single Romani representative in the Czech parliament. And that's a terrible mistake, because many educated Roma are asking for it. We want to be in parliament, we want to take care of our own affairs, but society isn't interested. Society still doesn't really know that it needs this. I keep going back to social exclusion because, as you said, Robert: What about these people? They can't help themselves, and that's what social exclusion is about. It's the needy who can't actually help themselves if they have no leaders and if the system somehow pulls them in and if the system, as I said, has little interest. So, I'd like to go back to what the so-called Romani problem is. It's a term I don't accept, but I want to use it to show that what is being referred to as the Romani problem, or even the problems of coexistence, is not something that is caused by the fact that we have socially excluded people here, a large percentage of which are Roma, but that the problem is also that the majority has no interest in Romani people. And the second part of that problem is that the Roma are not accepted. It's hard for them to come to terms with their identity because admitting one's Romani identity today is a risk. It's a stigma, and only those who are already at a certain level of education can bear that stigma. I'm saying that very few can actually afford the luxury of admitting their Romani origins. It's simply a stigma, and the public doesn't realize it, you know. I don't know if you remember when one prominent Czech artist, or even world artist, Kateřina Šedá, published the supposedly great book *Průvodce brněnským Bronxem* about our neighborhood of Brnox and received the Magnesia Litera prize for it. Society fawned over it. And the Roma were unhappy because she was making fun of them. And then even my non-Romani friends, who I otherwise like very much, didn't get it, couldn't understand it at all, and they said:"You've got some kind of complex, there's just no way, this here is a great book..." But look at the book. It's simply a mockery. It's having fun at the expense of the Roma, and my question is how the majority doesn't see this. This is absolute proof that there are two parallel worlds here that don't communicate with each other, and the Roma who are working for integration, the leaders, are trying to connect these parallel worlds and crying out: "We want to run for office, we want to be members of parliament, we want to take care of our own affairs." But the majority isn't listening to them.

RG Thank you for making this comment about Kateřina Šedá. I really appreciate it, because I have the exact same opinion, and I'm really angry that things like this even come out in society, and then these kinds of people are the most popular artists.

ÁR Robert, can I respond to the second part of what our colleague said, about Romani leaders and representation? Because I think that's an extremely relevant and important topic. It is incomprehensible and shameful when a country with a significant national minority doesn't have adequate representation of that minority in its political system, and I think that's a basic fact. Again, if we go back to Slovakia, since 1991 we have had a total of four or five representatives on the National Council in that entire period, and not even at one time. It has not yet been possible for a Romani person to hold a ministerial position, and yet the Roma make up almost ten per cent of the population. In the Czech Republic, it's less, but I still think it's a very significant community that should be represented.

JH And it's the largest minority in the Czech Republic.

ÁR Yes, and it may happen soon in Slovakia that it will be quite even between Hungarians and Roma, but it's not a competition and this is a very large ethnic community. But one thing you said—it's not that I have a problem with it, but I have a little bit of a different experience, and I have a lot of respect for community leaders of any nationality who are really trying to connect worlds. When minorities get some form of representation, then the representative, especially if it's a single person, tries to monopolize the representation, and at that point we have a problem because the minority closes in on itself. The parallel worlds not only do not connect, but they grow further apart. I think this is important to say, so, I'm not just recognizing that decisions regarding minorities should not be made without these minorities. Rather, I'm demanding that they not be. But at the same time, I condemn it when people say that only those from a particular minority should make decisions about that minority, because that also segregates, just from the other side.

RG I don't see it that way. When I first did ERROR, I also created an exclusive space in an inclusive institution, where no one but us had the right to enter, but I understand the other side as well. It's the restitution aspect of our work, the absolute distrust of allowing society into our spaces. When I first started creating ERROR—and now I'm mixing topics a bit—I met people who are multiply-marginalized, meaning they're excluded from society but also from their own families. Many of them live in tents and do any kind of work just to survive. This community has a huge amount of distrust for society because they are completely excluded, and so it also occurred to me that if, in dealing with this issue, we're going to open up the space to everyone, we first need to close it so that we can find intersections among ourselves. The problem I see is that although there are enough of us—and I know of people who would do this work—we don't know each other. Every month I hear about someone who is suddenly doing something similar to me, but we don't know each other. We need a space. Society has to give us a space where we can first connect to each other and hash it out. But we don't even like each other, we don't talk to each other. We talked about that a lot today, that we're there, but we want to split it with this society so that you're not the ones who are moving further away on the other side. To tell you the truth, the anger I have inside me comes from the awareness that I will never belong in this country. I'll never never be a part of it. I'll either be something less or something more, but I'll never be on the same level. And again, that's the question. Is this really the case? That these spaces—and this is more to you, Ábel—is it really the case that they need to be opened up, or do we also have the right, after centuries of colonization, to close the space for a while and start communicating among ourselves and healing our wounds?

ÁR You know, if you give me a question where the only option is whether you have the right, then no matter what you say, I have to answer yes. This question is falsely constructed that way. I think it's important to create safe spaces for minorities—I agree with that. And the question is, where are the borders of that space, who determines who is and is not in that space, and what do we do when that safe space appears safe from one point of view but unsafe from another? What do we do, for example, if we create strong minority local governments, and those governments, that is, ethnic minorities, start doing things against LGBT people within a closed, safe community? What do you do there? The moment you let people close themselves off, they can set their own rules. States are also just closed "safe spaces" for larger nations. When we start creating smaller ones within that, who is going to somehow control it so that those who are otherwise marginalized within the community don't end up with even worse problems than before. Classically, in England and other Western countries, when they gave more space to religious minorities to do their thing, it was very damaging for the women of those communities because they had more traditional, more patriarchal structures. I don't want to generalize, but I think you know what I'm getting at. Knowing the Romani communities, at least in Slovakia, if we increase their autonomy, who will protect LGBT people when we're talking about these things? It's a very, very delicate balance. We need to strengthen autonomy, but closure is always very dangerous for those who aren't a part of the mainstream community that will have autonomy over itself.

JH I may have understood your remark differently, Robert. The way I understood it is that you have some doubts. You feel a lack of mutual interaction among the doubly excluded Roma, even though they are non-binary. So, do you have the right to meet among yourselves and for no one from the majority to have a say in it? I think you absolutely have the right to do that because you have never had that here before. You owe it to yourselves to do it, in my opinion. So, I think you should have no doubt about that. And really, get together, enjoy what you never could. The Roma will exclude you. I know that—it's terrible. Facebook, yes, it's a sewer. But in spite of that, tendencies are visible there. And we have to face it: Not so much the middle generation, but particularly the older generation of Roma are really strongly affected by conservativism, and you probably won't get through to anyone there. But you have to give it time. And there are a lot of people—a lot of Roma—who are rooting for you today, so I think you have to go for it.

RG Certainly, I'm thinking more about these epistemic bodies that no one understands because only we have this episteme. For me, the epistemic body has an almost symbolic meaning—it's the knowledge of Romani bodies (corporeality) formed on the basis of lived events. It's really that experience that we can talk about, but we can only talk about it if these people are relieved of the problems they have, and so it's very difficult. Ábel and I have talked about this—how to connect if there is no real space in the implementation. Because as long as these systemically marginalized corporealities remain in unsafe spaces (such as complete poverty with no resources to heal sick bodies or improve the situation in Romani settlements), their episteme will not be heard. Talking about it without the academic, elitist level requires immense courage and a new space which is inclusive, non-academic, and non-elitist. I know we can't do it alone, which is why I asked you what strategies you suggest for this. Really, because as an artist, I can't cover this topic at all. I don't have any resources for it. But who do we ask, where do we go, and how do we trust a society that only accepts us when we are silent?

ÁR This microphone gets heavier and heavier as this discussion goes on. You always say a lot of things that could be unpacked, even word by word. For example, whether society only accepts the Roma if they are silent—that's an extremely important topic, but it's always like that with minorities. The moment a minority has any kind of demands, it's disloyal. "What are they doing here? They should be happy to live here at all. Why don't they leave?" So that's one topic, but that was peripheral to your big question. Well, my opinion is that, compared to other generations, we have a tremendous opportunity to communicate directly with people who are in marginalized life situations.

We are now seeing a massive democratization of the communication space, which has its advantages and disadvantages. We're currently discussing this in the context of a state-wide lockdown because some people get their information from conspiracy groups, so that's the dark side of this democratization of the communication space. The bright side is that everybody really can find people who are similar, and people who are similar need to be empowered to communicate, to have what we can call common spaces—so that they can exchange experiences. I can't advise you on this. No one can advise anyone on these matters. We need to generate that energy, that power, down there together. I did my fieldwork—I'm a sociologist, so that's what I call it—in southern Gemer in Slovakia, where we set up a network of activists. The network has this logic, that we always think about power over someone—I have power over you, or you have power over me. There's another form of power too, and Hannah Arendt says that it's when we get together and start putting pressure on things. That's the horizontal version of power—non-oppressive, non-violent, not over anyone, but the power to do something together. And I think that's how we need to empower excluded groups, excluded people. Let them come together, let's help them come together, but it's very, very sensitive. The more marginalized the position, the more difficult it is. And I'm not sure, when we're talking about multiple marginalization, if it's completely productive to always create a separate group for every nth marginalization. For example, when Vietnamese LGBT women in the Czech Republic have a problem, is it productive for those three women to get together and solve it on their own? No. We probably need to think about how to address one part, a second part, a third part of that larger marginalization. I really don't have a recipe, but what I will always say is that we need to create space for people to connect and work things out together—and to me, the less exclusionary, the less closed off to others, the better. And I'm certainly not going to bring up the issues of contemporary radical feminism, where people talk about who can advise whom among feminists, who is a real feminist, who is just a fake feminist, and things like that. It turns out that if we start cutting away and saying, "You're no longer this, neither are you," then we can create a sandbox where everyone looks the same—but is it productive? I'll just let that question float in the air.

RG Ms. Horváthová, your institution is very specific. Do you think you can cover and create interdisciplinary strategies between art and the real experience of your local community?

JH That's certainly terribly difficult, but what we try to do first of all is to offer information, especially to the majority, who lack information and are therefore held captive to stereotypes about Romani people. Apart from that, and in relation to the Roma, because we—and this is our vision—are equally directed toward the majority and toward the Romani minority—we don't focus more on one and less on the other—we try to open paths for the Roma to the roots of their own identity. It's what the Roma need in order to be able to live in this or any other society as equal partners and not have "complexes" and thus be able to open up the path toward engagement with the majority—because without coming to terms with one's identity, it is difficult to create equality. This is also my personal experience from adolescence, when I too had a complex because of my origins, and it was only coming to terms with it that offered me a kind of way forward. But going back to our museum, that's a very difficult question you asked me—or rather, task—but what we really want... We're simply a classical museum, a classical institution of memory, so on the one hand, for a long time there really was a deficit here in that the Romani people were not documented in any museum at all. It is well-known that although objects of Romani provenance could be found in many museums, especially in Slovakia, they were there incognito—they weren't there as Romani objects—and that was seen regularly before 1990. So that's what actually prompted us to start our own museum—it was missing. And today I'm sorry that we're still the only such a museum, because perhaps there should be this kind of museum of Romani culture in every large city where Romani and non-Romani people live together, and that has yet to happen. But this is exactly what the Romani people are talking about. For example Michal Mižu Mižigár, a history student at Central European University in Budapest, is now studying, I think, in Britain. We have a big interview with him in the second edition of the book *Amendar: Pohled do světa romských osobností* and he explains it so beautifully there, that actually throughout primary school and even secondary school he had a kind of complex because nobody spoke about the Roma. He felt this strange attitude that his teachers and classmates had toward him, and it wasn't until university, when he was studying Romani studies, that he was liberated for the first time because he suddenly heard about himself, his family, his culture, and he understood that Czech or Slovak children have this right in the first grade, but Romani children don't.

RG I'm still thinking about the center and actually about some real possibility for connecting the art world and art institutions which even today are—and I know this from my own experience—white. They're very dominant and don't allow that otherness into their own structures. How do we make those institutions inclusive so that we can actually be in them? And this is really just a commentary on what you said—that this knowledge is really needed, that it needs to be disseminated in society.

JH That's a tough question. This microphone really is heavy. I'd be happy to pass it to our colleague Mr. Ravasz, but this is what our museum is still struggling with. Although we're a state museum, frankly our position among state museums is not very complicated, because, of course, the ministries are full of officials who are just normal people who are probably about the same as most of the public. We know what the opinion polls are like, so maybe they're subconsciously affected by something called stereotyped thinking. And unfortunately, we feel it today and every day, because our museum's importance isn't generally accepted. We still have to fight so that we all realize, as it were, that the museum is important not only for the Roma but for the majority—and perhaps even more so for the majority than for the Roma.

ÁR So, it's difficult with institutions, because if we don't have any, that's obviously a problem. Then the first smaller, separate institutions are created—let them work it out among themselves, see you later, nobody cares. It's hard to disconnect, or rather, it's hard to change this situation, hard to invite non-Roma into a Romani institution, non-Hungarians into a Hungarian institution, and ghettoization is always a real threat. Then the minorities trickle into the standard institutions, and of course, first they get into the ones where the people who make up the institutions are already a little bit more open toward minorities. Then the first ones come, and they start making a fuss, asking "Why don't you give us more?" And then this, and then that, and then what happens is that the more tolerant ones find themselves under a massive barrage, and the idiots who would never let a living Roma into their institutions just sit and drink their coffee, satisfied because the ones who are supposed to be allies are fighting amongst themselves. It's an extremely difficult balance. Because yes, when someone from a minority is invited into a pro-majority institution, they shouldn't simply be grateful that they're there—they should lay claim to that space. But you also have to understand that on the other side there was probably also an effort to open up and find a space for cooperation, and I think that we have to gradually make all of our institutions, both minority and majority, more inclusive. For example, when we created a new fund in Slovakia in 2017 to support minority cultures, called Kultminor, that is exactly what we tried to combine. This means that every minority has its part, every minority has some money, and decisions about the money are made by the people from that minority. But we also made a section for intercultural projects so that it's not just about everybody shutting themselves in their own little pens and being there and not dealing with anything. We also made space for communication. If I had my way, it would be fifty-fifty—half for minority cultures and half for intercultural dialogue. Realistically, intercultural dialogue will never get that big of a share, but I think this is the way to go, and we also see it around the world—this is my big research topic—that we have a lot of good ideas at the local level in terms of intercultural issues and how to bring communities together, like some tips and tricks, for example, to bring parents of different nationalities together through their children and things like that. But we have to push, push, push this and be sympathetic to the other side of the argument and not be sympathetic to those who are intolerant and close their institutions.

RG Thank you, Ábel. We're reaching the end of our discussion, and I'm very glad that there are an awful lot of lingering open questions. It's a good incentive for us to meet again, and perhaps, in conclusion, I will give the floor to you. But first I want to say one very important thing that's on my mind—for me, it was very important in this project to find alliances, and I think about who those alliances are, whom to entrust with something so intimate, and that is why I am very glad that you are here and that you both accepted my invitation. I appreciate it very much, and mainly it really motivates me as a person to keep digging into these politics, these art politics, and to really remain intensively visible in our society, because I think art is a perfect tool and a very sensitive tool that we can use to deal with these things.

ÁR I think that was a very nice final word. I thank you for the opportunity to participate in this discussion.

JH I agree, and I was very honored that you invited me here. I would like to congratulate you again on winning the Jindřich Chalupecký Award, because from my perspective, it is a huge breakthrough. And I agree with you that art is the way.

This discussion took place on December 2, 2021 as part of the accompanying program of the Jindřich Chalupecký Award 2021 exhibition.

Why Am I so White?

Zai Xu

Overwhelming stress is reaching new highs every day. Minute by minute, I started to ignore it. But every now and then the stress reminds me that it is even stronger and more powerful than before. It started with the first news appearing. It was all over the internet. "There is a new disease spreading in China." It was the first time after a long period of calm, that stress returned. I wasn't sure what was happening. Probably like all of us. I was more confused than clear headed. One thing was sure: There was a new feeling of anxiety that I hadn't felt in a long time.

I was born with a color in a white society. I started to ignore my own skin. Sounds fine to me I would say, it should be normal to not care about my own skin color. There should be no reason to care. It became a problem when I started to lose the grasp of my own skin, with my own color, my culture, my identity—they started to slowly transform into something unfamiliar. Suddenly I started to forget who I am. It's not because I didn't care about my skin color. The difference between me and them. It's because I cared too much. I started to be alienated from myself. I was scared and intimidated.

Living with color in a white society is a full-time job. People around me make sure to always remind me that I'm not from here. We are not the same.

It started from the very beginning of my life. I was exoticized. They usually reminded me with small things. When I was a child, I didn't know that I was different from my classmates. There is a school play in kindergarten and I would really love to play St. Nicolas. I didn't know that only I was not fit to play him. I was only fit to play the devil, because I was darker than everyone else. I grew up with many more cases that I didn't understand. When I started to recognize the difference, I slowly started to choose to be the one without any color, like the people around me. I started to play the act that I always wanted to play.

Why am I so white? I remember that when I was around thirteen years old, I was bullied—I hated my skin and especially my eyes. I wanted nothing to do with the way I looked. I wanted to be white. I chose to be white the same way as I chose to ignore the stress. I had already forgotten my name, why couldn't I forget my skin?

There is a new disease appearing in China. When I first heard that I got chills down my spine. I was not afraid of the disease. I was not sad about the people who were going through hard surreal times. It was like I couldn't feel any emotions toward the outside world. I was full of other thoughts and just couldn't think about anything else. I became scared to go out in the street. I started to spend more and more time at home. At home where I was shielded against people. There was no quarantine yet. Going out became less and less joyful and being with other people became more unbearable. I still keep saying to myself, that there is nothing to be scared off. People won't be scared of me just because of the color of my skin. They won't judge me or hate me, will they? But they already were.

It all came in waves, a first wave, a second. I'm not writing about the virus but the anxiety that I felt. It all came hammering down, stronger and stronger.

The air became harder and harder to breathe as the disease spread from one place to another.

The disease is taking my freedom away day by day. I'm sitting outside in the park, smoking a cigarette on the way back from the grocery shopping. Why don't I feel like I used to feel? Why do they watch my every step? My skin is the only thing that is left, the only thing that is still visible. I feel naked. My skin that I was trying so hard to hide and forget.

In a conversation I had with my mother not long ago, she said that if everything is going to end up really bad and people would have to stand in the line for emergency aid, our family would be waiting at the end of the line. We would be lucky if we even get any support. I objected against her—I'm a Czech citizen. She answered, even though you are a Czech citizen, you would only be at the end of the line just in front of us. This part of the conversation keeps coming back to me and I can't stop thinking about it. Sometimes I still question it—it seems far-fetched and really hard to imagine. It seems far from reality, far from the progressive times we are living in. But despite everything, it's real for my mother. It is everyday life and the struggles that hide behind the curtains.

There is a memory that came back to me during the time of writing this text. When I was studying at elementary school, almost every other day I played outside near the school with some classmates. We were playing as ninjas, building bases from bushes, running around as warriors. One day we were playing on a steep hill—it was our base. It was the perfect location: There were some bushes where you could hide and the peak of the hill where you could see everything around you. I don't remember specifically how it actually escalated. But I remember the ache and how I cried. I think I wasn't physically hurt, but still I can feel the pain even today. I remember I was crying and telling everyone that I'm not like them. I'm not one of the Chinese. Do you think I like to be Asian? I was desperate and trying to distance myself from everything that could link me to my skin. I remember screaming I don't like China, I don't like Mao, screaming and avoiding the little things I knew about my origin. The little things I knew from watching television with my parents. I didn't really understand what it actually was. Only one thing was important to me. It was somehow connected to my skin.

The new disease has shed light on lot of things which used to be hidden. It brought back the memories that had gone away and made me remember the feelings that were almost forgotten. It's like how I used to eat sunflower seeds with my family. Cracking them open one by one. You are always going to find some spoiled ones.

At the beginning of February, I got a call from my school asking about the possibility of me getting the new disease. They were mapping out the situation across the board from school to school. The fear and ignorance overflowed from every part of the nation. Misunderstanding and lack of information made it worse. The mapping was mainly targeted towards foreign students. It was the beginning of a new semester and new students were arriving at school. The situation was escalating really quickly and everyone was trying to keep up. The only thing left to do was to react. In the fast chaotic turn of events, the hygiene station decided to target people coming from the risk areas. As a result of this decision and the previously mentioned context, a new door to stigmatization, stereotypes and also racism was opened. Instead of targeting people who have just been to the risk areas, they targeted everyone whose skin was different than theirs.

During the pandemic I slowly started to go out on a lot of walks. I couldn't stand being at home anymore even though I was scared. I mainly needed to wind down all of the rapid changes that had happened in the short period of time. So shocked that I didn't recognize myself. The walks calmed me down, I didn't know where I was heading to. Turning to the left or right where my mind went to. Some days I even walked through half of the whole city.

On several of those walks I was the only person on the street. I didn't notice anyone around—everyone was hiding in their shelters. It was the most apocalyptic view that I have ever witnessed. Sometime a car drove by me in a rush, like it was escaping from something. I really thought that I had woken up in a ghost town. It felt like everyone had left me.

It was like the disease had a skin also, skin that was similar to my own.

It was like I had a big dirty yellowish stain all over my body, that needed to be cleaned. Washed away the same way we started to wash our hands, very carefully and properly. The stain couldn't be hidden away using a face mask. It couldn't be hidden away even using my clothes. The one big dirty stain marked out who I am, marked out that I'm not like you, not the same. Marked out that I'm the sick one and the one who is below you. The one that doesn't deserve to be here.

Am I scared to visit a doctor? I should probably go and have my health checked. I should visit a psychiatrist, a dentist, my teeth are turning more and more yellowish. Everyone is still in panic mode right now, and you just feel the tension in the air. They just announced that you can start to visit hospitals again. I never liked visiting doctors, but I think I've never been scared of them. I could already imagine how people would look at me. What if they make a mistake? And I would be taken as a disease? Am I the disease? They would probably take me into the lab and test me, make experiments on me. It's going to be all over the news, we are now developing the vaccines from the sample of this yellow virus. Maybe not. That would be funny. What if they reject me? We don't want you here. You are the reason people are dying. Maybe I wouldn't even be allowed to enter. The hospital is virus free, free from me.

Overflowing with emotions and the small pieces of memories that are now gaining new meanings, I was left lost in the swirl of thoughts. I'm repeating the events that happened to me and trying to find peace of mind. Every now and then the search stops and I'm standing in front of myself with a breeze rising to my neck. I start panicking and going back to the place I started, the place that seems like the only place that gives me the temporal solace that I long for. My face disgusts me, my eyes disgust me. My skin is permanently tanned. My skin that I don't like. I look like I went to a tanning salon and went full on—give me everything you have. Yes, I will have this yellowish color please. After few weeks I would find out that the tan won't come off, and that it is permanent, that I'm permanently damaged. That would be also funny. At least in the story I was white. How the fantasy sometimes goes around and plays tricks on you.

Isn't it like that sometimes? People come and go, stuff that used to matter doesn't matter anymore. Sometimes when I hear people talking, you would see me as if I was suddenly frozen. My eyes would stare at a static point in front of me and my mouth would slowly start to smile, as if pieces of ice were melting away. Sometimes it feels like a lightning bolt just hit me.

"I have to say that your Czech is really good." Oh yeah, she just wanted to say something nice. It's cool. "You are not like them, those people who think that we would understand each other." Could it be me? Am I now finally white? I got approval from a white person. Not like those other people. I passed. After a while I start to laugh, like the is ice melting down entirely. It's not joy I'm feeling, at least I would not call it that. I laugh so strongly that I almost laugh my lungs out entirely. You may not hear it or see it but trust me, I'm laughing.

I would not call it joy, neither a joke that made me laugh. The tears are falling down from my eye and dripping into the pond. Suddenly there is darkness. I'm standing just in the middle of it. All around me there is nothing to see, and the pond starts to freeze like I was frozen before. It's cold out here, only my laughter makes me a little bit warmer. Wait, did you just call me? My eyes are going downwards; I cannot look into her eyes. I leave silently.

Isn't that funny. I was buying tobacco from her, the brand that I bought is called Golden Virginia. Pretty casual. You are not like them, those people who think that we would understand each other.

White, white, white, I would love to hear people calling me that, if they are already staring at me. How it can be that I feel so little but at the same time so big. I'm like a target that you just can't miss. Usually it is pretty casual, like I really don't notice it so often. Usually, people around me that are white notice it for me like one time a schoolmate said that in this project we all should speak in our own language. She pointed out that I should speak in Chinese. My friend was more offended than I was.

White, white, white… sometimes I think about being white. It should be pretty obvious from the text. I wonder who I would be if I were white. I'm thinking about different realities, different experiences, different me, a different present day. Would I have a totally different life? I would probably not write this text if I were white, maybe I would be a white liberal and write a text called "Why are you so white?" There are lot of memories that are coming back during the time I'm writing this and also I'm finding out that they have had a much bigger impact on my life than I thought.

When I'm bored, I usually spend my time on social media or dating apps. I don't think I'm looking for anything specific. I'm just killing time till I have better things to do. It's not unusual to meet, once in a while a group or a person that is really interested in you.

"I am looking for an Asian, top looking for sub." I kind of like to be a fetish in a way, at least someone like me. "Cute Asian boy riding his daddy's thick dick"—why does it matter if he's Asian or not. Asian, is it a sexual preference, do I also have a sexual preference based on race? I mainly slept with white people. A question of power, having power over someone. Living up to our colonial history, being the one in charge, enslaved in bed. Broken world, damaged by the dark history like the cute Asian boy dominated by the white daddy.

"You look like this K-pop singer." I think there's a point in life when you start to embrace it and not take things too personally. It's pleasurable in a world where you are usually the one that people look down to. Suddenly people are looking for you, they love you and they are obsessed with you.

Why am I so white? If I want to be loved, do I need to become yellow again?

Sometimes I find myself exploiting myself, sometimes I exploit my color. Sometimes it seems like it's the only way.

Shot, boom, another one dead, another one assaulted, humiliated, traumatized, depressed, anxious, scared for your own life. I've been looking out for myself again. Squishing my hand always when

I feel a danger is coming. I've been making assumptions like other people are maybe making assumptions about me. Stereotypes are in style lately. Profiling everyone I meet; everyone I'm going to meet. I know I'm probably overthinking it.

I don't think I talk too much. Once in high school a classmate told me that she would have liked me if I hadn't talked so much. I'm usually much more confused. Sometimes I would even say that look like I am totally apathetic towards the outside world. It's like a defense mechanism, ignoring stuff. Although being manic and talkative is also a defense mechanism. I remember that I used to find it easier to make fun of myself first than let other people take my place. I focused the attention away. It all was just for the good laugh. If I first humiliate myself, it becomes less of an attack. It became less hurtful. These reflections are starting to help me. But I'm not sure if I feel less vulnerable. Slowly I start to recognize all the internalized humiliation, different weapons and cages. Trapped inside of a hole dug by myself. Therefore, I guess I'm my own colonizer. Fear that conquered my whole body, the ache that stabbed me into the ground. The hate that stole everything away.

The Shape of Sports Diplomacy: Gelora Bung Karno, Jakarta, and the Fourth Asian Games

Robin Hartanto Honggare
Columbia University

By the time President Sukarno appointed New York-based architect Abel Sorensen to design the Indonesian Pavilion at the New York World's Fair 1964–65, around twenty Soviet architects and engineers were busy managing the construction of the Asian Games Complex—later named as Gelora Bung Karno—in Jakarta.[1] They had stayed in the capital since the construction of the sports complex began, in 1960, and remained so until 1962, the year it was inaugurated for hosting the Fourth Asian Games. The technical assistance was not the only connection between the complex and the superpower of the Communist bloc; the Soviet Union funded the construction of the Main Stadium and architects from the respective state helped design different venues within the complex.[2]

This foreign affiliation might sound counter-intuitive if we consider the Asian Games Complex as a proposition, as suggested by Sukarno himself, for bolstering the nation's pride. "Well, I would like to ask you now whether or not you are proud of having such a stadium like this," he asked the audience of one hundred thousand who attended the opening of the Main Stadium, "are you not proud of the fact that this tremendous stadium belongs to the Indonesian nation?"[3] A cynical mind could ask on the contrary, why we, as a nation, should be proud of another nation's creation.

Understanding the different architectural productions surrounding the Fourth Asian Games, however, demands an alternative reading of the architecture of nationalism. By the "architecture of nationalism," I refer to the common proposition that architecture participates in the formation of national collective subjectivities. Architecture produces the images, metaphors, and rhetorical turns from which national identities are expressed and the condition through which collective subjectivities are cultivated.

But by proposing an alternative understanding, I see national imaginaries through architecture less as an introverted domain. Rather than solely deciphering how architecture represents and symbolizes national identities, I incline to look both inward and outward: the ambition is to identify and theorize

1 Harul Zain, *Beberapa Aspek Keadaan Tenaga Kerdja Pada Projek Bangunan Asian Games* (Jakarta: Lembaga Penjelidikan Ekonomi dan Masjarakat Fakultas Ekonomi Universitas Indonesia, 1961), 26.

2 *Suluh Indonesia*, "Dokumen persetudjuan pembangunan kompleks Asian Games ditandatangani," November 23, 1959.

3 Sukarno, "Message by President Sukarno at the Opening of the Main Stadium in Senajan, Djakarta" (speech, Jakarta, July 21, 1962), Arsip Nasional Republik Indonesia, RA15, No. 405.

different modes through which architecture, in embodying the imaginaries, manifests nexuses between the national and the international. Understanding this worldliness of nationalism in architecture requires an intensive examination of the international geopolitics that situates any national architetural production. It involves reading architecture as diplomatic apparatuses, sites of negotiations, currencies of exchanges, exhibiting devices, and other manifestations of international relations that, conversely, helped foster the collective subjectivities of a certain nation. The architecture of the Fourth Asian Games, as this essay seeks to reveal, mobilized such reciprocity by taking advantage of the complex political condition of the global Cold War.

SPORTS INTERNATIONALISM

The intermingling between nationalism and internationalism in Indonesia could be traced back to the formation of the foundational philosophical theory of the state. Realizing the inseparability of both ideological concepts, Sukarno suggested in his influential speech titled "The Birth of Pancasila" that the second principle of the nation had to be internationalism, as a counterpart of nationalism—the first principle. Nationalism without internationalism, he said, could transform into chauvinism, while internationalism without nationalism could turn into cosmopolitanism.[4]

This interrelation was reflected in Indonesian nation-building policies during Sukarno's presidency, including through modern sport and international sporting events, such as the Asian Games. Olympism, the foundational philosophy of the modern Olympic games, reflects such spirit. Pierre de Coubertin, who helped reinvent the modern Olympics, regarded internationalism as a critical component to the games: "Internationalism as we understand it consists of respect for countries and the noble sentiment that stirs the athlete's heart when he sees his nation's colors being raised on the mast of victory."[5] The statement suggests a double play. On the one hand, Coubertin regarded sport as a means to build an international structure which encourages friendship and

4 Sukarno, "Lahirnya Pancasila" (speech, Jakarta, June 1, 1945), *Lahirnya Pancasila* (Jogjakarta: Penerbit Guntur, 1949), http://kepustakaan-presiden.pnri.go.id/uploaded_files/pdf/speech/normal/soekarno10.pdf.

5 Pierre de Coubertin, "The Trustees of the Olympic Idea," *Olympism: Selected Writings* ed. Norbert Müller (Lausanne: International Olympic Committee, 2000), 589.

peace between countries. This ambition is further encapsulated into the fundamental rule of the modern Olympiads: "All games, all nations." On the other hand, Coubertin also looked at sport as a potential instrument for producing national spirits. This aim can be achieved, among other possibilities, by organizing the collective participation of the athletes under the basis of the nation-state and by enunciating the nationalities of the athletes, as can be seen at the medal ceremonies in which national flags and anthems are the central properties. In light of this view, it is unsurprising that international sporting events had played critical roles for the newly independent states in Asia after World War II, not just for gaining international acknowledgment, but furthermore, as Stefan Huebner has argued in his recent work, for strengthening Asian nationalisms through the ideal of internationalism.[6]

Sukarno utilized the Games to help place the nation within the Asian community as well as within the world, as successfully hosting the games would lead to international recognition, and simultaneously foresaw the worldliness of it as an integral part of his nation-building project. He reemphasized thisview in the first piling ceremony of the Main Stadium:

> "In our efforts to build up a nation, in our nation-building which I said is carried out to establish a state respected by the whole world, to become a great nation respected by the whole world, I say that sport is one of the fields for nation-building. Then it is clear that if we want to become a nation respected by other nations in the world, if we are eager to have a state whose citizens are respected by the world, then it will be wise to pay attention to this matter of achievements."[7]

Given this agenda, the Fourth Asian Games became a complex site of national and geopolitical construction. This condition did not only pertain solely to the sporting matches, but further to the network of productions surrounding the Games: the opening and closing ceremonies, the cultural programs, the receptions, the media, the logo, the medals, the flags, the ephemera, and, as critical as the others, the architecture.

6 Stefan Huebner, *Pan-Asian Sports and the Emergence of Modern Asia, 1913–1974* (Singapore: NUS Press, 2016), 9.

7 Sukarno, "Speech by President Sukarno at the Ramming of the First Pile for the Main Stadium of the Asian Games" (speech, Jakarta, February 8, 1960), Arsip Nasional Republik Indonesia, RA15, No. 160.

"This area will soon be a modern sports complex," a voice-over described the scene of Nikita Khrushchev and Sukarno observing an architectural model of the Main Stadium. Dozens of reporters gathered around the two leaders with notebooks in their hands. The narrator continued his remark, "Russians call it the Luzhniki Stadium of Jakarta, as it resembles the Luzhniki Stadium in Moscow in size and style."[8]

The episode depicted the increasing alliance between Indonesia and the Soviet Union around the time of the Fourth Asian Games. The Soviet government provided a $12.5 million soft-loan to Indonesia for building the stadium. It was a strong symbol for the Indonesia-USSR bilateral relationship, which was non-existent before 1950. In the mid-1950s, the Soviet leadership began attempts to strengthen their relationships with, and to weaken Western influences over, Asian and African countries, including Indonesia as one of the dominant voices within the Asian-African community. Indonesia then became a premier site of Soviet aid and assistance. In 1954, the Soviet Union participated in Indonesia's second international economic exhibition and constructed the largest pavilion. This participation was followed up by the first trade pact between both states signed in 1956. High-level visits were greatly intensified afterward, including Sukarno's visit to Russia in 1956 and in 1961 and Nikita Khrushchev's ten-day visit to Indonesia in 1960, which was recorded by the narrated video. The funding for the stadium was a small, yet symbolical, account of the overall financial aid committed by the Soviet Union in 1960, which reached a total of around $700 to $800 million, more than half of which was dedicated to military credits.[9]

Given the significant contribution, the Soviet Union was present in many aspects of the Games, even though the country was not a member of the Asian Games Federation. During Khrushchev's visit, a ceremony at the driving of the stadium's hundredth pile was held, despite the fact that eleven days earlier the ramming of the first pile had already been

8 "Kunjungan PM Khrushchev di Indonesia," Arsip Nasional Republik Indonesia, DVD-FILM/2011, 660.

9 Larisa M. Efimova, "Soviet Policy in Indonesia during the 'Liberal Democracy' Period, 1950–1959," *Wilson Center*, November 8, 2011, https://www.wilsoncenter.org/publication/soviet-policy-indonesia-during-the-liberal-democracy-period-1950-1959; Guy J. Pauker, "The Soviet Challenge in Indonesia," *Foreign Affairs* Vol. 40, No. 4 (July 1962): 612–614; "Indonesia Considers Soviet Trade Pact," *New York Times*, September 25, 1954.

celebrated and executed by Sukarno. In the latter ceremony, Khrushchev was given the first chance to pull the ropes that would trigger the piling.[10]

The assistance from the Soviet Union, however, was not just financial. The Soviet government further provided architectural assistance to produce the stadium. The design team that represented the Architectural-Planning Department of Moscow—officially called Technoexport—produced a scheme that centered on the Main Stadium with eight main axes connecting other venues and supporting facilities. Furthermore, the team designed the Main Stadium for 100 thousand people, a badminton hall known as Istana Olahraga (the Sports Palace) with a capacity for ten thousand people, a swimming stadium for eight thousand people, an open field for hockey and athletics known as the Stadion Madya for 15 thousand people, and the Main Tennis Stadium for five thousand spectators. The rest was designed by the Indonesian team.[11]

Both parties enjoyed an exciting and productive cross-national collaboration. Translators were hired to mediate the two teams. During the construction process, Indonesian engineers and technicians learned as much as possible from the Soviets for future constructions. R. Semerdjiev, the principal architect of the Main Stadium who stayed in Jakarta during the construction, recalled that knowledge transfer was prominent: "in a short time, the Indonesians managed to master the equipment and machines...and comprehended the technological process for producing prefabricated reinforced concrete, which was new at that time." He also stated that "Close cooperation at the complex gave birth to a strong and profound friendship. Often, we were invited to houses or parties. At times, we went together for excursions to other places. At sports matches, evening gatherings, and art events held at the Soviet compound, Indonesian experts always took part."[12]

Due to this Soviet affiliation, many critics have related the design of the Main Stadium to the Luzhniki Stadium, but the resemblance to its sister in Moscow is based more on their visual impression than their

10 "Kunjungan PM Khrushchev di Indonesia," Arsip Nasional Republik Indonesia, DVD-FILM/2011, 660.

11 *Suluh Indonesia*, "Dokumen persetudjuan pembangunan kompleks Asian Games ditandatangani," November 23, 1959.

12 Harul Zain, *Beberapa Aspek Keadaan Tenaga Kerdja Pada Projek Bangunan Asian Games*, 26-28; Julius Pour, *Dari Gelora Bung Karno ke Gelora Bung Karno* (Jakarta: Grasindo, 2004), 185.

design. The stadiums, in fact, had many fundamental design differences. The Luzhniki Stadium did not have a projecting roof for spectators when it was built in 1955. Its current roof came after a renovation project in 1996. The Main Stadium meanwhile was designed with a cantilevered roof as its essential feature. The plan of Luzhniki is slightly square, while the plan of the Main Stadium is oval. The outer columns of the Luzhniki Stadium are free-standing, in opposition to the outer columns of the Main Stadium which are attached to its four-level floor planes.

Nevertheless, a stadium resembling other stadiums in the world was not what was expected of the Main Stadium. When the Fourth Asian Games preparation began in 1958, Sukarno had already stated that "the Asian Games Stadium must be greater and more tbeautiful than other stadiums." The stadium, as an actualization of Sukarno's nation-building project, was conceived to be superlative to help mobilize national pride. In achieving this ideal, Sukarno insisted, in discussion with the design team, that the roofing had to be a temugelang roof—a circular, cantilevered roof where its top part is interconnected structurally, thus resembling the shape of a bracelet. The Main Stadium utilized steel and aluminum sheets for the roofing materials, allowing the roof to project a very long span up to the front stands. Sukarno further requested that the seats must serve more than 100,000 people, therefore establishing the Main Stadium as one of the biggest football stadiums in the world by capacity at its time, probably only defeated by the Maracana stadium in Rio de Janeiro.[13]

Trained as an architect-engineer and having made a short career as one, Sukarno was well aware of the potential intersection between political rhetoric and architectural language. On the one hand, he utilized the techniques of political speeches to translate architecture into words, while on the other hand, he understood ways in which modes of architectural production could help materialize words into bricks. By exploiting superlatives, he interweaved internationalism within his national agenda for placing the nation as the beacon for building the new world he had continually imagined. "I have been around the world," Sukarno said at the opening ceremony of the Main Stadium, "I have seen the stadium in Rio de

13 *Asian Games IV Report: Volume 1* (Jakarta: The Organizing Committee for the Fourth Asian Games, 1963), 10, 42–44.

Janeiro, I have seen the stadium in Warsaw, I have seen stadium in Rome, I have seen stadiums in America, I have seen them in Mexico, I have seen them in other countries but oh, this Main Stadium of Jakarta is the best in the whole world! There is no other stadium in the world with this circular roof. The Rio de Janeiro Stadium is a bit bigger than ours, but it has no circular roof, and its construction is not as terrific as the construction of this stadium."[14]

BEYOND THE SPORTS COMPLEX

The Soviet Union was not the only country with which cooperation was held during the preparation for the Fourth Asian Games. The construction of road infrastructure, including the Jakarta Bypass and the "Semanggi" Cloverleaf Junction, provided another substantial development. The government of the United States and American oil companies helped provide the funding for the construction. There was a moment when Sukarno pushed Prime Minister Djuanda to challenge Ambassador Howard Jones: "Ask, doesn't America want to have legacies in Indonesia? If not, it's fine. Because Japan has, Russia also has legacies. But actually, I want loans from the United States to complete the construction of the cloverleaf junction."[15]

Acting more than as a showcase, the Jakarta Bypass and the Semanggi Junction had a direct impact on Jakarta's morphology on the macro level. The Jakarta Bypass changed Jakarta's urban structure through the addition of a new artery road connecting the Tanjung Priok seaport and Cawang on Jakarta's south side. This additional road provided the bacbone for the eastward growth of the city. The Jakarta Bypass also had a crucial role in creating west-east oriented spur routes in a city dominated by a north-south axis. Furthermore, the new infrastructure was not only utilized as transportation routes during the Games but also for other games facilities, such as marathons or cycling racetracks.[16] The Fourth Asian Games also opened the door for the completion of a structure that remains important as a landmark for Jakartans: Hotel Indonesia. Despite the fact that it had been conceived earlier, before Indonesia was chosen as the

14 Sukarno, "Message by President Sukarno at the Opening of the Main Stadium in Senajan."
15 Ria Hutabarat, "American Freeways in Indonesia," in *The Indonesian Town Revisited*, ed. Peter J.M. Nas (Münster: Lit Verlag; Singapore: Institute of Southeast Asian Studies, 2002), 65–66; Pour, *Dari Gelora Bung Karno ke Gelora Bung Karno*, 41.
16 *Asian Games IV Report: Volume 1*, 152, 219.

host, the Games had provided the momentum for its construction. Abel Sorensen designed the hotel, while the construction was handled by Tokyo's Taisei Construction Company and PT. Pembangunan Perumahan. The hotel was built using the Japanese war reparation fund, and some of the building materials were imported from Japan.

The most influential advancement enabled by the Games was arguably television transmission, which was initiated as a special mass media project under the Organizing Committee for the Fourth Asian Games. Before the Games, Indonesia did not have any television infrastructure. Maladi, who was the head of the organizing committee for the Games and also the Minister of Information, had been suggesting to Sukarno the importance of establishing television broadcasting since 1952. In 1959, Maladi insisted its significance by promoting the opportunity of providing coverage of the forthcoming Asian Games as a way to generate a sense of national pride and unity.[17] The television project finally received its green light from Sukarno in July 1961 and the Ministry of Information published an order to authorize a committee for the television preparation.[18]

Among the participating countries, only Japan (1953), The Philippines (1953), and Thailand (1954) had established television broadcasting services in their countries. Japan, owing to a rich experience in broadcasting the Third Asian Games held in Tokyo, 1958, provided tools and expertise to help set up television transmission in Indonesia. Eighteen technicians and production staff from Indonesia were sent for three months of intensive training with the Nippon Hoso Kyokai (NHK) in Japan, in early 1962. A team of eight Japanese engineers assisted in the design stages of the television studio and technical facilities planned for the Games complex. A technician and a reporter from NHK were also sent to help assist the Indonesian television team during the games.[19] Most of the equipment was imported from Japan. The trading company C-Itoh imported television broadcasting devices that were manufactured by the Nippon Electric Company to Indonesia for a lower price.[20]

17 Philip Kitley, *Television, Nation, and Culture in Indonesia* (Athens, Ohio: Ohio University Center for International Studies, 2000), 24–25.
18 Alex Leo, *Televisi di Indonesia: TVRI 1962-1972* (Jakarta: Direktorat Televisi Departemen Penerangan, 1972), 32.
19 Kitley, *Television, Nation, and Culture in Indonesia*, 22–30.
20 Leo, *Televisi di Indonesia*, 33–34.

Broadcasting activities were carefully considered in the design of the stadium. A shed for video compartments consisting of 40 booths for radio commentators, complete with modern radio equipment, was built on the upper part of the stadium.[21]

Hence, television broadcasting provided another intricate layer to the Games as a complex media event, as television broadcasting does not simply mean announcing the event, but further reproduces the place simultaneously. Media theorist Samuel Weber has written that television has to be understood not merely as to see and to hear, but to place before us—that is why we use the word "watching" television rather than "seeing" it. Television produces a surrogate for the body as it allows a certain sense-perception to take place simultaneously: in the place where the image and sound are "recorded", in the place where those images and sounds are received, and in the place in between, through which those images and sounds are transmitted. Therefore, in the case of a sporting event, television broadcasting does not simply represent the venue as background images; it further reproduces it into other places.[22]

Ten thousand television sets, consisting of 14-inch and 19-inch sets manufactured by Matsushita Electric, were ordered by the government before the Games to be distributed to different places, mainly on Java Island.[23] The Jakarta municipal government, in cooperation with the Gobel manufacturing company, assembled information counters around strategic locations in the city to provide information and news about the Games, including in streets, hotels, the airport, train stations, and commercial stores.[24] Games events were also relayed from Jakarta to Bandung, 180 kilometers away from the capital.[25] Local newspapers ran many television-related ads by different companies, from promoting a book on television, installation, and service, opening applications for television crews, to selling television sets.[26]

21 The Organizing Committee for the Fourth Asian Games, *3rd Progress Report to the Members of the Council of the Asian Games Federation* (Jakarta, 1962), 3.
22 Samuel Weber, "Television: Set and Screen," *Mass Mediauras: Form, Technics, Media* (Stanford, California: Stanford University Press, 1996), 117–118.
23 "10.000 Alat2 TV utk Indonesia," *Suluh Indonesia*, July 30, 1962, II.
24 "Perlengkapan2 TV untuk Information Counters," *Suluh Indonesia*, August 24, 1962, V.
25 "Djelas, Bersih, Tanpa Gangguan," *Suluh Indonesia*, August 28, 1962, III.
26 *Suluh Indonesia*, July 25, 1962; *Suluh Indonesia*, August 6, 1962; *Suluh Indonesia*, August 10, 1962; *Suluh Indonesia*, August 11, 1962; *Suluh Indonesia*; August 22, 1962; *Suluh Indonesia*, August 25, 1962; *Suluh Indonesia*, September 3, 1962; *Suluh Indonesia*, September 4, 1962.

The public nature of watching television during the Games was a unique experience. Philip Kitley observed that, although many television experiences began on the streets, the Indonesian case was qualitatively different. While in many countries viewers watched television through window shopping, in Indonesia thousands of residents jostled to see the black and white images of the games through public access sets rather than through retailers. Television, in this case, was not bound by the private world of domestic consumption but became collective experiences taking place in public domains.[27]

EPILOGUE

The Fourth Asian Games IV turned out to be one of the most controversial Asian Games. Indonesia purposefully excluded Israel and Taiwan. Three weeks before the games, Taiwan said that they had received no application forms, only a package of blank cards. The Israeli team had received nothing about Indonesian visas. Both countries, in the end, did not participate. Resistance came from members of the Asian Games Executive Committee, including from Guru Dutt Sondhi, who was regarded as the founding father of the Asian Games and also an influential committee member of the IOC. During the Games, a protest against Sondhi occurred in front of the Indian embassy, forcing him to leave the country early for his safety.[28]

Forms of punishment to the host were discussed by IOC, including changing the name of the Games so that it would not be admitted as the official Asian Games. The final decision was that Indonesia's IOC membership was suspended and the country was banned from participating in the Tokyo Olympics in 1964.[29]

Unsatisfied with the decision, Sukarno decided that Indonesia would resign from the IOC and create a counter-Olympics.[30] He named it the Games of the New Emerging Forces (GANEFO), a title that represented an even more transparent act of politicizing sports. The new emerging forces referred to

27 Kitley, *Television, Nation, and Culture in Indonesia*, 32.
28 Williard A. Hanna, "The Politics of Sport: Indonesia as Host to the 'Fourth Asian Games'," *Southeast Asia Series* Vol. X No. 19 (Hanover: American Universities Field Staff, 1962), 195–200.
29 "Indonesia dan Komite Olympiade Internasional," *Gelora GANEFO*, No. 1, August 17, 1963, 29–31.
30 "To Build the World of Sports Anew," *Indonesia* Vol. 3, 1963, 140–141.

the transnational community that he had conceived before, consisting of countries of the people of Asia, Africa, and Latin America, as well as socialist states.

"The IOC said, 'Sports are sports, do not mix sports with politics.' That is not true!... Now let us frankly say, sports have something to do with politics!" Sukarno said in a speech at the opening of the Preparatory Conference of GANEFO. GANEFO was held on November 10–22, 1963, a year after the Asian Games. In total, 48 countries participated in GANEFO, including China and the Soviet Union.[31]

GANEFO was a very ambitious attempt to replace the Olympic games and, in its larger picture, the United Nations. It was a polemical move, yet it also depicted Indonesia's persistence in decolonizing international institutions from the established powers and in bringing prominence to the newly independent states. The different architectural production that were mobilized for hosting the Asian Games and GANEFO embodied the spirit to stand as equals to the superpowers of the Cold War and to gain friendship with decolonized countries. They also provided a particular case in which the process of cultivating nationalism through architecture did not necessarily constitute an introverted domain. All in all, the Asian Games Complex and Jakarta, in that enthusiastic moment, epitomized the attempts by the state to produce national structures that welcomed the world.

This text was originally published in *mASEANa Project 2017. Modern living in Southeast Asia*. (Tokyo: DOCOMOMO Japan), 2018, 26-29.

31 Rusli Lutan and Fan Hong, "The Politicization of Sport: GANEFO – A Case Study," *Sport, Nationalism, and Orientalism*, 31.

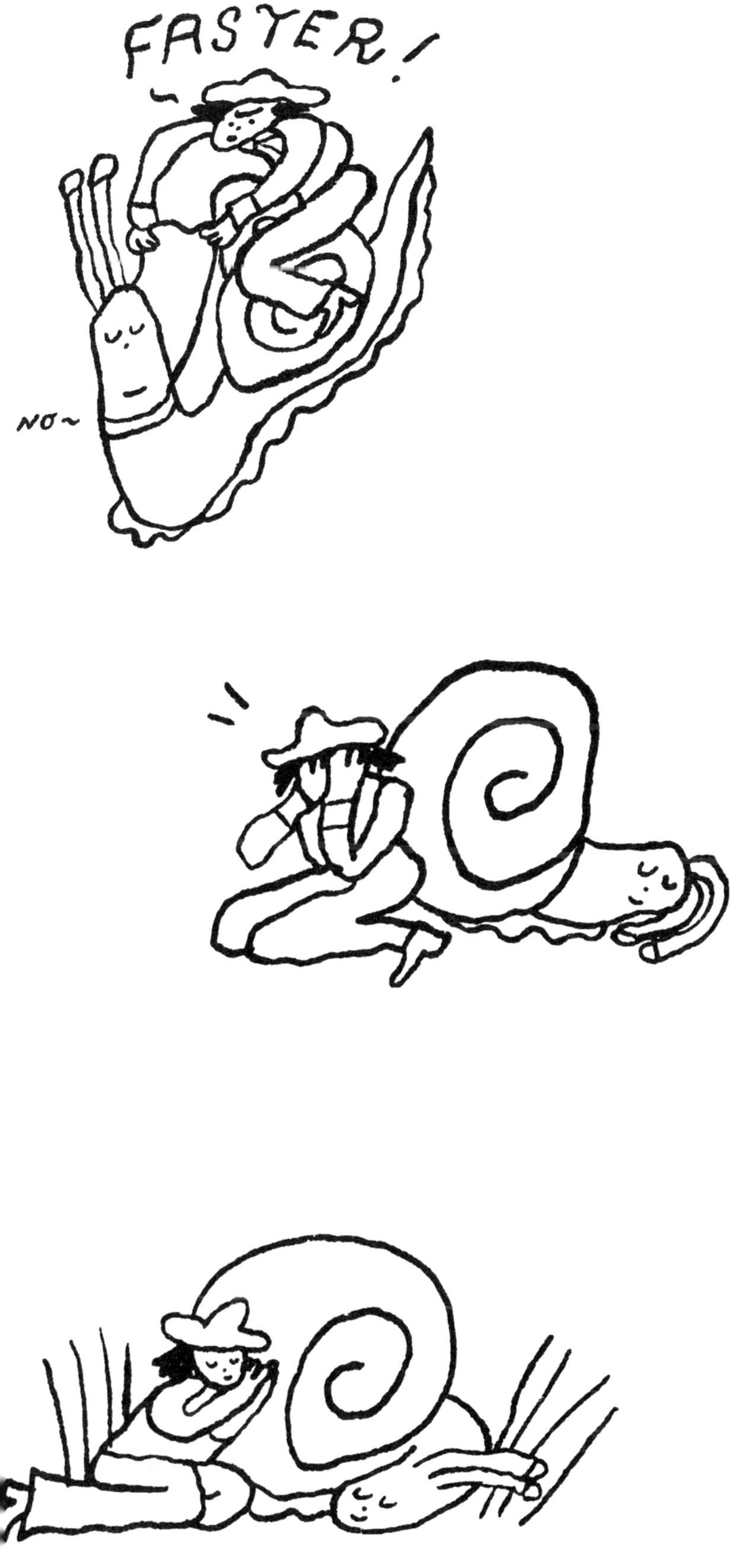FASTER!
NO~

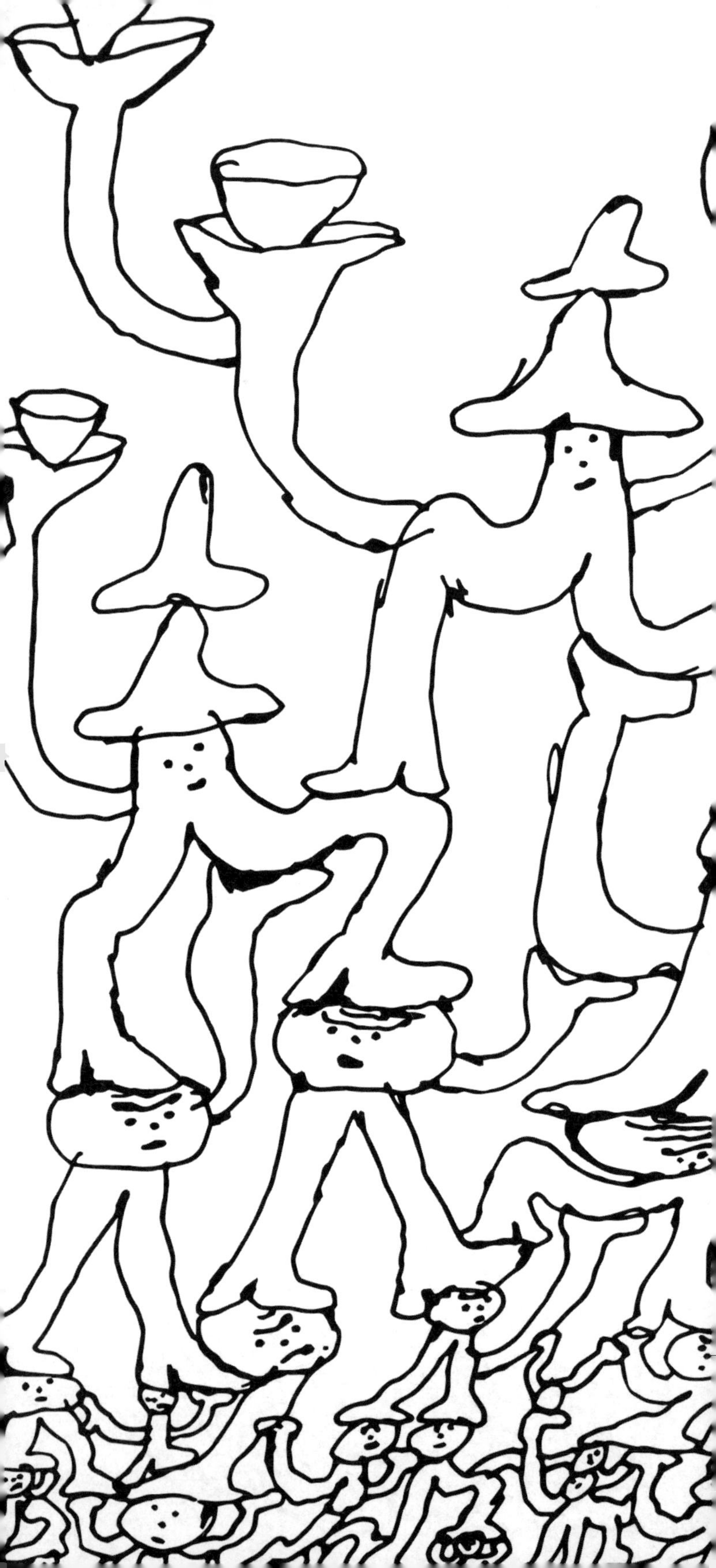

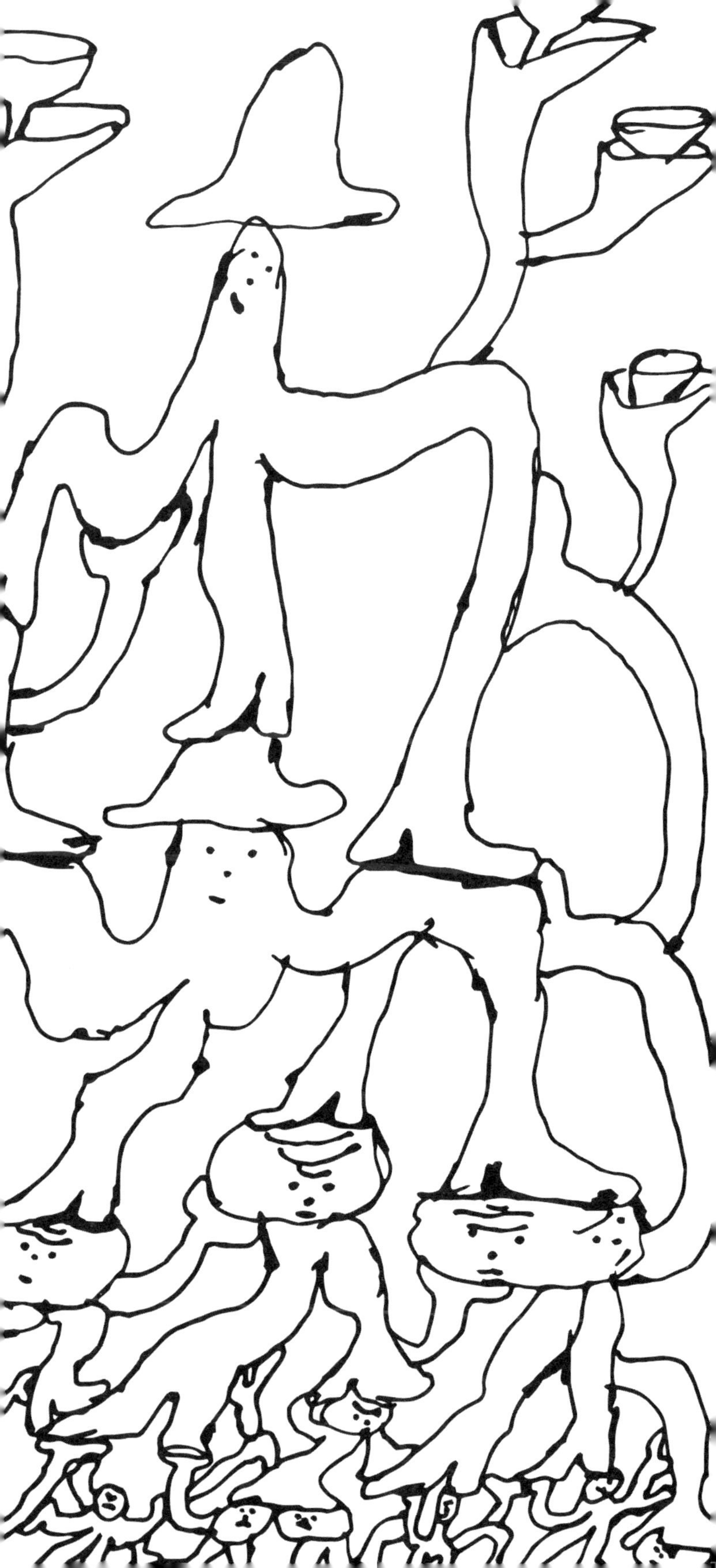

4

4

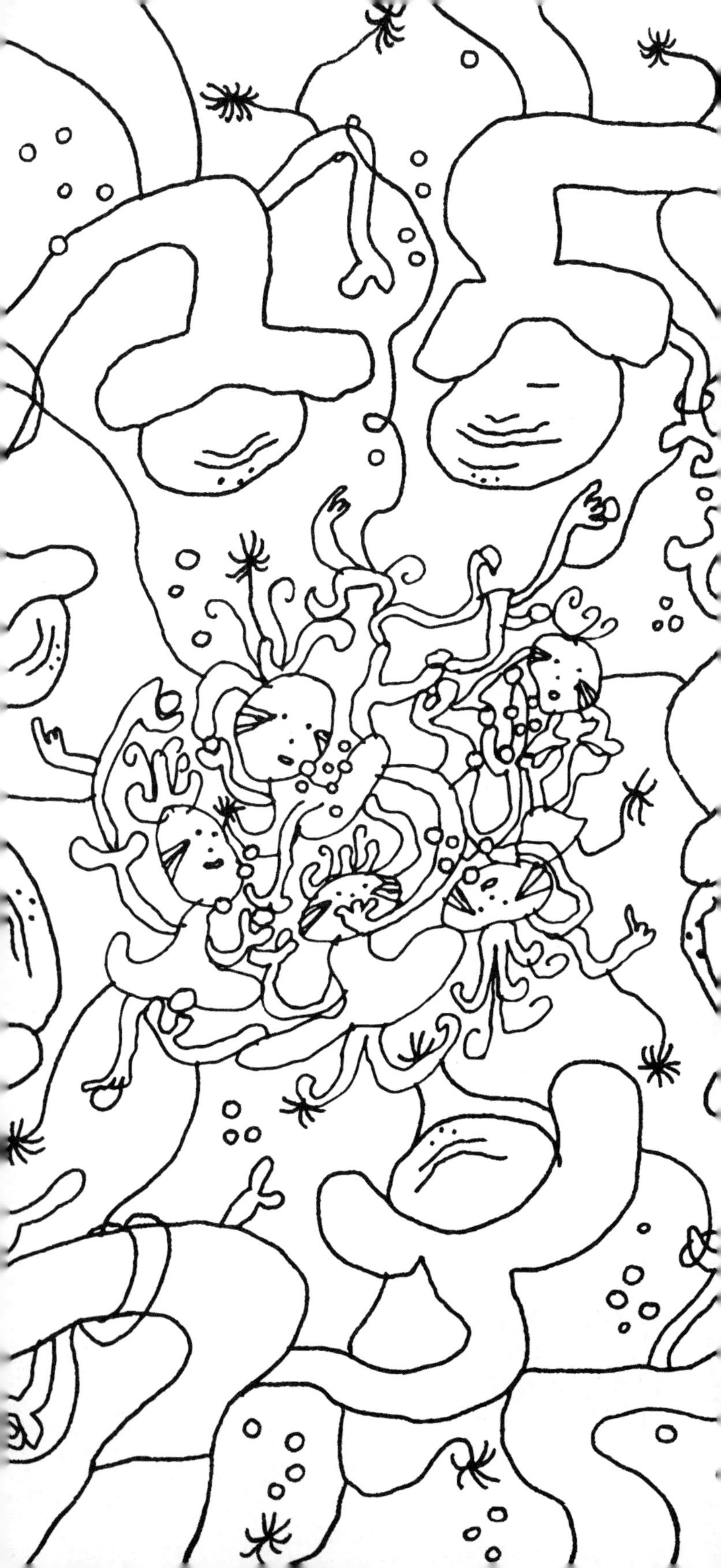

The Problem of Heritage:

Some Notes on Social Realism in Asia and the Limits of the Lukácsian Formulation

Ramon Guillermo
Center for International Studies
University of the Philippines, Diliman

In the late 1930s, the great Hungarian philosopher and literary critic Georg Lukács (1885–1971) exchanged some letters with the German novelist Anna Seghers (1900–1983) on the problem of "realism" in literature. Seghers initiated the correspondence because she felt a certain gnawing unease with Lukács's formulation of realism which she could not exactly put her finger on at the time.

A central issue of their discussion was the concept of the "immediacy" (*Unmittelbarkeit*) (or "spontaneity") of the artist's lived experience. This is not surprising because Lukács's insistent critique of immediacy and its various misunderstandings from a Hegelian standpoint is one of his most valuable contributions to a Marxist understanding of literature and art, especially on matters dealing with literary "realism." He correctly emphasized that the "basic experience" (*Grunderlebnis*) of a writer may seem "immediate" but that it is not actually so. His or her experience is always already mediated by his or her whole past. As he observed, "the entire conscious and unconscious life of the writer, his intellectual and moral labor in itself decides what the content of such an experience will be" (*Das ganze bewußte und unbewußte Leben des Schriftstellers, seine intellektuelle und moralische Arbeit an sich selbst entscheidet darüber, was der Inhalt eines solchen Erlebnisses sein wird*).[1] There is no such thing therefore as a purely immediate encounter with so-called "reality." However, moving from this level of spontaneous reception of the world towards rendering its various aspects into a "totality" which transcends the experience of capitalist fragmentation requires clarity in one's ideological position, which for Lukács was naturally a Marxist one.

While conceding the theoretical rigor behind his formulations, Seghers complained that Lukács did not seem to be forthcoming about whether his concept of realism applied only to the Europe of his time or to "realism in general" (i.e., "an orientation to the highest possible reality attainable at a particular time"). If it is the latter case, then she argued that one would have to admit that there existed quite a variety of "realistic" styles and creative methods which may seem "non-realistic" to someone accustomed only to a specific and historically bound concept of realism.

1 Georg Lukács, *Essays über Realismus* (Munich: Luchterhand, 1971), 356.

Seghers further pointed out that one could not decide offhand whether works were realist or non-realist without first "closely acquainting oneself with the social existence" of the artists concerned (*ihre gesellschaftliche Existenz in der Nähe kennenzulernen*). Probably sensing that a weak point in Lukács's concept of realism may be in the visual arts, she used painting as an example. For instance, referring to El Greco (1541–1614), she noted how his paintings faithfully captured the "colors of his country" (*die Farben seines Landes*) and "proportions of his people" (*Proportionen seiner Menschen*).[2] These images may seem fantastic, visionary, or "non-realist" (to a German perhaps) but this is only from the perspective of an outside viewer. Before any question of artistic method and the "overcoming of immediacy" (*Überwindung der Unmittelbarkeit*) can come in, Seghers emphasized that in the "immediate stage," "what matters is what it is in reality that makes an impression on whom" (*was in der Wirklichkeit auf wen Eindruck macht*). Seghers did not mean this in the exclusively individual and relativistic sense but quite clearly in terms of what she meant by the intersubjectively shared "colors" and "proportions" of their country. With this, she evidently referred not just to the simple objectivity of these colors and proportions but understood these as ways of perceiving the world through certain languages, cultures, and artistic traditions which can be understood adequately only if one takes the time to closely acquaint oneself with them. An artist's lifelong intensive labor, which is necessarily intimately related to the materials and traditions available to them, can deepen and enrich their spontaneous or immediate experience of the world, but also in a very specific way.

Seghers's misgivings may therefore be summarized as a feeling that Lukács's concept of realism does not fully take into account historical and cultural traditions which necessarily shape each particular artist's reception of the world. Whether this judgement is fair or not, it is evident that Lukács did have some rather flagrant blind spots. These surface most clearly in some of his few remarks on "Negro" sculpture which easily parallel Theodor Adorno's (1903–1969) notorious derogatory remarks on "Negro music."[3]

2 Lukács, *Essays über Realismus*, 350.
3 Theodor Adorno, *Gesammelte Schriften 17, Musikalische Schriften IV* (Berlin: Suhrkamp Verlag, 1982).

For instance, Lukács wrote to Seghers:

> "Auch hier ergänzen sich die scheinbar polaren Gegensätze: die pseudomarxistische Enge, die alles nicht unmittelbar Proletarisch-Revolutionäre aus der deutschen Geschichte gestrichen hat, steht auf demselben Niveau wie die geschmäcklerische Enge des »Avantgardismus«, die Negerplastik und Phidias, Irrenzeichnungen und Rembrandt auf dasgleiche Niveau stellt, ja womöllich jene bevorzugt."[4]
>
> (Likewise, what seem to be polar opposites complement one another: the pseudo-Marxist narrowness that would erase from German history everything which is not immediately proletarian and revolutionary stands on the same level as the tasteless narrowness of the "avant-gardism" which puts on the same level Negro sculpture and Phidias, the drawings of the insane and Rembrandt, even preferring them where possible.)

One can see how on the one hand, Lukács fiercely and quite correctly defended the literary and artistic heritage (*Erbe*) of Europe against those on the Left who would reject these as "non-proletarian" and thoughtlessly surrender them to the bourgeoisie. On the other hand, he criticized the "kitschy narrowness" of the avant-garde which would put on the same level "negro sculpture" (*Negerplastik*) with the Greek sculptor Phidias and the "drawings of the insane" with Rembrandt. With some discomfort, one sees here how Lukács casually puts "Negro" sculpture "on the same level" as the "drawings of the insane" (he is here probably referring to dada or surrealist art) while seeing any misguided aesthetic appreciation of these as symptomatic of the general lack of taste within the avant-garde. Lukács is indignant that anyone could even think of comparing the incomparable Greeks with "Negroes" (as if the African continent possessed only one culture). To show any signs of "preferring the latter over the former could only be a display of childish and perverse obstinacy. He therefore traced a straight line from so-called "Oriental art" (*die orientalische Kunst*) and "Negro sculpture" to what he presumed to be the "decadent" European "anti-realistic" or "anti-portrayalist" (*antigestalterisch*) tendencies of his time. Naturally, this

4 Lukács, *Essays über Realismus*, 361.

attitude could be traced at least as far as Hegel, but it does not necessarily mean that all Hegelians or Marxists, especially those living more than a century later, would necessarily have thought this way. For instance, Seghers was not as quick as Lukács to dismiss the artistic strivings of her contemporaries as symptomatic of a foolish infatuation with Oriental or Negro art.

One gathers from these remarks that Lukács considered the bourgeois European artistic heritage to be the uniquely valid basis for any future socialist society. Seghers would perhaps have argued that if one went beyond one's narrow prejudices and truly attempted to closely acquaint oneself with African artistic traditions, each with their own unique sense of color and proportion, one would be able to perceive the realist impulses of the societies behind them. The problem with Lukács is that the mediations which generate the "spontaneous" grasp of the artist of his or her reality turn out to be strictly European. For him, it seems that it is a given that any genuine artist's experience of the world must be mediated by exclusively European languages, cultures, and artistic traditions and nothing else. These have become so transparent to Lukács, perhaps one of the last European mandarins, that he can no longer think or even experience anything outside of them. For him, European civilization and art, starting with the Greeks, represent the pinnacle of human achievement and cultural refinement. Anything else would therefore have appeared to him infantile, grotesque and primitive. He thus equated the ultra-Left rejection or surrender of the classical European heritage with the "reactionary" embrace of non-European "Oriental" (particularly, Japanese) and "African" traditions. Naturally, such remarks could today only be viewed as racist. But since Lukács could not seriously be racist on an intellectual plane, one could attribute these opinions to the stubbornly insular European narrow-mindedness which is not at all unique to him. Even "progressive" Europeans like Jürgen Habermas who certainly could not be accused of racism exhibits this complete self-absorbed complacency of Europe and total disregard for the world outside it.[5] Given these prejudices, Lukács is able to totally ignore the question of how socialist and communist

5 Peter Dews,ed., *Autonomy and Solidarity. Revised Edition. Interviews with Jürgen Habermas* (London: Verso, 1992), 183.

movements outside of Europe would be able to "inherit" the European heritage of realism despite the fact that the imposition of such stringent and narrowly European cultural standards on Asia, Africa, and South America would have required the most thoroughgoing European linguistic and cultural colonialism and imperialism.

However, Seghers was also correct in sensing that Lukács's notion of mediation already points beyond, towards a more satisfactory way of understanding and redefining "realism" and "social realism." It appears, following Seghers's argument, that the problem with Lukács is that he did not apply mediation consistently and rigorously enough as a concept in artistic production. If he had done so, he would have come to the materialist conclusion that sense of "realism" in any historical, cultural, and social context would have to be mediated by the languages, cultures, and artistic traditions that any particular artist finds themself immersed in at any given time in history. Lukács's resistance was probably due to an uneasy awareness that such a concession would undermine the coherence of some of his theoretical formulations.

It is in this context that the Chinese revolutionary leader Mao Zedong's "Talks at the Yenan Forum" (1942) became a crucial turning-point. Mao underscored the importance of inheriting (继承 *jìchéng*) and critically absorbing (批判 地 吸收 *pīpàn de xīshōu*) the artistic and literary heritage (遺產 *yíchǎn*) from both "ancient" Chinese traditions and from foreigners.[6] Though he criticized those who indiscriminately imitated (模仿 *mófǎng*) these sources, he also emphatically opposed the outright and indiscriminate rejection of both Chinese and foreign traditions in the development of Chinese revolutionary culture and literature. Mao's particular formulation implied that any kind of "realism" (現實主義 *xiànshízhǔyì*) would not only have to borrow from European models but would also have to be filtered through or mediated by Chinese language and culture as well as by China's rich literary and artistic traditions beginning from ancient times. The results of such a process cannot be foreseen in advance and obviously cannot be judged based solely on their conformity, or lack thereof, with any preexisting models which Lukács

6 Mao Zedong, 在延安文艺座谈会上的讲话 (*Zài yán'ān wényì zuòtán huì shàng de jiǎnghuà*). *Marxists Internet Archive*. www.marxists.org/chinese/maozedong/marxist.org-chinese-mao-194205.htm

proffers from the great European classical traditions. Putting literary "realism" concretely in practice in China would give it Chinese characteristics which would inevitably distinguish it from the canonical realist European works. As Seghers put it, realism in China would have to portray the "colors" and "proportions" of that particular country and its people. Mao's decisive intervention on this question meant that the concept of "realism," and especially of its more politically radical form, "social realism," would be mediated through the Chinese experience in the revolutionary theory and practice of countries in Southeast Asia like the Philippines and Indonesia. For instance, in the fifties and early sixties, Indonesian progressive artists enthusiastically embraced these insights from Mao. This can be observed in the "Mukkadimah" (Preamble) of the Leftist cultural organization LEKRA (*Lembaga Kebudayaan Rakyat* [Institute of People's Culture]) from 1959.[7] In the "Mukkadimah," the artists of LEKRA declared their pride in having a "diverse" (*beragam*) and "rich" (*bernilai*) national culture. They urged the acceptance, albeit critically, of the "heritage of our ancestors" (*peninggalan-peninggalan nenek-moyang kita*) as well as the careful study of "classics from any country in the world" (*hasil-hasil klasik maupun dari bangsa lain yang mana pun*). By combining these sources, they hoped to be able to "creatively carry forward the great tradition" (*meneruskan secara kreatif tradisi yang agung*) of their country towards a new and liberated national culture. "Carrying forward" this "great tradition" (*tradisi yang agung*) therefore implied that any type of "realisme" or "realisme sosialis"[8] in Indonesia would have to be contextualized vand synthesized within pre-existing literary and cultural traditions.

The Philippine counterpart to LEKRA, the Panulat para sa Kaunlaran ng Sambayanan (Writing for the Progress of the People, PAKSA) also produced similar statements in 1971.[9] PAKSA was heavily influenced by Mao's statements on culture and art. However, it is noticeable how much more reticent and less confident the pronouncements of PAKSA are in terms of

7 Eka Kurniawan, *Pramoedya Ananta Toer dan Sastra Realisme Sosialis* (Yogyakarta: Jendela, 1999), 160.
8 Pramoedya Ananta Toer, *Realisme Sosialis dan Sastra Indonesia* (Jakarta: Lentera Dipantara, 2003).
9 *Rebolusyonaryong panunuring masa sa sining at panitikan: Mga dokumento ng 1971 ng Panulat para sa Kaunlaran ng Sambayanan (PAKSA) at Nagkakaisang Progresibong Artista-Arkitekto (NPAA)* (Manila: Kalikasan Press, 1992).

extolling the cultural "heritage" of the Philippines. In a collection of documents titled "Revolutionary Mass Criticism in Art and Literature," there is just a short section on "katutubong sining" (which literally means "native art" but is translated in the same document as "folk art").[10] It recognized that the "masses" are more familiar with folk art because it is part of their everyday lives. However, even as it continues to be popular because of the patronage of the masses, the ruling classes would like to marginalize the people's folk art and promote instead art forms which are "distant from the people." It is telling that instead of characterizing "folk art" as a "heritage" of the people, it is instead described as what has been "left behind" (*yaong nananatili*) after the European colonizers had tried to stamp out all traces of it (*yaong nanatili sa kabila ng pagtatangka ng kolonyalismong Espanyol na wasaking lahat ang bakas ng ating katutubong sining*). Interestingly, the Indonesian word "peninggalan" as employed in the LEKRA Preamble can mean both "heritage" and "remains" (or remnants) but the Tagalog phrase "yaong nanatili" can only mean "what remains" or "what has been left behind." The different attitude of Filipinos to their cultural "heritage" as compared with the Chinese and the Indonesians may be symptomatic of its particular colonial history. However, there have been moves more recently to correct this, for example, the art critic and historian Alice Guillermo wrote that, "The people's living traditions shape the common identity and thus are not to be regarded as mere "residue" of earlier periods or modes of production to be eventually superseded in the course of historical development."[11]

What is most striking about the Philippine case, at least in the area of visual arts, is the fact that concrete artistic production within the broad category of "social realism" is no longer simply confined within what has conventionally been called "realism." Here, it is as if Seghers's examples from painting in her debate with Lukács, suddenly become topical in the writings of Guillermo. According to the Filipino critic:

> "The social realist trend which developed [in the Philippines] was not based on any particular style but on common progressive principles.

10 *Rebolusyonaryong panunuring masa sa sining at panitikan: Mga dokumento ng 1971*, 103.

11 Alice Guillermo, "Mao Zedong's Revolutionary Aesthetics and its Influence on the Philippine Struggle," Rev Asg, *Selected Articles on Cultural Revolution in the* Philippines (Quezon City: Alay Sining, 2013), 41.

> The artists produced work in a variety of styles, including expressionism, surrealism, even conceptual art in different media or in mixed media. Among these figurative styles, realism was only one of them. But whatever style they were in, their subject and content reflected the socio-political conditions of Philippine society, although not done in the realist style of recording reality and being strictly faithful to observed material detail. It seemed that the variety and inventiveness of the modernist style made flexible by the artists could produce more striking images in their discovery of expressive form. Form itself assumed a semiotic meaning-conveying capacity and approached the desired fusion of form and content."[12]

With this summary, Guillermo describes Philippine visual arts practice over the span of several decades. This practice has definitively separated "social realism" from "realism".[13] It may seem paradoxical that "social realism" has no longer become "realist," but the point here is similar to Seghers' earlier argument that what may seem "non-realist" to a German cultural mandarin may in fact be "realist" for those who live in countries immersed in different colors and proportions. "Social realism" in the Philippines is therefore no longer "realist" in the narrow sense of slavishly following classical European models of realism as prescribed by Lukács. As Guillermo, emphasized, the supposedly "non-realist" forms associated with modernism have themselves become the most appropriate means of "representing" the content of "reality." She therefore advocated an open realism which has been freed from the shackles of its origins and which allows artists to draw from local and foreign artistic and cultural traditions in order to create works which can more effectively represent the socio-political conditions of their own societies. One sees here the full implications of the Maoist injunction to learn to synthesize one's own cultural traditions with those that are foreign which breaks the bounds of Lukácsian Eurocentrism. It actually goes beyond even Seghers' limited plea for a realism which recognizes the unique individuality, in terms of

12 Alice Guillermo, "Mao Zedong's Revolutionary Aesthetics," 45.

13 Alice Guillermo, *Protest/revolutionary Art in the Philippines, 1970–1990* (Quezon City: University of Philippines Press, 2001); Alice Guillermo, *Social realism in the Philippines* (Manila: Asphodel, 1987).

“colors” and “proportions,” of different nations. In this way, social realist practice transcends national limits and becomes a cosmopolitan and “internationalist” artistic practice which strives nonetheless, and very crucially, to remain rooted in the popular struggles of the masses.

A Racialized Homo Sovieticus

Dorota
Jagoda Michalska

The category of "race" rarely occurs in research on the post-communism period which ensued at the turn of the 1990s in Eastern Europe. Current historical narratives concerning the region focus mainly on such methodological concepts as "nation", "religion", "democracy" or "liberalism". To this, the category of "class" should also be added, which constitutes a fundamental point of reference for a younger generation of scholars who critically address the implementation of capitalism in the region.[1] Despite the multiplicity of existing research perspectives on post-communism, race seldomly appears as a key analytical term to scrutinize the dynamic of the changes that took place after 1989.[2] My text aims to both address and conceptualize this void. The starting point for my considerations is a belief that Eastern Europe is deeply complicit in the global matrix of colonial power. Indeed, despite an absence of overseas conquests, the area is very much part of global histories of modernity shaped by transnational conceptualizations of race.[3] Such a perspective has been put forward in research on Scandinavian countries, former Yugoslavia and the Baltic states, which—even if they did not own colonies overseas themselves—constituted part of the world-system, where colonialism played a crucial role.[4]

In my essay I would like to propose the analytical category of "racialized homo sovieticus" as a useful term to shed light on the racial aspect of post-communist transformations. The term *homo*

1 Tomasz Rakowski, *Hunters, Gatherers, and Practitioners of Powerlessness: An Ethnography of the Degraded in Postsocialist Poland,* (New York: Berghahn, 2016), Jane Hardy, *Poland's New Capitalism* (London: Pluto Press, 2009), Aleksandra Leyk, Joanna Wawrzyniak, *Cięcia. Mówiona historia transformacji* (Warsaw: Krytyka Polityczna, 2021), Roman Frydman, Kenneth Murphy, eds., *Capitalism with a Comrade's Face. Studies in the Postcommunist Transition,* (Budapest: Central European University, 1998), Ekrem Karakoc, *Inequality After the Transition*. (Oxford: Oxford University Press, 2018), Anders Aslund, *How Capitalism Was Built: The Transformation of Central and Eastern Europe, Russia, the Caucasus, and Central Asia*, (Cambridge University Press, 2013), Béla Greskovits, *The Political Economy of Protest and Patience: East European and Latin American Transformations Compared*. (Budapest: Central European University Press, 1998).

2 See: Interview with Marina Gržinić, Tjaša Kancler, Piro Rexhepi, "Decolonial Encounters and the Geopolitics of Racial Capitalism", *Feminist Critique. East European Journal of Feminist and Queer Studies* 3, 2020 (pp. 13–38). Important exceptions are Anikó Imre's articles: "Whiteness in Post-Socialist Eastern Europe: The Time of The Gypsies, The End of Race," in: *Postcolonial Whiteness. A Critical Reader on Race and Empire*, ed. Alfred. J. Lopez (NY: Suny Press, 2005), Anikó Imre, "Global Entertainment and the European 'Roma Problem'", *Third Text*, 20:6/2006, pp. 659–670, Anikó Imre, "Postcolonial Media Studies in Postsocialist Europe" *Boundary* 2 41, no. 1 (2014): 113–34.

3 Catherine Baker, *Race and The Yugoslav Region. Postsocialist, Post-conflict, Postcolonial?* (Manchester: Manchester University Press, 2018), 2–7.

4 See: Krisitn Loftsdóttir and Jensen Lars, eds. *Whiteness and Postcolonialism in the Nordic Region: Exceptionalism, Migrant Others and National Identities,* (Farnham: Ashgate, 2012), Violeta Kelertas, *Baltic Postcolonialism,* (Leiden, The Netherlands: Brill, 2006), Magdalena Naum and Jonas M. Nordin, *Scandinavian Colonialism and the Rise of Modernity. Small Time Agents in a Global Arena,* (New York: Springer, 2013), Suvi Keskinen, Salla Tuori, Sara Irni, Diana Mulinari, eds. *Complying with Colonialism. Gender, Race and Ethnicity in the Nordic Region,* (London: Routledge 2016).

sovieticus emerged in the 1990s in Eastern Europe to distinguish and describe a certain social group largely constituted by members of the former working class. The expression had an unambiguously pejorative meaning to it: the liberal discourse labeled homo sovieticus as an inert individual, unable to adapt to the new political regime, dependent on welfare and functioning as burden to the remaining part of society in transition—the middle class in particular. Those people were labeled—and stigmatized—as those responsible for a standstill in the process of evolution towards capitalism, as those who do not live up to the new, capitalist work standards, have a sense of entitlement, are characterized by alcoholism, a propensity for theft and other allegedly pathological behaviors. As Polish sociologist Monika Bobako has observed, the social group thus formed demonstrated distinct features of "racialization," i.e., envisaging class and social differences as biological and immanently present in a certain social class.[5]

The key point of reference for my essay are writings on whiteness and its ambivalent status in Eastern Europe. Critical analyses of whiteness account for a crucial body of research on race issues: these reflections stemmed from the groundbreaking texts by various scholars and writers including W.E.B Dubois, James Baldwin and Toni Morrison.[6] Essential to our geographic perspective are the books by the American, Marxist historian David Roediger—*The Wages of Whiteness. Race and the Making of the American Working Class* (1991), and *Working Towards Whiteness. How America's Immigrants Became White: The Strange Journey from Ellis Island to the Suburbs* (1998), which are a pioneering scrutiny of racialization processes, to which the subsequent immigration waves in the United States were subjected starting from the 19th century.[7] Roediger demonstrates how minorities, including the Irish, Italian or Polish, were perceived as not entirely white by the American Anglo-Saxon Protestant population.

5 Monika Bobako, "Konstruowanie odmienności klasowej jako urasawianie. Przypadek polski po 1989 roku," *Biblioteka Think Tank Feministycznego*, http://www.ekologiasztuka.pl/think.tank.feministyczny/articles.php?article_id=555.

6 W. E. B. Du Bois, *Darkwater. Voices from Within the Veil* (London; Verso, 2016), James Baldwin, *The Fire Next Time*, (London: Penguin, 2018), Toni Morrisson, *Playing in the Dark: Whiteness and the Literary Imagination*, (New York: Vintage Books, 1993).

7 David Roediger, *Working Towards Whiteness. How America's Immigrants Became White: The Strange Journey from Ellis Island to the Suburbs*, (New York: Basic Books, 2005), David Roediger, *The Wages of Whiteness. Race and the Making of the American Working Class*, (London: Verso 2007).

Thus, the scholar positions whiteness not as an essentialist category, but as a contstruct operating on a broad spectrum, within which white as well as "less white" peoples are to be found. What is seminal from Roediger's perspective is that the "class" and "race" categories are deeply intertwined, which brings an important diagnosis in the context of the racialization of class differences that took place in Eastern Europe at the turn of the 1990s.

In what follows, I will consider three main categories—labor, time and space—which led to emergence of the racialized homo sovieticus figure in the post-communist region. This choice results from a conviction that it was those fundamental categories that led to the shaping and implementation of the global colonial matrix following 1989. The first of the three categories—labor—allows homo sovieticus to be placed in the field of the liberal economic system-world, which emerged following the Cold War. The second term—time—is connected to the changing experience of temporality and post-communist historical narratives, which defined the region as "backward" and "lagging behind". The last term—space—highlights the changing status of land in Eastern Europe of the 1990s, and it relates to the privatization of farmland and the emergence of Special Economic Zones. It is at the junction of those three axes that the figure of the racialized homo sovieticus emerged, which—even if tightly connected to the local context and conditions—belongs to the global histories of colonialism and their long duration throughout the centuries.

I.

The term "homo sovieticus" was first introduced in 1981 by Soviet philosopher Alexandr Zinoviev to describe a specific subjectivity, which developed during the late communist period in the USSR.[8] However, in Poland the concept was made popular in the early 1990s thanks to the writings of Polish priest Józef Tischner which appeared in several liberal newspapers such as Gazeta Wybrocza.[9] In his view,

8 Aleksandr Zinoviev, *Homo Sovieticus,* (London: Paladin, 1986).

9 See: Piotr Sztompka, "The Ambivalence of Social Change in Post-Communist Societies," *Czy koniec socjalizmu? Polska transformacja w teoriach socjologicznych*, ed Anna Śliż et al., (Warsaw: Wydawnictwo Naukowe Scholar, 2008), Piotr Sztompka, *The Sociology of Social Change.* (Oxford: Wiley- Blackwell, 1993), Józef Tischner, *Etyka solidarności i Homo Sovieticus* (Krakow: Społeczny Instytut Wydawniczy Znak, 1992).

homo sovieticus embodied all the alleged sins of the former communist system such as cynicism, nepotism, lack of responsibility, inertia, dishonesty, propensity for breaking the law and helplessness. The figure was presented as a major obstacle, preventing Poland's full accession to Western Europe, for it came to represent the antithesis of European modernity understood as a linear narrative hinging upon the category of progress, capitalist development, rationality and individualization. In this context the anthropologist Michał Buchowski states that the figure of the homo sovieticus was "orientalized" by neoliberal writers by presenting him as the antithesis to the modern subject.[10] Significantly, this neocolonial form of racialization was largely propagated by the local intelligentsia which was fully supportive of the new neoliberal order. Indeed, we might consider this a form of internal colonialism which served as an ideological tool to reinforce the class system. Nonetheless, it seems to me that the category of "orientalization" does not suffice to describe this racialization process. What appears far more apt is introducing the "race" category, understood as a role/position under the capitalist economy and the system of global production.

In order to shed some light on the racialized character of the homo sovieticus, I would like to refer to Cedric J. Robinson's monumental work titled *Black Marxism. The Making of the Black Radical Tradition* (1983), which attempts to rewrite modern Western history by placing at its center the category of race.[11] The diagnoses included in the book bear significant importance for conceptualizing the racialized character of the European peripheries. By referring to a variety of disciplines ranging from political theory, through philosophy and history to cultural studies, Robinson puts forward that the notion of race was invented in Western Europe prior to the encounter between inhabitants of Europe and Africa or the New World. The category was created with the emergence in the 15th century of the new capitalist regime with the purpose to discipline and subjugate lower classes which included wage laborers, peasants, serfs, slaves, vagabonds and beggars[12]. Robinson claims that the first "blacks" in Medieval Europe were Tatar, Greek,

10 Michał Buchowski, "The Specter of Orientalism in Europe: From Exotic Other to Stigmatized Brother," *Anthropological Quarterly* 3(79), 2006: 463–482.
11 Cedric J. Robinson, *Black Marxism: The Making of the Black Radical Tradition*, (London: Penguin, 2021).
12 Ibidem. 22.

Armenian, Slavic, Irish as well as Chinese slaves. They worked as house servants but they were also used for farming, on sugar plantations (such as the ones in Medieval Italy) and in mines.[13] Robinson labels this historical stage as "intra-European slavery" and claims that it lay the groundwork for the later human slavery on the Atlantic.[14] Contrary to the traditional Marxist narrative, which regards capitalism as an opportunity to leave the darkness of feudalism, from the very beginning Robinson describes the emergent system as a vehicle for enslavement, violence, exploitation, and death, whose major tool is racialization and differentiation of various social groups. The author writes:

> "As the Slavs became natural slaves, the racially inferior stock for domination and exploitation during the Middle Ages, as the Tatars came to occupy a similar position in the Italian cities of the late Middle Ages, so at the systemic interlocking of capitalism in the 16th Century, the peoples of the Third World began to fill this expanding category of a civilization reproduced by capitalism."[15]

The central notion that Robinson puts forward is "racial capitalism," which can also shed light on the processes taking place in Eastern Europe in the 90s. According to the scholar, the term reflects the nature of the emergent capital, which has a "tendency not to homogenize but to differentiate—to exaggerate regional, subcultural, and dialectical differences into "racial" ones."[16] How did the process look in the countries of the former Eastern Bloc? In the early 90s a series of brutal economic reforms were conducted with a view to dismantle the Soviet centrally planned economy and implement capitalist measures. One effect of these transformations was a skyrocketing unemployment rate, which reached 20% in Poland in 2002.[17] Cuts in welfare led to aggravated levels of poverty.[18] In this context, the homo sovieticus stigma aimed to neutralize the political agency of the

13 Ibid. 15.
14 Ibid. 16.
15 Ibid. 27.
16 Ibid. 34.
17 Stopa bezrobocia Rejestrowanego, Główny Urząd Statystyczny, https://stat.gov.pl/obszary-tematyczne/rynek-pracy/bezrobocie-rejestrowane/stopa-bezrobocia-rejestrowanego-w-latach-1990-2021,4,1.html.
18 David Ost, *The Defeat of Solidarity: Anger and Politics in Postcommunist* Europe (Ithaca: Cornell University Press, 2005). See also: Ryszard Szarfenberg, *Ubóstwo i wykluczenie społeczne w Polsce – pomiar, wyjaśnianie, strategie przeciwdziałania,* (Warsaw: Fundacja ICRA, 2012), Wojciech Woźniak, *Nierówności społeczne w polskim dyskursie politycznym*, (Warsaw: Wydawnictwo Naukowe Scholar, 2012).

formerly powerful working class. Indeed, they ceased to be perceived as full-fledged citizens struggling for the right to a dignified life: instead they were described as a social stratum characterized by a sense of entitlement fighting for the preservation of their past privilege.[19] At the same time, the impoverished working class in Eastern Europe turned out to be an important economic resource as a stock of cheap labor in the new capitalist order. With a reference to the Marxist notion of "primitive accumulation" as an indispensable stage in the development of capitalism we can state that in the case of Eastern Europe the cheap work force, deprived of rights, subsisting on the verge of extreme poverty was the primary asset. It was them that accounted for the local "form of capital": an energetic resource serving the purpose of propelling forward the new economy.

The system that emerged in the 1990s can be analyzed as a manifestation of "racial capitalism" described by Robinson and other scholars including W.E.B Dubois and Eric Williams[20]. Several social and class processes that occurred after 1989 can be envisaged in racial terms. On the one hand, we encountered the aspirations held by the middle class and intelligentsia to fully join Europe which was perceived as an embodiment of "whiteness". On the other hand, there was an ongoing process of racialization of the working class as the "raw" material upon which the new capitalist system was founded. Those changes stemmed from the re-inclusion of Eastern Europe into the global market after 1989, from which it was largely excluded under the communist regime. The region was admitted as a periphery abundant in cheap labor, a site of low-taxed production and an attractive market outlet.[21] It is noteworthy to highlight that the peripheral positioning of Eastern Europe should be considered in the long-term perspective as its economic status was largely shaped as early as the 16th century. In was then that the modern system-world was formed and the dynamics between centers

19 Wojciech Woźniak, "From Underclass To Homo Sovieticus: Human Constraints Towards Modernization," *Praktyka Teoretyczna*,13/2014.

20 See: Eric Williams, *Capitalism and Slavery*, (Chapel Hill: The University of North Carolina Press, 1994), W. E. B. Du Bois, *The World and Africa and Color and Democracy*, (Oxford: Oxford University Press, 2007).

21 Ivan Berend, *Central and Eastern Europe, 1944–1993: Detour from the Periphery to the Periphery*, (Cambridge: Cambridge University Press, 1999).

and (semi)peripheral regions established.[22] The changes occurring in the 1990s in fact meant returning to the centuries long configuration, where Eastern Europe played a predefined role.

II.

The concept of time is one of the most relevant social categories, which determine the life, identity, memory and culture of a given community. It is far from a constant category: on the contrary, it is subject to continuous transformations dictated by changing ideological, religious or economic systems. Simultaneously, from the very beginning time has always been the site of conflict and clashing visions of the world. It also played a fundamental role in the colonization process: starting from the 60th century the West strived to impose its comprehension and measure of time on the remaining part of the world.[23] The Western category of time—perceived as rationalist and mechanistic—was to supersede indigenous practices deemed "irrational," "chaotic," "unprecise," and "subjective."[24] Native people were presented as deprived of an "objective" sense of time, which led to an alleged laziness, lack of productivity and punctuality, as well as lack of initiative. The colonial authority operated on a series of dichotomous divisions, which rendered the natives irrefutably Other—also in temporal terms. The process, in Edward Said's words, led to "help[ing] the mind to intensify its own sense of itself by dramatizing the distance and difference between what is close to it and what is far away."[25] The race category has an immanently inscribed time component in itself. People of color were often perceived as lagging "behind the times."[26]

22 Marian Małowist, *Europa i jej ekspansja w XIV–XVII wieku [Europe and its expansion in the 14th–17th centuries]*, (Warsaw: Wydawnictwo Naukowe PWN, 1993), Witold Kula, *Historia, zacofanie, rozwój*, (Warsaw: Czytelnik, 1983), Anna Sosnowska, *Explaining Economic Backwardness: Post-1945 Polish Historians on Eastern Europe*, (Budapest: CEU Press, 2019).

23 Giordano Nanni, *The Colonisation of Time: Ritual, Routine and Resistance in the British Empire*, (Manchester: Manchester University Press, 2012). See also: Vanessa Ogle, *The Global Transformation of Time: 1870–1950*, (Cam. Massachusetts: Harvard University Press, 2015), Stephen E. Hanson, *Time and Revolution Marxism and the Design of Soviet Institutions*, (Chapel Hill: The University of North Carolina Press, 2000), David S. Landes, *Revolution in Time. Clocks and the Making of the Modern World*, (London: Penguin, 2000).

24 Giordano Nanni, *The Colonisation of Time: Ritual, Routine and Resistance in the British Empire*, 3–15.

25 Edward Said, *Orientalism*, (New York: Pantheon Books, 1978) 55.

26 Charles Mills, "The Chronopolitics of Racial Time", in *Time & Society* 29(2) (2020): 297–317.

How can these observations relate to the post-communist period? At first, we can see that the time rhetoric became one of the main instruments for defining and ordering the new reality. From the outset the area was labeled as "backward" and lagging behind the standards of Western Europe.[27] As envisaged by Western consultants (such as the neoliberal economist Jeffrey Sachs) as well as local elites the region was at a different—earlier—stage of development. That is why the implementation of political and economic reforms was often accompanied by the "catching up with the West" rhetoric. This ideological position entirely overlooked the fact that the reforms did not in the least lead to Eastern Europe joining Western Europe on an equal position. On the contrary, the applied measures turned the region into the backyard of the system-world, where exploitation of cheap labor provided by the racialized homo sovieticus played a central role. Even though this discourse eventually became subjected to critical analysis, it has not been explored in racial terms. However, there are undeniable similarities in the way that "backward" inhabitants of Eastern Europe were characterized in the 1990s and the rhetoric of colonial racialization of the Other as in the case of indigenous people from American or Australian native communities.[28] In none of these cases did the "backwardness" rhetoric base on impartial evaluation but it became a tool that legitimated conquest policies or implementation of Western political and economic solutions. In order to describe the ideological nature of time researchers introduced the term "chronopolitics," which draws a direct connection between temporal regimes and their political objectives.[29] It is a broad term that encompasses diverse social processes ranging from the macro level (historical politics) to micro (quotidian life). As the Caribbean philosopher Charles W. Mills maintains, race becomes a global matrix of power because of chronopolitics:

> "The chronopolitical discourse of empire centres Europeans as the most temporally advanced race on the planet, ready to assume the burden of leading to civilization those with the capacity

27 Boris Buden, *Transition to Nowhere: Art in History After 1989*, (Berlin: Archive Books, 2020).
28 Thomas McCarthy, *Race, Empire, and the Idea of Human Development*, (Cambridge: Cambridge University Press, 2009).
29 George Wallis, "Chronopolitics: The Impact of Time Perspectives on the Dynamics of Change," *Social Forces* 49(1)/170: 102–108.

to progress, even as assimilated inferiors, or if necessary to exterminate or at least remove from the path of progress those lacking this capacity."[30]

Western temporality is termed as unambiguously objective and white, whereas the remaining part of the world lives in the shadow of what we might call "time of color." In the post-war era this rhetoric was replaced by the division of states into "developed" (the capitalist core countries), "developing" (semi-peripherical countries) and "backward" (peripherical countries), which often laid the ground for imperialist American foreign policy and military interventions.[31] What can be used to exemplify the colonial chronopolitcs in the case of a racialized homo sovieticus? I have already mentioned the "catching up with the West" rhetoric. Another instance refers to the changes in the way work is performed and how production is organized, which ensued following the implementation of the neoliberal "shock doctrine" and free market.[32] The reforms announced the need for profound transformations in the work regime as the homo sovieticus was dubbed lazy, slow, and lacking in any discipline. One of the instruments to rectify the situation was keeping track of time. Task fragmentation was introduced and a set time period was prescribed for their implementation. Working conditions in Polish Amazon warehouses can be quoted as one of the most drastic examples of colonial chronopolitics. Employees work longer shifts and receive a few times lower wages than their German counterparts. The most brutal example of exercising control in Amazon's workhouses in Poland is fixing a particular time limit expressed in minutes under which workers are required to perform every action like starting and finishing a task (7 minutes) or taking a break (15 minutes).[33] A system of trackers that monitor the work pace supervise employees' productivity, and the workers are expected to meet the set time limits. This system results from the matrix of the managerial,

30 Charles Mills, "The Chronopolitics of Racial Time", 307.

31 Neda Atanasoski, *Humanitarian Violence: The U.S. Deployment of Diversity*, (Minneapolis: University of Minnesota Press). See also: Celso Furtado, *The Myth of Economic Development and the Future of the Third World*, (Cambridge: Cambridge University Press, 1974).

32 Naomi Klein, *The Shock Doctrine: The Rise of Disaster Capitalism*, (London: Penguin, 2008), Isabella M. Weber, *How China Escaped Shock Therapy. The Market Reform Debate*, (London: Routledge, 2021).

33 Patrycja Otto, "Praca w Amazonie to kołchoz. Główna zasada to: wykorzystać, przemielić i wyrzucić," *Dziennik Gazeta Prawna*, https://serwisy.gazetaprawna.pl/praca-i-kariera/artykuly/1214408,praca-w-amazon-polska.htmlpublished 13 August 2018.

colonial authority, which perceives Polish workers as unable to meet the expected standards of capitalistic production without strict policing measures.

III.

Land constitutes one of the key elements of colonial subjugation. This is especially true in the case of "settler colonialism"—a type of domination that aims to take over indigenous land and pass it to white settlers.[34] This is the case of Australia and North America, where indigenous land was seen as *terra nullius*: an empty space, without owners, awaiting ownership by Western settlers.[35] Scholars have pointed out that "settler colonialism" was tightly bound with the changing property law, which starting from the 16th century moved away from communal ownership and shifted towards individual rights.[36] Natives were held to be inherently "primitive" and "savage" and thus unable to hold any property. That is why, "in the process of settler colonialism, land is remade into property and human relationships to land are restricted to the relationship of the owner to his property."[37] This has led some historians such as Ellen Meiksins Wood, among others, to claim that it was land and changing modalities of farming that lay the groundwork for the developing modern capitalist regime.[38]

How to translate these considerations to the realities of post-communist Eastern Europe? What changes occurred in the land status and how did they impact the emergence of a racialized homo sovieticus? The fall of the soviet regime was followed by dynamic transformations in agriculture. These entailed the privatization and restitution of property, as a result of which state ownership as well as cooperative-held property was reduced to the

34 See: Lorenzo Veracini, *Settler Colonialism: A Theoretical Overview*, (New York: Palgrave Macmillan, 2010), Lorenzo Veracini, *The Settler Colonial Present*, (New York: Palgrave Macmillan, 2012), Patrick Wolfe, *Settler Colonialism and the Transformation of Anthropology: The politics and poetics of an ethnographic event*, (London: Bloomsbury, 1999).

35 Patrick Wolfe, "Land, Labor, and Difference: Elementary Structures of Race" *The American Historical Review* 106, no. 3 (2001): 866–905.

36 Ibid. 869.

37 Eve Tuck and K. Wayne Yang, "Decolonization Is Not a Metaphor," *Decolonization: Indigeneity, Education, & Society*, Vol.1, No.1 (2012): 3.

38 Ellen Meikins Wood, *The Origin of Capitalism. A longer View*, (London: Verso, 1999), Spencer Dimmock, *The Origin of Capitalism in England, 1400–1600*, (Chicago: Haymarket Books, 2015).

benefit of individual farmers.[39] In 1990 in Hungary an approximate 75% of farmland belonged to farming cooperatives, whereas in 2011 80% was privately held. Thus, over a period of 20 years the proportion was completely reversed.[40] The dynamics bear strong similarities to the historical process of land enclosure in the late Middle Ages which involved the appropriation of "waste" or "common land" by landowners which until then had been considered collective property of the inhabitants of nearby villages. This sparked mass protests, regarded as one of the first forms of rebellion against the emergent capitalism. Land enclosure took place both in Western Europe and in the New World from the 16th to 17th century and, according to scholars, accounted for one of the key transitional stages from the feudal to the capitalist economy.[41] A similar process of land enclosure/privatization occurred in Eastern Europe in the 1990s and led to the disappearance of state-owned/collective forms of ownership and to the emergence of private agricultural land. While some protest took place against those policies, it never reached a wider audience, remaining rather isolated and fragmented.

Perhaps the most striking example of land enclosure in Eastern Europe after 1989 was the establishment of Special Economic Zones (SEZ)—administrative territorial units, where business was to be run on preferential terms. The zones in question were specifically created to attract Western investors and foreign capital. SEZ offer, among other benefits, income tax reliefs and attractive premises with already developed infrastructure. In Poland there are 14 zones of that type, and several others were instituted in post-Soviet Lithuania, Belarus, and Ukraine. SEZ can be perceived as a spatial articulation of colonial capitalism where breaches of workers' rights occur on a regular basis, there is a ban on union organizing and state control is completely absent. This spatial dimension of colonialism was described by Achille Mbembe in the following way:

> "*Colonial occupation* itself was a matter of seizing, delimiting, and asserting control over a physical geographical area—of writing on

39 Jerzy Bański, "Zmiany własnościowe użytków rolnych w wybranych krajach Europy *Środkowej*," Wieś i Rolnictwo, 1(174) /2017. Wyjątkiem stanowiła Polska oraz Jugosławia, w których w latach 80tych prywatna własność ziemska stanowiła ok 80% całości.
40 Ibid. 10.
41 See: Patrick Brantlinger, *Barbed Wire: Capitalism and the Enclosure of the Commons*, (London: Routledge, 2017), Brett Christophers, *The New Enclosure*, (London: Verso, 2018).

> the ground a new set of special relations. The writing of new spatial relations (territorialisation), was, ultimately, tantamount to the production of boundaries and hierarchies, zones and enclaves; the subversion of existing property arrangements; the classification of people according to different categories; resource extraction, and, finally, the manufacturing of a large reservoir of cultural imaginaries. [...] Space was therefore the raw material of sovereignty and the violence it carried with it."[42]

The establishment of SEZ in Eastern Europe resonates with the process described by Mbembe where colonial relations are spatialized thanks to interlocking processes of land seizure and border demarcation. This leads to the establishment of strict hierarchies that classify people accordingly to a system of racialized differences with preestablished spatial coordinates.

CONCLUSION

The aim of my text was to re-inscribe Eastern Europe onto the global map of racial relations that began to take shape starting from the 17th century. This modern world-system was profoundly shaped by race relations which were often the basis of political, economic and ideological relations between metropoles and peripherical areas. Such an outlook allows us to consider Eastern Europe through the prism of long-duration, a methodological perspective which claims that any given region has been shaped by centuries-long processes and dependencies. Several Polish historians such as Marian Małowist, Witold Kula, Anna Sosnowska, and, more recently, Jan Sowa have claimed that it is exactly this historical perspective that permits precisely locating the exact moment when Eastern Europe started to diverge from the Western model of modern development.[43] While in the 16th century core countries moved toward wage labor, in Eastern Europe we witnessed the phenomena of "second serfdom" which saw the peasants in Poland, Ukraine, Hungary, and Bohemia increasingly

42 Achille Mbembe, *Necropolitics*, (Durham: Duke University Press, 2019), 25–26

43 Marian Małowist, *Europa i jej ekspansja w XIV–XVII wieku [Europe and its expansion in the 14th–17th centuries]*, (Warsaw: Wydawnictwo Naukowe PWN, 1993), Witold Kula, *Historia, zacofanie, rozwój*, (Warsaw: Czytelnik, 1983), Anna Sosnowska, *Explaining Economic Backwardness: Post–1945 Polish Historians on Eastern Europe*, (Budapest: CEU Press, 2019), Jan Sowa, *Fantomowe ciało króla: peryferyjne zmagania z nowoczesną formą*, (Warsaw: Wydawnictwo UNIVERSITAS, 2011).

subjugated to their landlords. This has led to a disproportionate development of agriculture at the expense of industry and handicraft which were to shape the upcoming reality of modernity in Western Europe. From then on, Eastern Europe was to increasingly rely on cheap forms of labor which are by some historians compared to the system of black slavery and plantation production in the New World.[44] Indeed, as a sort of intellectual provocation, we might wonder if the figure of the racialized homo sovieticus might not also be perceived in terms of "blackness." While there are striking historical differences between how race operated within the context of the African diaspora and Eastern Europe peripheral status, it is also of the utmost importance to underline the many similarities which exist between how the two subaltern groups have been constructed within a global setting. Hence my proposal to introduce the category of race in relation to class realities in Eastern Europe is not only linked to post-communist economic structures but is instead deeply rooted in centuries-long processes which have led to the emergence of modernity and its global matrix of power.

44 Michał Rauszer, "Chłop-niewolnik? Pańszczyzna w perspektywie antropologii historii," *Lud (Lublin)* 101 (2018): 107. See also Kacper Pobłocki, *Chamstwo,* (Warsaw: Wydawnictwo Czarne, 2021).

Being-in-the-Room Privilege: Elite Capture and Epistemic Deference

Olúfẹ́mi O. Táíwò

> "I abandoned the pitch because I don't think I'm the right person to write this story—I have no idea what it's like to be Black ... I can send you the Google doc with my notes, too?"

I flinched inwardly. It was an innocent and properly motivated offer: Helen, a freelance journalist, was offering to give up something for me, stemming from her concern to live out an ethos of racial justice. But I worried that it was also a trap.

Even setting aside the mistake about the power dynamics of the conversation (I am Black, but also a tenure-track professor), there was a problem here that I had seen many times before. Behind the assumption that I had experiential insight she lacked was the recognizable cultural imprint of a much discussed, polarizing perspective on knowledge and politics: standpoint epistemology.

If you consider a textbook definition of standpoint epistemology, it may be hard to see the controversy around this idea. The *International Encyclopedia of Philosophy* boils it down to three innocuous-sounding contentions:

1) Knowledge is socially situated
2) Marginalized people have some positional advantages in gaining some forms of knowledge
3) Research programs ought to reflect these facts.

Liam Kofi Bright argues persuasively that these contentions are derivable from a combination of 1) basic empiricist commitments, and 2) a minimally plausible account of how the social world affects what knowledge groups of people are likely to seek and find.

So, if the problem isn't the basic idea, what is it?

I think it's less about the core ideas and more about the prevailing norms that convert them into practice. The call to "listen to the most affected" or "center the most marginalized" is ubiquitous in many academic and activist circles. But it's never sat well with me. In my experience, when people say they need to "listen to the most affected," it isn't because they intend to set up Skype calls to refugee camps or to collaborate with houseless people. Instead, it has more often meant handing conversational authority and attentional goods to those who most snugly fit into the social categories associated with these ills—regardless of what they actually do or do not know, or what they have or have not personally experienced. In the case of my conversation with Helen, my racial category tied me more "authentically" to an experience that neither of us had had. She was called to defer to me by the rules of the game as we understood it. Even where stakes are high—where potential researchers are discussing how to understand a social phenomenon, where activists are deciding what to target—these rules often prevail.

The trap wasn't *that* standpoint epistemology was affecting the conversation, but *how*. Broadly, the norms of putting standpoint epistemology into practice call for practices of deference: giving offerings, passing the mic, believing. These are good ideas in many cases, and the norms that ask us to be ready to do them stem from admirable motivations: a desire to increase the social power of marginalized people identified as sources of knowledge and rightful targets of deferential behavior. But deferring in this way as a rule or default political orientation can actually work counter to marginalized groups' interests, especially in elite spaces.

Some rooms have outsize power and influence: the Situation Room, the newsroom, the bargaining table, the conference room. Being in these rooms means being in a position to affect institutions and broader social dynamics by way of deciding what one is to say and do. Access to these rooms is itself a kind of social advantage, and one often gained through some prior social advantage. From a societal standpoint, the "most affected" by the social injustices we associate with politically important identities like gender, class, race, and nationality are disproportionately likely to be incarcerated, underemployed, or part of the 44 percent of the world's population without internet access—and thus both left out of the rooms of power and largely ignored by the people in the rooms of power. Individuals who make it past the various social selection pressures that filter out those social identities associated with these negative outcomes are most likely to be in the room. That is, they are most likely to be in the room precisely because of ways in which they are systematically *different from* (and thus potentially unrepresentative of) the very people they are then asked to represent in the room.

I suspected that Helen's offer was a trap. She was not the one who set it, but it threatened to ensnare us both all the same. Broader cultural norms—the sort set in motion by prefacing statements with "As a Black man ..."—cued up a set of standpoint-respecting practices that many of us know consciously or unconsciously by rote. However, the forms of deference that often follow are ultimately self-undermining and only reliably serve "elite capture": the control over political agendas and resources by a group's most advantaged people. If we want to use standpoint epistemology to challenge unjust power arrangements, it's hard to imagine how we could do worse.

***

To say what's wrong with the popular, deferential applications of standpoint epistemology, we need to understand what makes it popular. A number of cynical answers present themselves: some (especially the more socially advantaged) don't genuinely want social change—they just want the *appearance* of it. Alternatively, deference to figures from oppressed communities is a performance that sanitizes, apologizes for, or simply distracts from the fact that the deferrer has enough "in the room" privilege for their "lifting up" of a perspective to be of consequence.

I suspect there is some truth to these views, but I am unsatisfied. Many of the people who support and enact these deferential norms are rather like Helen: motivated by the right reasons but trusting people they share such rooms with to help them find the proper practical expression of their joint moral commitments. We don't need to attribute bad faith to all or even most of those who interpret standpoint epistemology deferentially to explain the phenomenon, and it's not even clear it would help. Bad "roommates" aren't the problem for the same reason that Helen being a good roommate wasn't the solution: the problem emerges from how the rooms themselves are constructed and managed.

To return to the initial example with Helen, the issue wasn't merely that I hadn't grown up in the kind of low-income, redlined community she was imagining. The epistemic situation was much worse than this. Many of the facts about me that made my life chances different from those of the people she was imagining were the very same facts that made me likely to be offered things on their behalf. If I *had* grown up in such a community, we probably wouldn't have been on the phone together.

***

Many aspects of our social system serve as filtering mechanisms, determining which interactions happen and between whom, and thus which social patterns people are in a position to observe. For the majority of the 20th century, the U.S. quota system of immigration made legal immigration with a path to citizenship almost exclusively available to Europeans (earning Hitler's regard as the obvious "leader in developing explicitly racist policies of nationality and immigration"). But the 1965 Immigration and Nationality Act opened up immigration possibilities, with a preference for "skilled labor."

My parents' qualification as skilled laborers does much to explain their entry into the country and the subsequent class advantages and monetary resources (such as wealth) that I was born into. We are not atypical: the Nigerian American population is one of the country's most successful immigrant populations (what no one mentions, of course, is that the 112,000 or so Nigerian Americans with advanced degrees is utterly dwarfed by the 82 million Nigerians who live on less than a dollar a day, or how the former fact intersects with the latter). The selectivity of immigration law helps explain the rates of educational attainment of the Nigerian diasporic community that raised me, which in turn helps explain my entry into the exclusive Advanced Placement and Honors classes in high school, which in turn helps explain my access to higher education ... and so on, and so on.

It is easy, then, to see how this deferential form of standpoint epistemology contributes to elite capture at scale. The rooms of power and influence are at the end of causal chains that have selection effects. As you get higher and higher forms of education, social experiences narrow—some students are pipelined to PhDs and others to prisons. Deferential ways of dealing with identity can inherit the distortions caused by these selection processes.

But it's equally easy to see locally—in this room, in this academic literature or field, in this conversation—why this deference seems to make sense. It is often an improvement on the epistemic procedure that preceded it: the person deferred to may well be better epistemically positioned than the others in the room. It may well be the best we can do while holding fixed most of the facts about the rooms themselves: what power resides in them, who is admitted.

But these are the last facts we should want to hold fixed. Doing better than the epistemic norms we've inherited from a history of explicit global apartheid is an awfully low bar to set. The facts that explain who ends up in which room shape our world much more powerfully than the squabbles for comparative prestige between people who have already made it into the rooms. And when the conversation is about social justice, the mechanisms of the social system that determine who gets into which room often just *are* the parts of society we aim to address. For example, the fact that incarcerated people cannot participate in academic discussions about freedom that physically take place on campus is intimately related to the fact that they are locked in cages.

Deference epistemology marks itself as a solution to an epistemic and political problem. But not only does it fail to solve these problems, it adds new ones. One might think questions of justice ought to be primarily concerned with fixing disparities around health care, working conditions, and basic material and interpersonal security. Yet conversations about justice have come to be shaped by people who have ever more specific practical advice about fixing the distribution of attention and conversational power. Deference practices that serve attention-focused campaigns (e.g., we've read too many white men, let's now read some people of color) can fail on their own highly questionable terms: attention to spokespeople from marginalized groups could, for example, direct attention away from the need to change the social system that marginalizes them.

Elites from marginalized groups can benefit from this arrangement in ways that are compatible with social progress. But treating group elites' interests as necessarily or even presumptively aligned with full group interests involves a political naiveté we cannot afford. Such treatment of elite interests functions as a racial Reaganomics: a strategy reliant on fantasies about the exchange rate between the attention economy and the material economy.

Perhaps the lucky few who get jobs finding the most culturally authentic and cosmetically radical description of the continuing carnage are really winning one for the culture. Then, after we in the chattering class get the clout we deserve and secure the bag, its contents will eventually trickle down to the workers who clean up after our conferences, to slums of the Global South's megacities, to its countryside.

But probably not.

***

A fuller and fairer assessment of what is going on with deference and standpoint epistemology would go beyond technical argument and contend with the emotional appeals of this strategy of deference. Those in powerful rooms may be "elites" relative to the larger group they represent, but this guarantees nothing about how they are treated in the rooms they are in. After all, a person privileged in an absolute sense (a person belonging to, say, the half of the world that has secure access to "basic needs") may nevertheless feel themselves to be consistently on the low end of the power dynamics they actually experience. Deference epistemology responds to real, morally weighty experiences of being put down, ignored, side-lined, or silenced. It thus has an important non-epistemic appeal to members of stigmatized or marginalized groups: it intervenes directly in morally consequential practices of giving attention and respect.

The social dynamics we experience have an outsize role in developing and refining our political subjectivity, and our sense of ourselves. But this very strength of standpoint epistemology—its recognition of the importance of perspective—becomes its weakness when combined with deferential practical norms. Emphasis on the ways we are marginalized often matches the world *as we have experienced it*. But, from a structural perspective, the rooms we never needed to enter (and the explanations of why we can avoid these rooms) might have more to teach us about the world and our place in it. If so, the deferential approach to standpoint epistemology actually prevents "centering" or even hearing from the most marginalized; it focuses us on the interaction of the rooms we occupy, rather than calling us to account for the interactions we don't experience. This fact about who is in the room, combined with the fact that speaking for others generates its own set of important problems (particularly when they are not there to advocate for themselves), eliminates pressures that might otherwise trouble the centrality of our own suffering—and of the suffering of the marginalized people that *do* happen to make it into rooms with us.

The dangers with this feature of deference politics are grave, as are the risks for those outside of the most powerful rooms. For those who are deferred to, it can supercharge group-undermining norms. In *Conflict is Not Abuse*, Sarah Schulman makes a provocative observation about the psychological effects of both trauma and felt superiority: while these often come about for different reasons and have very different moral statuses, they result in similar behavioral patterns. Chief among these are misrepresenting the stakes of conflict (often by overstating harm) or representing others' independence as a hostile threat (such as failures to "center" the right topics or people). These behaviors, whatever their causal history, have corrosive effects on individuals who perform them as well as the groups around them, especially when a community's norms magnify or multiply these behaviors rather than constraining or metabolizing them.

For those who defer, the habit can supercharge moral cowardice. The norms provide social cover for the abdication of responsibility: it displaces onto individual heroes, a hero class, or a mythicized past the work that is ours to do now in the present. Their perspective may be clearer on this or that specific matter, but their overall point of view isn't any less particular or constrained by history than ours. More importantly, deference places the accountability that is all of ours to bear onto select people—and, more often than not, a hyper-sanitized and thoroughly fictional caricature of them.

The same tactics of deference that insulate us from criticism also insulate us from connection and transformation. They prevent us from engaging empathetically and authentically with the struggles of other people—prerequisites of coalitional politics. As identities become more and more fine-grained and disagreements sharper, we come to realize that "coalitional politics" (understood as struggle across difference) is, simply, politics. Thus, the deferential orientation, like that fragmentation of political collectivity it enables, is ultimately anti-political.

Deference rather than interdependence may soothe short-term psychological wounds. But it does so at a steep cost: it can undermine the epistemic diaspora in North America. And the 1908 Industrial Exhibition hosted a village of Abyssinians who showed off "primitive" products that contrasted with the modern production of Czech industrial companies.

These exhibitions' anthropological sections also presented supposedly scientific information on the biological characteristics of the Czech nation, illustrated by a series of supposedly typical Czech, German, and "gypsy" skulls, plus other osteological materials, photographs of "typical Czechs," and statistical data. Such events were possibly the first place where visitors might hear that Czechs and Slavs were a part of the "white race." In this way, they learned to look at the world through the lens of modern racial theories.[10]

Other modern institutions presented non-European cultures to domestic audiences in a similar manner, though not necessarily with the explicit use of the concept of race. To this day, probably the best-known example is the Náprstek Museum in Prague. Originally founded as a museum of modern industry, from its beginnings the museum also included examples of "primitive" craft production. Thanks mainly to generous donations from the aforementioned Czech explorers, this part of the museum's exposition eventually predominated, and so an exhibition of industrial production was transformed into what to this day is a relatively important ethnographic museum.[11]

If, on the basis of these considerations, it is possible to speak of the colonial complicity of members of the Czech national movement—meaning a kind of concordance on the part of local elites with notions of the superiority of the "white" man and "white" civilization—we must also acknowledge the Czech nation's very specific position in its relationship to imperialism and, by extension, to the question of colonialism. Czech explorers (and later also tourists) often describe the dark sides of colonial rule, meaning the injustices committed by European colonizers against the non-European populace. This criticism was directed primarily at the German engagement in eastern (Tanzania, Rwanda, Burundi, Mozambique) and southeastern (Namibia) Africa and in New Guinea. Josef Durdík, Emil Holub, and others nevertheless also

10 Filip Herza, "Anthropologists and Their Monsters: Ethnicity, Body, and Ab/Normality in Early Czech Anthropology," *East Central Europe* 43, no. 1–2 (2016): 64–98.
11 Křížová, "Koloniální sny."

spoke relatively openly about the negative aspects of colonial rule in the Dutch and British colonial holdings. And finally, various individuals spoke out publicly as active supporters of national liberation movements against colonial rule. For instance, in the second half of the 19th century, Ferdinand Blumentritt, director of Litoměřice's *gymnázium*, maintained contacts with the Filipino writer José Rizal, a leading representative of the movement for the Philippines' independence from Spain.[12]

Criticism of colonialism often resonated with how local elites saw their own situation within the Habsburg monarchy. The alleged oppression of the Czech national movement in the "prison of nations" may also have led Czechs to symbolically identify with at least some colonized and oppressed nations. One example is the distinct popularity of the North American "Indians," whose tragic fate was evocatively captured by the poet Josef Václav Sládek after he returned from his travels throughout North America in the late 1860s and early 1870s.[13] As for other non-European populations, especially those in Africa and Asia, any similar level of solidarity and identification was absolutely unimaginable.

In their position towards the existence of colonial empires and colonialism in general, local elites are probably best described as being convinced of a certain level of exceptionalism. On the one hand, the members of the Czech national movement identified with the idea of the superiority of Euro-American civilization and undoubtedly profited from the existence of the colonial system's economic and power structures; on the other hand, the Czech lands' ties to these structures were indirect and thus less conscious. And finally, the local form of colonial exceptionalism contained certain (albeit limited) possibilities for Czechs' symbolic identification with the colonized populations on the basis of a subjectively felt oppression within Austria-Hungary. In the end, this dimension of Czech colonial exceptionalism may have led to the conviction that Czechs were exceptionally predisposed to an alternative form of colonial expansion that would differ from the supposedly inhumane British or German colonialism. The notion of a humanist,

12 Ladislava Gažiová, "Nitroglycerin v granátovém jablku," Artalk.cz, January 20, 2020, https://artalk.cz/2020/01/20/nitroglycerin-v-granatovem-jablku/.

13 See Josef Václav Sládek, "Na hrobech indiánských," *Ruch: Almanach omladiny československé* (Prague: I. L. Kober, 1870), 138–143; and Josef Václav Sládek, *Americké obrázky a jiná prósa*, ed. Ferdinand Strejček (Prague: J. Otto, 1914).

democratic colonialism based on Czechs' experience of "national bondage" and their alleged natural democratic nature played a key role in international attempts at the establishment of formal Czechoslovak colonies. Here it should be added that colonial exceptionalism was not just a Czech phenomenon but that it found broader expression throughout the Danube monarchy and East-Central Europe in general.

Austria-Hungary, which in the late 19th century found itself increasingly marginalized as a power and which, unlike Germany or Belgium, had not participated in the colonization of Africa, developed its own version of colonial exceptionalism.[14] In this context, the multiethnic monarchy was presented as a state with extensive experience ruling an ethnically diverse mosaic of multiple populations. The various groups' specific interests within this monarchy were allegedly balanced by the neutral authority of the emperor, who was charged with looking after all his subjects in an impartial manner. According to some people at least, the Habsburg monarchy was thus well predisposed for colonial rule—an argument made, for instance, in relation to its occupation of Bosnia and Herzegovina.

And finally, Poland developed its own version of colonial exceptionalism in the interwar era. Like its Czech neighbors, Poland pointed to its historical experience of national suppression and foreign rule, which supposedly qualified Poles to be better, more cultivated colonizers of non-European populations in the future.[15]

INTERWAR AND POSTWAR CZECHOSLOVAKIA

While Poland after the First World War partially realized its colonial fantasies or at least seriously tried to do so,[16] in the interwar period the Czechoslovak the colonial lobby never moved beyond bold plans and ambitions. But this does not mean that it should be ignored.

The idea of the future Czechoslovakia making colonial claims appeared in the domestic press as early as during negotiations regarding the postwar

14 Ginelli and Mark, "Decolonising the Non-Colonisers."

15 Marta Grzechnik, "The Missing Second World: On Poland and Postcolonial Studies," *Interventions* 21, no. 7 (March 19, 2019): 998–1014.

16 Poland's interwar projects involving targeted migration and the creation of ethnic enclaves in South America and several African countries were recently described in detail in Piotr Puchalski, *Poland in a Colonial World Order: Adjustments and Aspirations, 1918–1939* (London: Routledge, 2021).

world order. According to some, as an ally of the Entente, the newly founded state should claim the right to some of the colonies taken from the defeated powers. Most frequently mentioned in this regard was Togo in western Africa, although other German colonies such as Papua New Guinea were proposed as well.[17] Support for the idea of Czechoslovak colonial expansion was found among individuals from across the political spectrum. One of the main representatives of the Czechoslovak colonial lobby was the national socialist (no affiliation with the German National Socialists) Jan Havlasa, who had been a participant at the Paris Peace Conference. The idea of colonial engagement also enjoyed significant support among former legionnaires and within the circle of the first Czechoslovak prime minister, Karel Kramář. In this case, potential colonization was associated with the planned international intervention against Soviet Russia that, if successful, could potentially be followed by Czech and Slovak colonists settling the fertile regions of central Asia.[18] In fact, the Bank of the Czechoslovak Legions (a.k.a. Legiobanka) was one of several Czechoslovak financial institutions to support the idea of colonization or, more specifically, the use of domestic capital abroad.

In the interwar period, these individuals and banks—and even the Czechoslovak state itself—launched a number of initiatives that in one way or another promoted colonial expansion. Perhaps the most significant of these was the founding of the Institute for Emigrational and Colonizational Economic Relations within the Masaryk Academy of Labor. Established in 1923 by Rudolf Pilát, director of the market division at Živnostenská Banka, over the course of the interwar years this institution became the center of Czechoslovakia's colonial lobby.[19] Its representatives attempted, through various state institutions, to change existing migration laws in order to facilitate the creation of Czechoslovak colonies abroad. Unlike Jan Havlasa and other proponents of postwar colonial expansions, however, they did not envision the creation of overseas colonies

17 The idea of taking over German Togo was promoted, among others, by the geographer Stanislav Nikolau and the journalist Jan Reichman. Papua New Guinea figured among the proposals made by Jan Havlasa and the entrepreneur Rudolf Cicvárek. See Ivo Vasiljev, "K snahám české buržoazie o získání kolonií v době buržoazní ČSR," *Češi v cizině* 3, Stanislav Brouček (Prague: Ústav pro etnografii a folkloristiku AV ČSSR and Státní zahraniční ústav ČSSR, 1988), 139–192.

18 Ibid.

19 Stanislav Brouček and Ivo Vasiljev, "K charakteristikám československé vystěhovalecké politiky mezi dvěma světovými válkami," *Český Lid* 72, no. 2 (1985): 71–80.

in the form of territories formally controlled by the Czechoslovak state. Instead, colonies would be founded by leasing or purchasing suitable lands on the territory of a foreign state that would then be offered, under favorable conditions, to Czech and Slovak settlers. In the future, the ethnically compact enclaves thus created in, for instance, South America would act as markets for Czechoslovak industrial products or as a source of natural resources and other commodities. Although they would not involve formal colonial rule, the arguments made in support of such Czechoslovak colonies differed very little from the way in which colonization was seen in classical colonial empires. These considerations also included the same notion of "spreading the white race" at the expense of so-called primitive races and nations that one could find in the arguments of Czechoslovak proponents of colonization. From the very beginning, the idea of a more just and more democratic colonialism "à la Czechoslovakia" thus ironically involved a conviction in the superiority of the "white race." Here, too, the belief in Czech and Slovak exceptionalism was an effective form of self-deception rather than an unquestionable fact.

In any case, these interwar Czechoslovak colonial fantasies were never realized. Proposals for the annexation of one of Germany's former colonies were not implemented, and the activities of the Czechoslovak Colonization Society, founded in 1928 by members of the Emigration Institute, did not meet with much success. Its activities were limited by the restrictive migration policies enacted by a number of countries during the interwar years and, later, by the Great Depression. Essentially the only territory where Czechoslovak colonial ambitions were realized was Subcarpathian Ruthenia, a region in today's western Ukraine that international postwar treaties awarded to the newly founded republic in 1919.

The debate as to whether and in what ways Subcarpathian Ruthenia was an internal colony of Czechoslovakia has yet to be conclusively decided. The region was given to the newly founded republic on the basis of international treaties and with the approval of local elites and the significant Ruthenian diaspora in the United States. On the other hand, for its entire twenty-year existence, the Czechoslovak province of Subcarpathian Ruthenia was governed by an administration that consisted almost exclusively of Czech officials, and although the local inhabitants enjoyed the same civil rights as in other parts of the country, demands for the region's full autonomy were never met. Czechoslovak politicians and officials argued that the local population had not yet reached the level of civilizational development necessary for full political responsibility. For many members of the Czechoslovak colonial lobby, the republic's far east represented a kind of alternative to overseas colonization. Indeed, the fertile lowlands along the Hungarian border saw the establishment of colonial settlements that as a rule were inhabited by Czechs and Slovaks, many of them former legionnaires. Czech entrepreneurs and financiers expanded eastward as well, and much attention was paid to the region's natural and mineral resources: timber, rock salt, and Carpathian oil deposits.

In many aspects, Czechs' view of Subcarpathian Ruthenia understandably resembled their relationship to Slovakia. However, while Slovaks were considered a part of the Czechoslovak nation, in the eyes of the Czech public Ruthenians were a separate group in terms of both ethnicity and level of civilization. For most Czechoslovaks, the eastern part of the republic was an exotic region inhabited by picturesque, backwards people. For these reasons, the region was often referred to as Czechoslovakia's Orient, Bosnia, or Palestine, or even as "darkest Africa."[20] The civilizing mission undertaken by Czechoslovakia's government institutions and other organizations or individuals with the aim of securing the "good" and "progress" of the Ruthenian nation can thus be seen as a kind of colonial project, one that was significantly influenced by the notion of colonial exceptionalism. On the one hand, Czechoslovak officials denied frequent accusations that they were acting like colonizers in the region, but at the same time their democratic "civilizing mission" was guided by the logic of paternalism and the notion that the Ruthenians were ethnically or even racially different from them.

The Czechoslovak presence in western Ukraine ended in 1939. After the war, the region became a part of Soviet Ukraine, and Czechoslovakia itself ended

20 Stanislav Holubec, "We Bring Order, Discipline, Western European Democracy, and Culture to this Land of Former Oriental Chaos and Disorder: Czech Perceptions of Sub-Carpathian Rus and its Modernization in the 1920s," *Mastery and Lost Illusions: Space and Time in The Modernization of Eastern and Central Europe*, ed. Wlodzimierz Borodziej, Stanislav Holubec, and Joachim von Puttkamer (Munich: De Gruyter Oldenbourg, 2014), 203–225.

up within the Soviet sphere of influence. As a part of the socialist camp, the Czechoslovak state adopted, at least in theory, the rhetoric of anti-imperialism and the struggle for the liberation of the colonized nations. The ease with which anti-colonial sentiments were adopted was quite probably due to the existing tradition of colonial exceptionalism. Examples of distancing oneself from imperialism and expressions of solidarity with subjugated nations—but also paternalistic attitudes towards and the exoticization of non-European cultures—can be found in the travelogues and books written by Miroslav Zikmund and Jiří Hanzelka.[21]

Socialist Czechoslovakia's various activities in Africa—which had been an important export market for the country's industry since the interwar era—were accompanied by a similar rhetoric. As a smaller country that laid claim to an anti-imperialist tradition, Czechoslovakia truly was able to more easily establish diplomatic and trade relations with the newly decolonized countries.[22] In the 1950s and 1960s, Czechoslovakia was one of the main suppliers of weapons, ammunition, and aviation technology to countries on the African continent. In the era's complicated international situation, these supplies not only went to "friendly" socialist countries, but also often ended in the hands of their enemies. For instance, Czechoslovakia intervened in the civil war in Nigeria by selling weapons and planes to the central government in Lagos while simultaneously supporting the liberation movement in the secessionist region of Biafra, where it also sent humanitarian aid.

The economic and diplomatic activities of Czechoslovakia and other Eastern European states in Africa declined significantly after 1968. The topic nevertheless remains a little studied subject, although increased research interest in recent years means that we can soon look forward to many new findings.[23] For instance, Łukasz Stanek recently looked at the activities of Eastern European architects and construction companies in the newly decolonized African states in the 1970s and 1980s. According to Stanek, the market environment that they

21 Anna Chejnová, "Reprezentace jiného v cestopisech Zikmunda a Hanzelky," master's thesis (Prague: Charles University, Faculty of Humanities, 2020).
22 Philip E. Muehlenbeck, *Czechoslovakia in Africa, 1945–1968* (Basingstoke: Palgrave Macmillan, 2016).
23 E.g., James Mark, Artemy M. Kalinovsky, and Steffi Marung, eds., *Alternative Globalizations: Eastern Europe and the Postcolonial World* (Bloomington: Indiana University Press, 2020).

encountered there later contributed to these companies' successful transformation after the collapse of the command economy in Eastern Europe.[24] The process of decolonization, he thus argues, indirectly influenced the shape taken by capitalism in Central and Eastern Europe.

CONCLUSION

Stanek's argument invites us to briefly consider how the colonial past outlined above is reflected in the current situation in the Czech Republic and the other post-communist countries. What has remained of the isolated activities and often unrealized colonial ambitions of Czech and Czechoslovak elites? Local museums still exhibit items variously plundered during the colonial era: ethnographic collections, human and animal remains, plants, minerals, and a whole range of visual representations, maps, paintings, and photographs. But can the local colonial legacy be considered outside surviving artifacts of material culture? For instance, could the constant flow of migrants from Subcarpathia in search of work be interpreted as a legacy of Czechoslovakia's interwar colonialism just as the country's large Vietnamese community is the legacy of socialist-era migration policies?

It seems to me that the most vital part of local colonial culture remains the denial of its existence and the belief that the Czech lands historically played no or only a minimal part in colonial rule and that they were always on the side of the "ruled." Czech colonial exceptionalism undoubtedly is not as strong as its Polish variant. In other words, the way Czechs think about state socialism or earlier history does not use colonialism to condemn the power and influence of the Soviet Union or Austria-Hungary. And yet, it is my opinion that a belief in colonial exceptionalism is in some way reflected in contemporary debates in the Czech Republic. I am thinking primarily of the continued denial that the Czech Republic was in some way historically involved in the structures of colonial rule, which would mean that the country is not responsible for the many crises resulting from the legacy of colonialism. This denial was perfectly illustrated during the migrant crisis, which many people considered—and still consider—a problem that seemingly

24 Łukasz Stanek, *Architecture in Global Socialism: Eastern Europe, West Africa, and the Middle East in the Cold War* (Princeton: Princeton University Press, 2020).

does not concern the Czech Republic. Similarly, the local tradition of racism tends to be viewed more as a modern import than as the legacy of, among other things, the local colonial past. And finally, even the tendency to stick one's head in the sand when discussing the need to regulate the world economy in the face of the looming environmental catastrophe may be the result of long-term myopia and the denial of coresponsibility for the state of the world.

In recent years, high-ranking officials from a number of European states, including Britain, France, and Germany, have apologized for the crimes their countries committed during the colonial era. Should Czechs, too, apologize for their part in slavery and the colonial past, as the historian Dušan Třeštík provocatively asked at the beginning of the millennium?[25] I personally believe that such gestures can be of symbolic significance, although I understand and partially share the views of critics. Without concrete measures for rectifying past and current injustices, such gestures could easily remain mere talk. Precisely for this reason, I see great importance in a more thorough understanding of the colonial past, one that will help us to realize the limits of our own way of thinking in the present and thus liberate our imagination in order to consider a better future.

25 Dušan Třeštík, "Britové se omluví za otroctví. Čeká nás to také?," *Lidové noviny*, March 29, 2007, https://www.pressreader.com/czech-republic/lidove-noviny/20070329/281522221637650. It should be added that Třeštík was not just thinking of modern slavery, but also early medieval slavery in central and eastern Europe, which contributed to the rise of the Přemyslid state.

Forced Sterilization of the Marginalized: A Global Issue

Gwendolyn Albert

According to a 2019 data booklet published by the United Nations, the most prevalent contraceptive method among women worldwide today is sterilization.[1] This raises the question: How many of those sterilizations were chosen freely by a person who fully understood what it involved?

The apparently neutral term "sterilization" generally refers to two kinds of medical events. The first use is as a generic name for the surgical procedures of tubal ligation and vasectomy, both of which block the usual routes through which eggs or sperm are physically released so they can travel through the reproductive organs. According to a 2014 interagency statement from the World Health Organization and five other UN bodies,[2] if informed consent is given to such surgery, and if it is correctly performed in a proper clinical setting up to professional standards, then it is considered effective at bringing the reproductive capacity of the patient under all but total control due to its irreversible nature, and it is also considered safe. The second kind of event usually referred to as sterilization is one where a medical intervention undertaken for a different purpose has the secondary effect of also permanently curtailing the natural flow of reproductive material. The outcome for the patient in either kind of sterilization is the same: without medical assistance, a man would no longer be able to impregnate a woman and a woman would no longer be able to conceive a child.

When either kind of sterilization is performed without the individual's free, full and informed choice and consent, then it is a forced sterilization (also sometimes termed "coercive"[3] or "involuntary"[4]). According to international human rights oversight bodies and various courts, forced sterilization violates more than one human right, such as the right to decide on the number and spacing of one's children, the right to health, the right to information, and the right to privacy. Forced sterilizations also violate the ethical principles that should govern the profes-sional provision of health care: the principle of beneficence,

1 "Contraceptive Use by Method 2019." https://www.un.org/development/desa/pd/sites/www.un.org.development.desa.pd/files/files/documents/2020/Jan/un_2019_contraceptiveusebymethod_databooklet.pdf

2 OHCHR, UN Women, UNAIDS, UNDP, UNFPA, UNICEF and WHO. "Eliminating forced, coercive and otherwise involuntary sterilization: an interagency statement." https://www.unaids.org/sites/default/files/media_asset/201405_sterilization_en.pdf

3 Especially when involving third-party persuasion of a person, whether using incentives or threats.

4 This term refers to any medical procedure that renders a legally incompetent person permanently infertile.

the injunction to "first do no harm," and respect for the autonomy of the individual. In some cases, they also implicate the Convention on the Prevention and Punishment of the Crime of Genocide.[5]

Governments worldwide have imposed arbitrary requirements on the conditions under which patients are able to autonomously decide whether or not to choose sterilization as a permanent method of contraception, often through coercive policies designed to regulate birth rates among certain groups. Such governments have been condemned by international human rights oversight bodies for allowing forcedm-sterilizations to happen, including by states where such violations are proscribed by law. Doctors also forcibly sterilize intersex[6] and transgender[7] persons. In some legal systems, transgender persons must undergo sterilization to obtain official documentation listing their preferred gender, while obstetricians perform cosmetic surgery on intersex persons' reproductive organs as soon after birth as possible. Such procedures are frequently performed without the informed consent of the infant's legal representatives, rendering these persons sterile later in life. This medical malpractice has been ruled a human rights violation by courts and international human rights oversight bodies.

When those who wield power treat groups or their individual members as either inferior or insignificant, that means they are marginalizing them. They are predefining who belongs at the center of society and will be most able to access opportunities and share power, and who belongs on the periphery of society, where their ability to act, their access to opportunity, is curtailed and they are rendered powerless and voiceless. As a means of social control, marginalization is undertaken for the purpose of creating centers of affluence and power and peripheries of poverty and powerlessness, both at the level of the groups and their individual members.

5 "Convention on the Prevention and Punishment of the Crime of Genocide, 1948," https://www.un.org/en/genocideprevention/documents/atrocity-crimes/Doc.1_Convention%20on%20the%20Prevention%20and%20Punishment%20of%20the%20Crime%20of%20Genocide.pdf

6 Intersex is a term describing bodies that do not conform biologically to the female/male distinction. It is a naturally occurring variation and does not usually cause any problems for the person in health or medical terms.

7 A transgender person is a person whose gender identity, the personal sense of one's own gender, does not correspond with their birth sex.

Forced sterilization has been used as an instrument of marginalization worldwide, even as it has been touted as an alleged solution for poverty.[8] Professionals in the fields of health care and social welfare have forcibly sterilized persons who have been categorized by authorities as disabled,[9] members of an ethnic group (particularly indigenous groups),[10] impoverished, or as members of a religion.[11] In low-resource settings, forced sterilizations often happen under dangerous and unhygienic conditions, and those performing them also fail to provide any follow-up care, resulting in frequent deaths.

A BRIEF (AND SELECTIVE) HISTORY OF FORCED STERILIZATIONS

It is increasingly acknowledged by historians that the development of contraception in the early 20th century was, from its inception, intertwined with the eugenics movement's attempt to "breed" human beings to eliminate undesirable traits and promote desirable ones.[12] Especially in the aftermath of the population losses sustained during the First World War (1914–1918) many European governments became concerned about repopulation and the "quality" of their future citizens (and soldiers). At this time, some provinces in Canada and some states in the USA ran programs that forcibly sterilized thousands of people selected through eugenic criteria. After the Second World War, family planning accelerated even as eugenics fell out of favor after the Nazi genocide against the Jews and Roma in Europe, and advances in comprehending human heredity have revealed how simplistic it was for certain traits to have once been understood as genetically inherited. However, the proscription on eugenic rhetoric did not change the idea that misery and poverty could be alleviated just by preventing the birth of more poor people, and that has justified the promotion of sterilizations,

8 Matthew Connelly, *Fatal Misconception: The Struggle to Control World Population*, (Cambridge, MA: Belknap Press, 2010).

9 Such persons may or may not be deprived of legal capacity; when they are, their sterilization is called "involuntary." Such cases will not be described here, but given the stigmatization of various ethnic groups, ableism and eugenic thinking may play a role in forced sterilizations even of persons not diagnosed with any disability as a medical matter.

10 Jennifer Leason, "Forced and coerced sterilization of Indigenous women," *Canadian Family Physician*, July 2021, no. 67 (7) 525–527; DOI: https://doi.org/10.46747/cfp.6707525

11 This frequently overlaps with an ethnic or national identity as well, as in the case of the Uyghurs discussed herein, who are Muslim.

12 Matthew Connelly, *Fatal Misconception: The Struggle to Control World Population*, (Cambridge, MA: Belknap Press, 2010).

along with temporary forms of birth control, by the Global North to the Global South. Key tenets of eugenic thinking thus persist in the forced sterilizations that we see underway globally in the 20th and 21st centuries.

The first country to undertake eugenically motivated forced sterilizations was the USA, and representatives of Nazi Germany are said to have been inspired by its example. The people initially targeted were categorized as allegedly "mentally defective." The first state to propose and adopt such legislation was Indiana in 1907, followed by California and Washington in 1909. The 1927 Supreme Court decision *Buck v. Bell* upheld the forced sterilization of intellectually disabled patients in Virginia. In 1937 such a law was also enacted in the territory of Puerto Rico and not repealed until 1960. Oregon's program lasted until 1983, with the last forced sterilization in 1981. California, Oregon and Virginia have publicly apologized for these programs. Ultimately 27 of the 50 states had such laws, and in Washington they remain in effect. Courts also order sterilizations as part of sentencing, such as a 2014 Virginia plea deal where a man convicted of child endangerment agreed to a vasectomy. In 2020, illegal hysterectomies were performed in Georgia on the migrants being held at a particular U.S. Immigration and Customs Enforcement (ICE) center. It is also still lawful in many states for girls living with either mental or physical disabilities to be subjected to hysterectomies or to surgical removal of their breast buds when their legal guardians request this.

In Japan, a leprosy prevention law was adopted in 1907 to segregate lepers and forcibly sterilize them; the legislation was updated in the 1930s and 1950s to continue the practice. Legislation in 1940 forcibly sterilized people on a eugenic basis and legislation in 1948 clarified that persons alleged to have a "genetic predisposition to commit crime" were to be forcibly sterilized. In 2019, Japan's Supreme Court upheld the requirement for transgender persons to have their reproductive organs removed when seeking legal recognition of their preferred gender, resulting in their compulsory sterility.[13]

13 https://www.hrw.org/news/2021/10/12/trans-man-fights-japans-sterilization-requirement

In Europe, besides Nazi Germany, Sweden enacted a eugenics program including forced sterilizations in 1934 and abolished it in 1976. Compensation was paid to some victims in the 1990s, including some Romani women. Transgender persons who wanted to update the gender in their state-issued identification were required to be sterilized in Sweden until 2012. In 2017 the Government announced it would compensate the transgender people forced to undergo sterilization under that requirement.

In comparison, the former Czechoslovakia launched its own sterilization programs during the 1960s. In 2021, the Czech Republic signed into law[14] a compensation process for anybody forcibly sterilized between 1966 (when it was still part of Czechoslovakia) and 2012, when legislation was amended to require a waiting period between when a sterilization is requested and when it is performed. The compensation is the outcome of an investigation begun by the Public Defender of Rights (the ombudsman) in 2004 of complaints from Romani women that they had been sterilized without their informed consent. Elena Gorolová, the spokesperson for these women, has worked with the author since 2006 on this advocacy.

The ombudsman's Final Statement[15] reported on how the communist regime incentivized sterilization as a birth control method. Social workers targeted Romani women with incentives that were either negative (threats to institutionalize their existing children if they didn't comply) or positive (usually financial) to coerce them into it, including by misleading them as to its irreversibility. This wrongdoing was reported on at the time by dissident human rights advocates in the late 1970s and early 1980s, and the incentive programs themselves were brought to an end after the transition to liberal democracy in 1990.[16] Parallel to the incentive effort, however, women, including non-Romani women, were also being sterilized without their informed consent during Caesarean deliveries, especially during second Caesarean deliveries. That kind of forced sterilization continued not just after the 1990 transition, but also into the first

14 Act No. 297 (2021)

15 "Final Statement of the Public Defender of Rights in the Matter of Sterilisations Performed in Contravention of the Law and Proposed Remedial Measures, Office of the Public Defender of Rights," 2005, https://www.ochrance.cz/uploads-import/ENGLISH/Sterilisation.pdf

16 See the contributions to the special issue of *Romano džaniben* (2019/2) dedicated to this history, https://www.dzaniben.cz/publication.html?m=0002b666e412d85f9121a8ee0ee4a2900105&t=2014902

decade of the 21st century. Many of the women were misinformed after the fact that their sterilization had been "life-saving." Since 1966, hundreds if not thousands of women have been subjected to forced sterilization in these various ways on Czech territory.[17]

Like the Czech Republic, Slovakia was also part of Czechoslovakia until becoming independent in 1993, and the incentivizing of sterilizations under communist rule proceeded there as it did in the Czech lands. The impact in Slovakia is, however, likely to have been much more extensive, as the Romani population there is much larger and their state of marginalization is much more intense than in the Czech Republic.[18] In 2003, ongoing forced sterilizations there were reported, as was discrimination against Romani women in segregated maternity wards and cases of what is today termed obstetric violence.[19] Official backlash against the report was severe at the time.[20] Several cases were brought by Romani plaintiffs in these matters. After domestic courts failed them, the European Court of Human Rights then ruled against Slovakia and ordered compensation.[21] In November 2021 the Government of Slovakia made the historic move of apologizing for the forced sterilizations, in language acknowledging that Romani women in particular have been harmed as part of the attempted regulation of the birth rate of "socially vulnerable layers of society".[22] Compensation for most of those affected has yet to be paid.

In the Global South, impoverished men and women are targeted for sterilization through similar incentive programs that have run for decades. In Bangladesh, the average number of sterilizations between 1965–1978 grew from 600 to 50,000

17 The author has been involved in advocating for redress about this issue since 2004.

18 *Roma Civil Monitor*, https://cps.ceu.edu/sites/cps.ceu.edu/files/attachment/basicpage/3172/c1-slovakia.pdf

19 "Body and Soul. Forced Sterilization and Other Assaults on Roma Reproductive Freedom in Slovakia," Center for Reproductive Rights, 2003, https://reproductiverights.org/body-and-soul-forced-sterilization-and-other-assaults-on-roma-reproductive-freedom/

20 "Slovak Investigation Covers Up Human Rights Abuses," Center for Reproductive Rights, 2003, https://reproductiverights.org/slovak-investigation-covers-up-human-rights-abuses/

21 V. C. vs. Slovakia, Application No. 18968/07, Final Judgment, 8 November 2011. http://hudoc.echr.coe.int/eng?i=001-107364 ; N. B. vs. Slovakia, Application No. 29518/10, 12 June 2012, Final Judgment, published September 12, 2012, https://hudoc.echr.coe.int/eng#{„dmdocnumber":[„909446"],"itemid":[„001-111427"]}; I. G. and others vs. Slovakia, Application No. 15966/04, Final Judgment, November 13, 2012, published April 29, 2013, https://hudoc.echr.coe.int/fre#{%22itemid%22:[%22001-114514%22]}

22 "Slovak Government Apologizes for Illegal Sterilizations, Lawyer and Plenipotentiary for the Romani Community Say Compensation Must Follow," Romea, 2021, http://www.romea.cz/en/news/world/slovak-government-apologizes-for-illegal-sterilizations-lawyer-and-plenipotentiary-for-the-romani-community-say

per month.[23] In 1982, doctors and field workers were required to perform at least two tubal ligations and two vasectomies monthly in order to be paid at all until 1.4 million sterilizations had been completed within two years.[24] By 1983, 40,000 official recruiters were employed in this effort.[25] Access to food subsidies was also limited just to those women who could prove they had been sterilized.[26] Studies have reported deaths during or after these procedures due to respiratory arrest caused by oversedation, hemorrhage, the contraction of tetanus, or post-operative infections.[27] In some cases, doctors in Bangladesh have also reportedly sterilized women without their knowledge during gastrointestinal surgery.[28] Promotion of sterilization to Rohingya refugees from Myanmar is said to be underway there as well.[29]

China's one-child policy,[30] in and of itself a serious human rights violation,[31] was imposed in 1978. Amnesty International reported that parents of one-child families are forcibly sterilized to make sure they will not conceive again, even though such forced sterilizations contravene Chinese law.[32] In 2005 the BBC reported that national authorities had acknowledged such local violations.[33] In 2016, China moved to a two-child policy and the sterilization rates reportedly declined, but not in the Xinjiang Uyghur Autonomous Region.[34] Mass forced sterilization was reported from Xinjiang in 2019 and 2020 as part of

23 Atiqur Rahman Khan and Ingrid E. Swensen, "Acceptability of male sterilization in Bangladesh: its problems and perspectives," *Bangladesh Development Studies*, no. 6 (2) (1978).

24 Alamgir Mohiuddin, United Press International, 14 December 1982. "The Bangladesh government plans a mass voluntary sterilization of ... " archived at https://www.upi.com/Archives/1982/12/14/The-Bangladesh-government-plans-a-mass-voluntary-sterilization-of/3265408690000/

25 William Claiborne, "Bangladesh's Midwives Promote Birth Control," *Washington Post* (January 28, 1983).

26 Maria Mies and Vandana Shiva, *Ecofeminism* (1993)

27 M.J. Rosenberg,. R.W. Rochat, J. Akbar, P. Gould, A. R. Khan, A. Measham and S. Jabeen, "Sterilization in Bangladesh: mortality, morbidity, and risk factors," *International Journal of Gynecology and Obstetrics*, no. 20(4) (August 1982): 283–291

28 Nozrul Islam, "Healthcare in Bangladesh: only sterilization and vasectomies are free," May 19, 2011, https://www.asianews.it/news-en/Healthcare-in-Bangladesh:-only-sterilization-and-vasectomies-are-free-21608.html

29 https://www.theguardian.com/world/2017/oct/28/bangladesh-to-offer-sterilisation-to-rohingya-in-refugee-camps

30 The one-child policy was a Chinese government plan executed between 1980 and 2015 by restricting many families to a single child.

31 The one-child policy is considered a violation of the human right to determine the size of one's family, see note 6 above.

32 Amnesty International, "Thousands at risk of forced sterilization in China," April 22, 2010, https://www.amnesty.org/en/latest/news/2010/04/thousands-risk-forced-sterilization-china/#:~:text=Authorities%20in%20southern%20China%20must,Amnesty%20International%20said%20on%20Thursday.

33 "China 'acts on forced abortion'." BBC, September 20, 2005, http://news.bbc.co.uk/2/hi/asia-pacific/4262890.stm

34 David Stavrou, "A Million People Are Jailed at China's Gulags. I Managed to Escape. Here's What Really Goes on Inside," Haaretz. 2019, https://www.haaretz.com/world-news/2019-10-17/ty-article-magazine/.premium/a-million-people-are-jailed-at-chinas-gulags-i-escaped-heres-what-goes-on-inside/0000017f-e216-d804-ad7f-f3fe73670000.

the genocide underway there.[35] China's authoritarian rule and strict censorship make information difficult to confirm about this and other human rights abuses.

In Peru, beginning in 1995, the Fujimori administration forcibly sterilized Aymara and Quechua indigenous people with funds from Japan's Nippon Foundation, the UNFPA (The United Nations Population Fund), and USAID (The United States Agency for International Development). In response to outcry, in 1998 a USAID representative told US legislators that campaigns to promote tubal ligation and vasectomy were going to stop there. The program stopped as a whole in 2000. In 2011, the Inter-American Commission on Human Rights ruled that these cases amounted to crimes against humanity and the Attorney General reopened an investigation into them. In 2018 the first class action lawsuit involving 1,306 people, five of whom had died of the surgeries, began and has yet to conclude. Obstacles reportedly include unavailability of interpreters for the plaintiffs.

WHAT DO THESE CASES HAVE IN COMMON?

What all of these examples have in common is the elite nature of the perpetrators and the sustained investment of energy, money and time into forcing sterilizations as part of state policy. The performance of either a tubal ligation or a vasectomy is a complex endeavor, usually requiring a trained surgeon, other health care workers, medical equipment, an intake system for patients—and the bureaucracy of a recruitment program by paraprofessionals in cases where incentives are offered.

The second parallel has to do with justice systems. Even in countries where the potential for rights abuses related to sterilizations was understood by those drafting the laws to regulate these procedures, such as in China or the former Czechoslovakia, violations both of the law and of rights have happened locally and have apparently been tolerated by the state. In the case of the former Czechoslovakia and its successor states, prosecutors have rarely involved their offices with such cases, and in Slovakia when they did so, it was to threaten to prosecute the human rights defenders. Another commonality has to do with

35 "China cuts Uighur births with IUDs, abortion, sterilization," Associated Press, June 29, 2020, https://apnews.com/article/ap-top-news-international-news-weekend-reads-china-health-269b3de1af34e17c1941a514f78d764c

the continuous nature of these abuses irrespective of the kind of governmental rule. After the transition to liberal democracy in Czechoslovakia, the incentives for sterilization were no longer offered, but forced sterilizations continued. Bangladesh has gone in and out of military rule, seemingly without any effect on its policies in this regard. Even authoritarian China, despite promulgating its much clearer regulations for the one-child policy in 2002,[36] was unable to stop forced sterilizations being undertaken by local officials in different parts of the country—and apparently does not intend to stop them happening to the Uyghurs in Xinjiang.

Charges of genocide are brought by the international community in cases involving spectacular violence, but tubal ligation is usually performed in the inner sanctum of a hospital by professionals who often believe they are helping the woman involved and who may genuinely be unaware that if she did not freely choose and consent to that operation, they are grossly violating her rights. The Peruvian cases above may be the only ones that have been identified as crimes against humanity to date.

Although the postwar framing of the concept of genocide does include preventing births within a group as one definition of that crime, it only applies to certain kinds of groups: ethnic ones, national ones, "racial" ones or religious ones. If we were to broaden the grounds for genocide to include the group of people impoverished through social marginalization, we would quickly understand how frequently this crime has been committed globally through forced sterilizations and how many have been involved in conspiring to commit it, directly and publicly inciting its perpetration, and are complicit in it. More progress must be made not just on compensating victims but instructing members of the medical profession in how they can maximally comply with human rights when providing reproductive health care services.

36 Stavrou, 2019

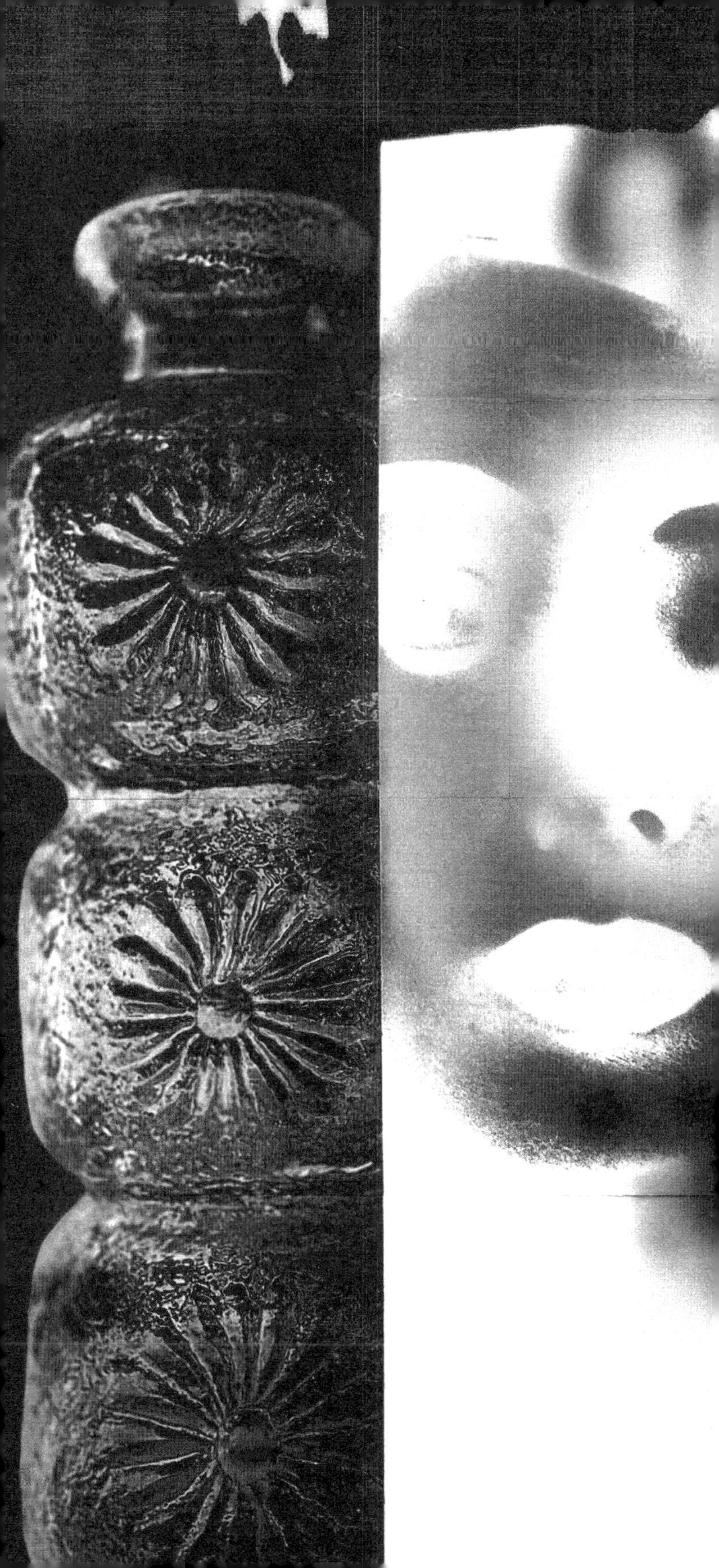

quarterly for culture
43/2020

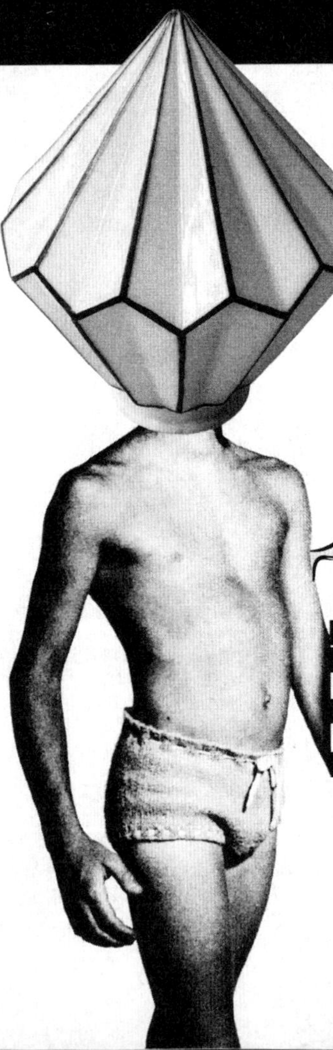

PIŽMO

support for non-believers

43

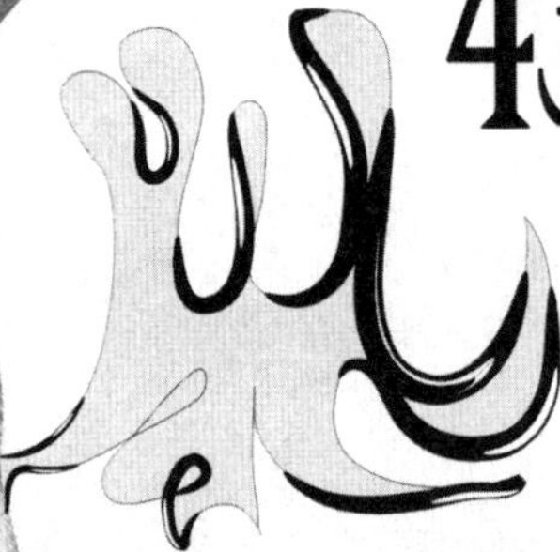

Determined to Break Something

You wanted them for the rest of your life,
But you don't love them.
You knit them scratchy clothing.
They already know what's what.
You broke it with portents of doom.
For life and death.
Farting in a woolen swimsuit.

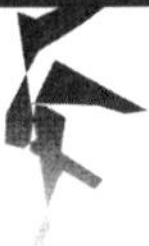

Likeness Is a Really Unpleasant Thing

When I drive, I quickly leave the place where they were lying
Where they practiced adopted lies
Exorcised the chosen with drivel about the likeness of the master
Determined their offspring, whom they own, O woe
Moments of yearning in memory
Fucking Mother with human remains

I overtake
By the gate I call
I am here
You are there
Open up

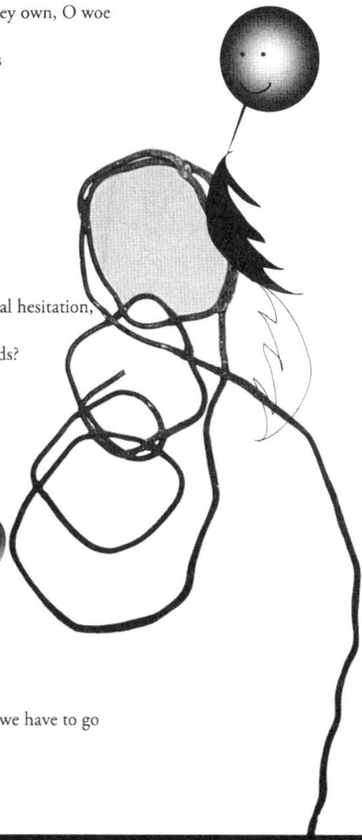

To Evoke a Story

You are burning and the result is a dual hesitation,
Difficult fellow citizens arrive.
Do they have something on their heads?
They do.

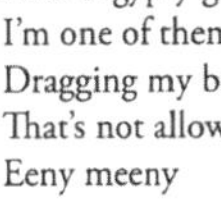

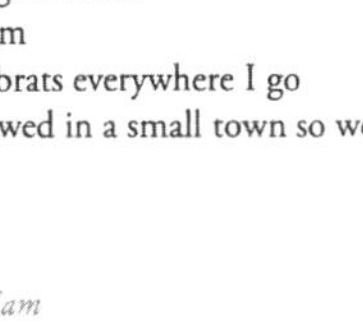

Miny Moe

Lots of gypsy girls shout
I'm one of them
Dragging my brats everywhere I go
That's not allowed in a small town so we have to go
Eeny meeny

text/ilustr.: Sráč Sam

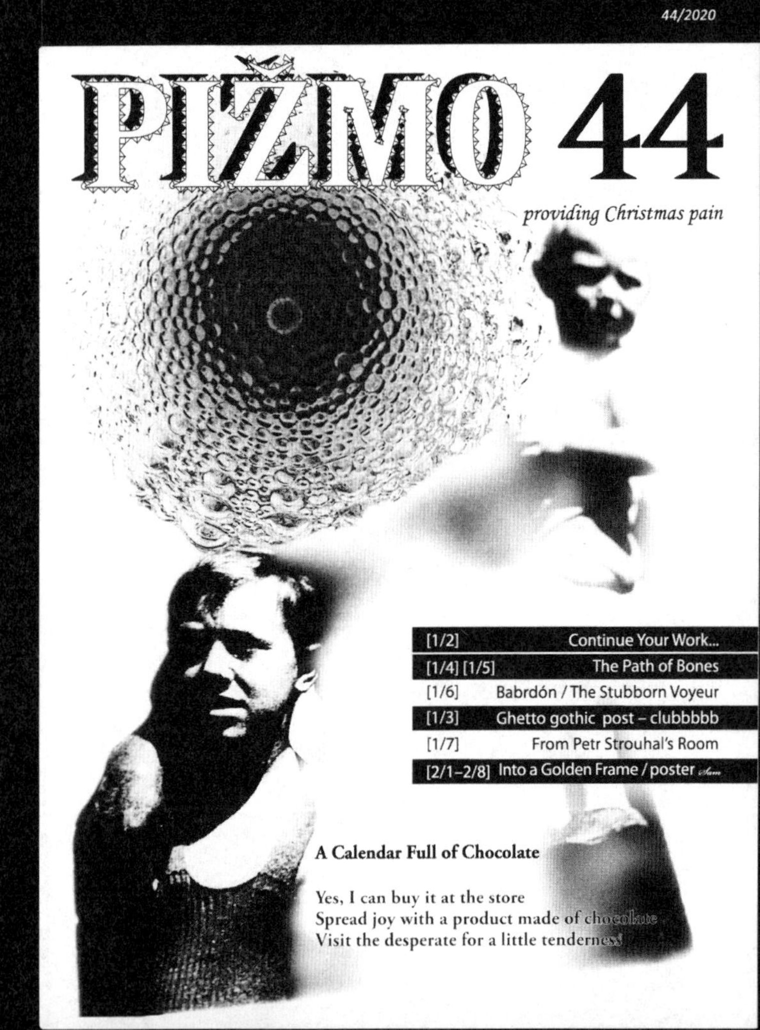
44/2020
PIŽMO 44
providing Christmas pain
[1/2] Continue Your Work...
[1/4] [1/5] The Path of Bones
[1/6] Babrdón / The Stubborn Voyeur
[1/3] Ghetto gothic post – clubbbbb
[1/7] From Petr Strouhal's Room
[2/1–2/8] Into a Golden Frame / poster
A Calendar Full of Chocolate
Yes, I can buy it at the store
Spread joy with a product made of chocolate
Visit the desperate for a little tenderness

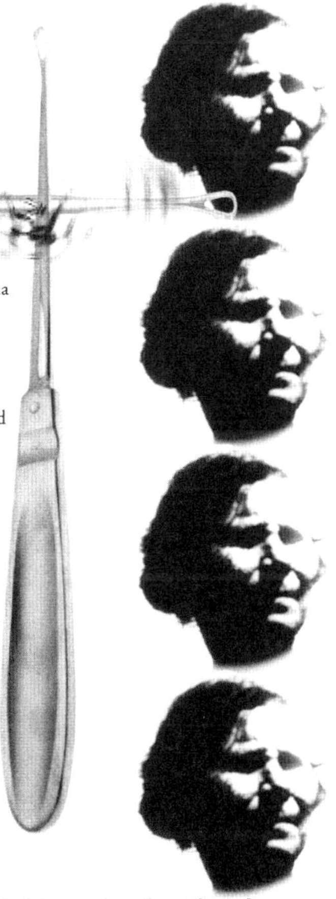

Universal Joy

We pretend nothing is wrong
I'm always putting things somewhere
Taking away and adding
I photographed my family

The floor is cold
I can't get used to it
We learn the start of dying
I don't know where you are
Thanks for writing a text message, Kristina

Curette

Liturgical constructs
You rejoice, you hellish brat
The library of commandments has survived
The womb is mine
Even on Christian holidays
Does that bother you?
Get used to it

Seekers and Gatherers

We don't want to shoot
We're not really good with a knife, either
It's not plundering if we use a rake
And we'll have time for each other
While picking blueberries

You should've looked down as well
You really should have looked
You might have found it
All you had to do was look properly
Now your neighbor has it in his basket
And we're stuck peeling slippery jacks

I spent all day and all night crying by that box,
dan, ewelín, ura

text/ilustr.: Snéž Sam

6

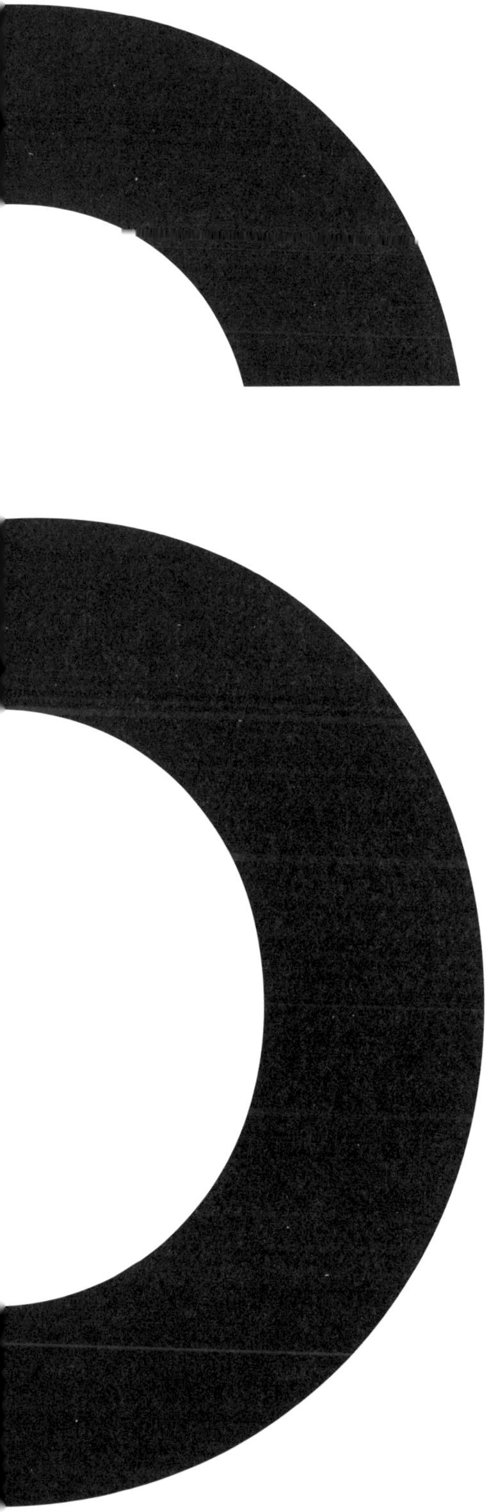

45/2021

PIŽMO 45

pursuing a fear of banal situations

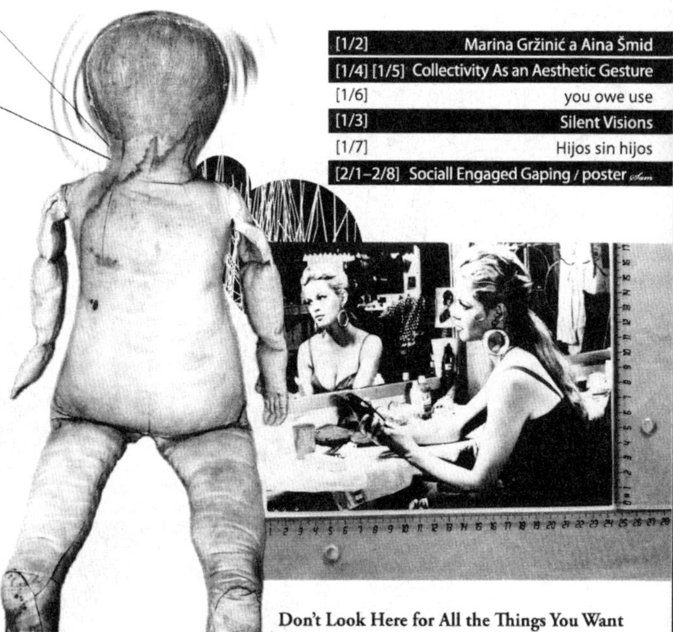

Don't Look Here for All the Things You Want

What hand are you touching me with?
The dirty one?
Don't do that.

Confidentially

On a normal day, my beloved loafs about
She does it quickly
So it looks like she's working hard
She pretends to be exhausted

She willingly rises when she senses
That she can show off
She senses a reward for her effort
She calculates gratitude
And confidentially shares secret contacts

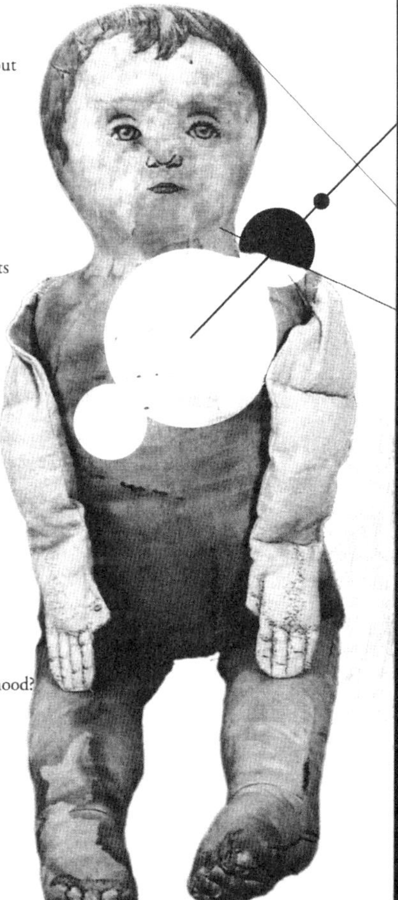

Slight Pressure

You tend to hold back
At the expense of ecstatic calamity
You're good at controlling your body
Another serious mistake
For which you can appreciate yourself

For a Pleasant Atmosphere

Pavla Sceranková told Kristína
Láníková to confess.
To reveal something.
What influence does that have on my mood?
If it's supposed to be bad, then good.

I've never kissed Pavla,
Although she's as beautiful as Kristina.
I've never even met her and have never
Had anything in common with her.

Except for Kristina

text/ilustr.: Sráč Sam

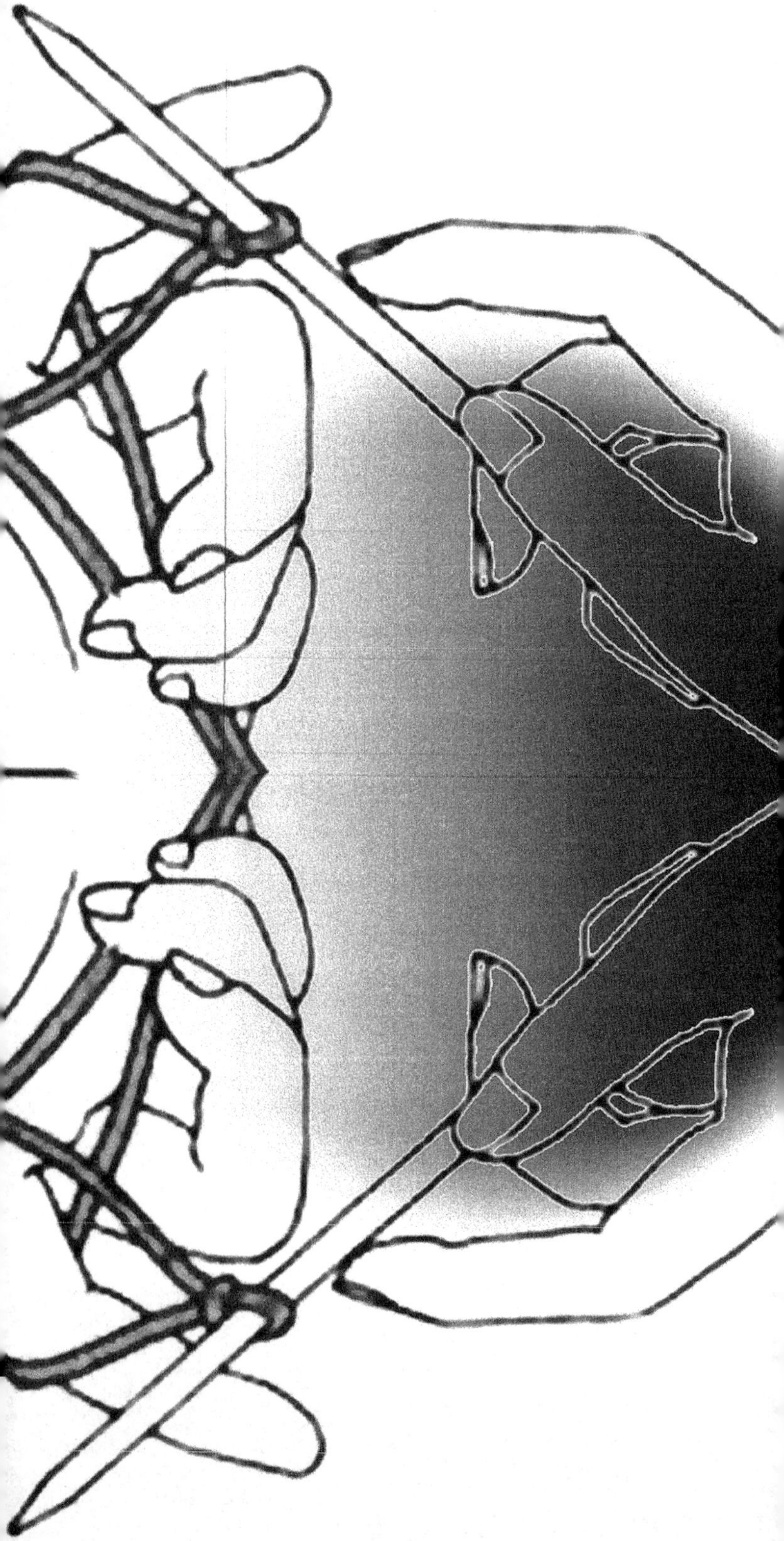

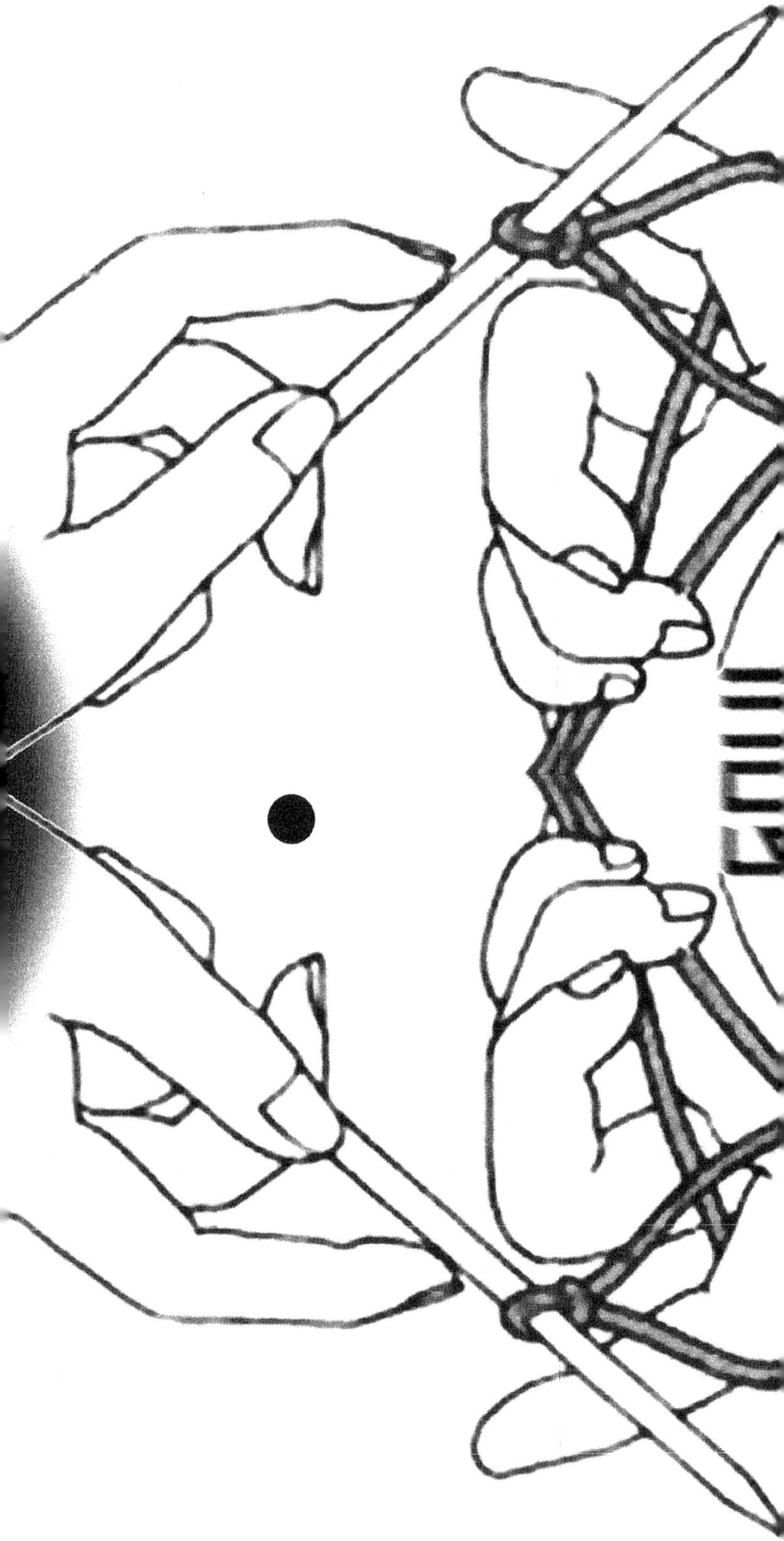

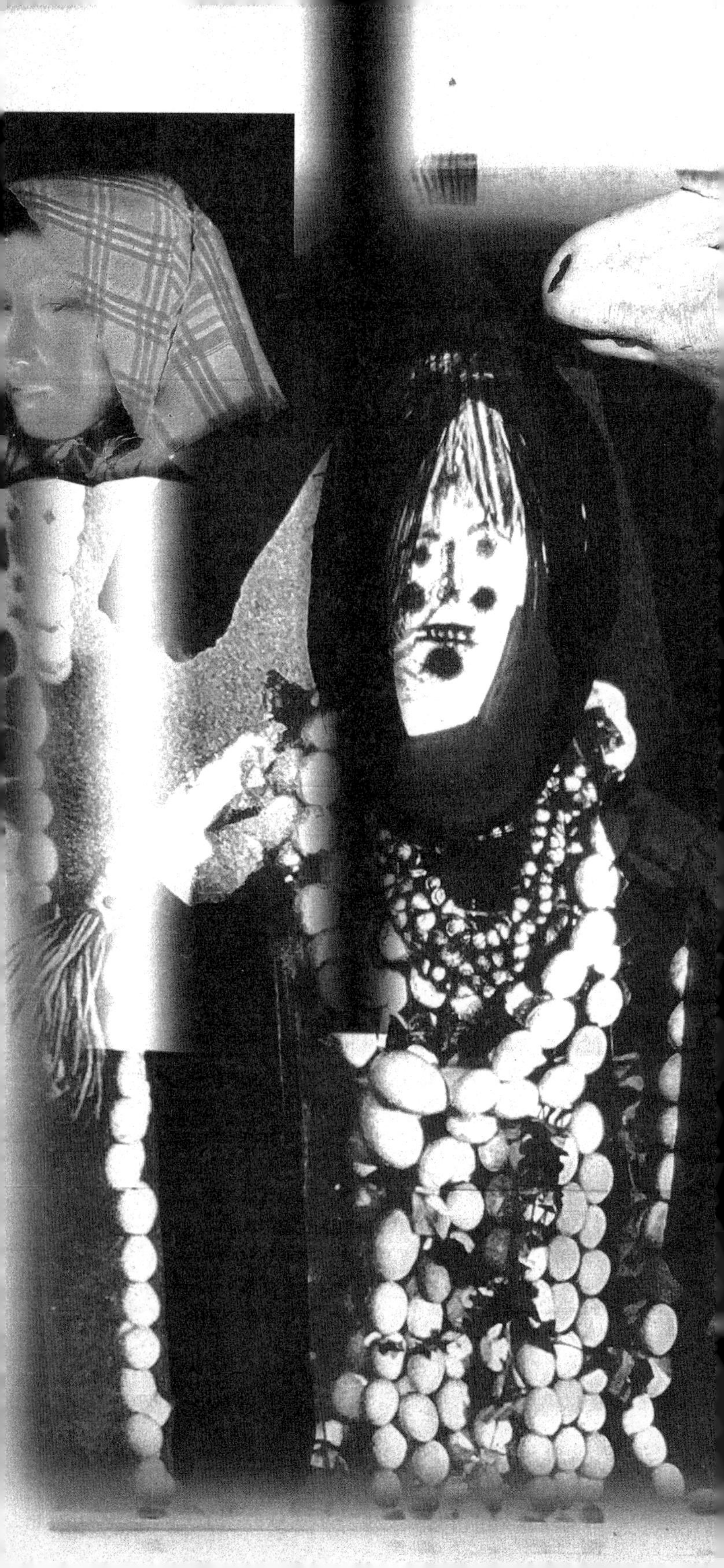

The Aesthetics of Poverty:

A Rationale of the Design For the Philippine People's Theater 1973–1986

Brenda V. Fajardo
Professor Emeritus
Department of
Art Studies
University of the
Philippines, Diliman

In its pioneering phase, the founder of the Philippine Educational Theater Association (PETA) envisioned a Philippine national theater. During the 1950s and 1960s, theater in the Philippines was either traditional, in relation to the Catholic calendar, or school-based, which meant plays in English. The articulated vision for PETA was to develop a national theater with original plays and in the national language. PETA was defined by the changing economic, political, social, and cultural realities, and by the 1970s through the 1980s this national consciousness was heightened to include a growing nationalist sentiment.[1]

PETA has its repertory company, the Kalinangan Ensemble, and it also has an educational unit now referred to as the School of People's Theater. In the 1970s, its artists went to various communities to give theater workshops that helped build a national theater movement, converging in two MAKIISA festivals, held at Raha Sulayman and later the Christ the King Seminary Compound in Quezon City, where theater productions came from all over the nation. Thus, during the martial law years, theater became a potent vehicle for political expression. This was further inspired by two significant theorizing moves: the adoption of Nicanor G. Tiongson's *Repleksiyonng Pangangailangan ng Nakararami* (RPN) and the development of the orientation artistry-organization framework (OAO) as criteria for the planning and evaluation of PETA's performance as a theater company.[2]

PETA has always considered developing a people's theater aesthetics. Following the OAO framework, it articulated in 1983 the following goals:

- Orientational
  PETA strives to raise the level of national and social consciousness among its artists and members as well as among the audienceor public.
- Artistic
  It devotes itself to (1) the growth of a Filipino- and people-based theater aesthetics as well as to experimentation and subsequent development of theater forms and styles inspired by Filipino and Asian theater tradition and materials; and (2) the training and honing of the artistic and technical skills and talents of drama artists in various

1 Laura Samson, Brenda Fajardo, Cecilia Garrucho, Lutgardo Labad, and Ma. Gloriosa Cabangon, *The Story of PETA: 1967–2007*, (Manila: PETA, 2008), 17–28.
2 Samson, Fajardo, Garrucho, Labad and Cabangon, *The Story of PETA*, 29–46.

aspects of theater arts and stage production, including educational theater and research.

- Organizational
  It initiates and supports the establishment of theater groups in schools, communities, and institutions that, like itself, shall be committed to the promotion of a national culture.[3]

In the 1970s, many of its productions were exploratory in nature. There were original plays, adaptations, and a series of absurd plays. Although it was primarily conscious of developing Filipino plays, it did not forget to include classic works in each theater season. By the 80s, it became even more conscious of the plays to produce whether original or adaptations and always relevant to current socio-political conditions.

THE AESTHETICS OF POVERTY

PETA is known for its commitment to the development of a people's theater that mirrors Philippine social realities—a people's theater for empowerment, a potent agent toward personal and societal transformation. Thus, PETA has used its creative ability to survive in spite of its perennial poverty.

The Philippines is a poor country. This is a reality from which we Filipinos should not escape, if only because its acceptance is the first step to survival. Then and now, conditions have not changed. In the late 70s, the concept of the "aesthetics of poverty" came about, articulated by PETA in its scenic designs and became a working philosophy. This practice was adopted by PETA long before it was labeled as such. It was a result of long years of creating forms for theater under conditions of poverty, inside and outside the company.

Aesthetics of poverty implies that there is a sense of beauty which belongs to people who live in conditions of material deprivation. There are concepts of color, line, space, texture, rhythm, and movement that are conditioned by particular natural, cultural, and social environments. It results from a particular quality of life that is conditioned by its reality. Cutting down the expenses, however, was not the main point. It was the new way of seeing the actualities of life—the various shades and combinations of colors that are seen daily in heaps of garbage and forms of attrition;

3 Samson, Fajardo, Garrucho, Labad and Cabangon, *The Story of PETA*, 135.

the various tones of browns and grays seen on the skin of sunburned people, the broken down houses, and the shanties; the patches of color that peep out of once polychromed jeepneys—revealing a world heretofore unknown. Colors and textures of found objects that reflected these realities were used for the sets; symbolic representations in the costumes, props, and the like were carefully chosen for their meaning. The approach not only expressed the truth, it also provided authentic aesthetic experience not only for its viewers but also for the creating artists. It was possible to capture the patina of time and become more sensitive to the aesthetic qualities of local materials thereby increasing our powers of expression.

Mistakes have been committed time and again. Some productions have costly designs despite limited budgets. In the past, these mistakes have caused our designers and directors to reexamine their work in relation to the vision for a Philippine theater. How can an artist claim to be socially responsible when he mounts high-cost productions during times of deprivation?

A direct result of this questioning during those years became an unspoken company policy: to produce designs on as low a budget as possible, using the least expensive and readily available materials. This economic limitation, in turn, proved to be of vital importance to the evolution of the company's "aesthetics of poverty." Design concepts were discussed and adjusted to financial limitations so that the PETA designer of those times gradually became realistic and practical, always keeping one eye on the limited budget.

Ironically, although not totally unexpected, the limitations brought out the resourcefulness and creativity among the design practitioners in finding solutions to problems. There were endless possibilities of working with commonly-used and inexpensive materials. These were explored, producing works that have been both economical and aesthetic.

SPACE

The aesthetics of poverty was practiced when PETA staged its productions at the Dulaang Raha Sulayman at Fort Santiago, Intramuros. For almost four decades, the Dulaang Raha Sulayman was PETA's theater space during the dry season, moving to indoor spaces during the wet season. It is an open theater and three dimensional, with heavy stone and brick-inlaid walls seen from all sides of the space. By itself, it provided an atmosphere that was grounded in history.

In 2005, PETA built a theater center which houses an indoor theater space, the PHINMA Hall. The design concepts have differed because of the nature of the space. But PETA directors, who have been so used to the Raha Sulayman space, still conceive plays in a three-dimensional manner, no matter its planar orientation.

DESIGNING FOR PETA

During the martial law years, PETA had a pool system according to certain aspects of theater work. There was a writers' pool, a music pool, a technical pool, and a design pool, etc. It meant working collectively so that its members could contribute ideas to the production concept. A team of designers were selected for a particular production and together they worked on scenic design, costumes, props, and so on. There was always a lead designer who put the ideas together and supervised the work.

Being fundamentally a people's theater, its members had varying degrees of artistic training and capability. Some had academic training but most were non-professionals equipped only with natural talent and an inclination for the theater arts. Thus, the pool system worked with each member contributing individual strengths to the pool's work. In the process, they learned from each other.

Preparation included research and understanding the premise of the play, as well as the writer's and director's intent. These helped the designers to conceptualize and integrate their own ideas and translate them into visual terms.

Design concepts and forms are evoked and emerge from the basic structure of the play, the theater space, the concept and style of the director. There is a great advantage when everyone on the production team knows the play and the director's staging concept. Designing become challenging and urgent but easier.

The design team starts by reading and analyzing the script. Images from the script are collected and considered. Then, each one is asked to work on the images. The group meets often to share individual ideas. Some ideas are rejected, others selected.

Selected ideas are discussed and worked on to generate more concepts which are then presented to the director. After a concept is formed, smaller teams are formed to work on the details of the design. The group finalizes the concept and synchronizes the different aspects of design. Though seemingly laborious and circuitous, this process has actually strengthened the working relationship and the internalization of the principles of the aesthetics of poverty.

APPROACHES TO DESIGN

The experience of designing collectively has led to different types of theater designs. This, along with the exploration of cultural forms in search of a distinctively Filipino form, has resulted in what is seen as a "PETA style." This paper will focus on the visual aspects of theater, manifested in PETA productions from the early 1970s to 1986. It is in the visual medium that the concept of the "aesthetics of poverty" is largely explored. As a working philosophy it was adopted by PETA during those periods when finances were scarce and production processes were not as complex. The following examples will give an idea of how the design was approached in the various plays of the period.

ACCORDING TO THE DIRECTOR'S TECHNIQUE AND SPECIFICATIONS

The director who uses a workshop technique in mounting a production often uses improvisation. The actors become active participants in the creative process and have a direct hand in evolving the play's form. Improvisation would include costuming and props making. Everyone looks for and uses ready-made or found objects, using them to create new images. The role of both the director and the designer is that of aesthetic coordinators, monitoring the totality of the work wherein every member of the cast and crew contributed their individual creativity. This approach needed careful handling, for it is easy to find junk but difficult to create art from junk. Sensitivity, selectivity, and discrimination are necessary and the assigned lead designer provides the necessary guidance.

There are problems encountered in the use of this approach. Sometimes a director tells the designer that ten acting areas are needed. Since the budget is limited, a solution is to use portable space modules. Such modules could be placed within the staging area. Since the Raha Sulayman theater was among ruins, there were many possibilities for creative staging, as in the case of *Bayaning Huwad/Fake Hero* (1967 and *Joe Hill* (1979) where the fort's window arches, ramparts, adjacent chamber areas, ladders, etc., were utilized. Sometimes an acting area is constructed but the director decides to remove it because of limitations of the lighting equipment or a lack of coordination between the set-designer and the light-designer. Thus both designers need to consult the director along the way to avoid unnecessary expense. A thorough study of the area, establishing certain acting spaces and levels before implementing the design, is important.

THE USE OF BACKDROPS IN CAPTURING THE ESSENCE OF THE PLAY

Scenic paintings (backdrops) have been used to establish settings. In *Kabesang Tales/Chieftain Tales* (1975), the painted backdrops were utilized not to establish particular scenes but to create a sense of history, functioning as "historical backdrops." Carefully selected photographs and documents of the period were enlarged into sepia murals that provided a patina of history. These enlarged historical documents in the form of faded sepia murals combined with costumes of muted colors and spare props resulted in a total design of a three-dimensional historical document, likened to a life-size diorama.

Three-dimensional backdrops were used for the Brechtian plays *Ang Hatol ng Guhit na Bilog/Caucasian Chalk Circle* (1977), and *Ang Buhay ni Galileo/Galileo Galilee* (1980). The backdrops were an assemblage of actual materials. For the former, forms of attrition such as tarnished metal sheets, old rubber tires, and found pieces of lumber provided the textural qualities that complimented the play as a whole. For the latter, images exploring the role of the scientist in the advancement or destruction of life was created. Recalled images from the works of Leonardo da Vinci, Francisco Goya, a news photo from *Time* magazine, and quotations taken from the text of the play were juxtaposed like fragments of news and images, of thoughts and feelings, echoing the questions and anxieties posed by the play, presenting a visual stream of consciousness.

THE USE OF COMMON MATERIALS IN CAPTURING THE ESSENCE OF FORM

It was in working with PETA's guest director and mentor Frit Bennewit who directed *Hatol*, *Galileo*, and *Macbeth* (1984) that designing for PETA became more meaningful and challenging. It was while working with him that PETA developed a particular scenic style and helped me to articulate the principles of the aesthetics of poverty.

Bennewit introduced a working method and attitude that recognized the individual concept of the designer while integrating the director's own ideas, thus establishing the importance of a strong rapport and working relationship between the director and designer as the play is conceptualized together. The approach underscores the importance of the two artists listening to each other in collaboration to bring out significant ideas and meanings.

With *Galileo*, Bennewit mulled over the situation of the limited budget and problems with costuming. It was not necessary for costumes to be historically authentic, he proposed. After some brainstorming, Bennewit and the designer came up with the use of yards of cloth stained in inexpensive cloth dye to render the hue and tinge of antiquity to the material. These clothing materials were solicited from steam laundries. As a result, the costumes had the look of being oxidized and the patina provided visual unity to the forms. The actors wearing the robes of stained cloth looked sculptural on stage. Colors symbolized the characters they were playing. The monks wore white, the Cardinals had a grayish pink to blood-stained red, the Duke in royal yellow, the little monk in humble gray, and so on. The colors established social class and character. Designing for plays by Brecht taught us the art of improvising, using found materials.

Similar techniques and styles were further explored in PETA's production of Shakespeare's *Macbeth*. The problem was to project the setting of the play without making it alien to our own experience. Natural materials such as hemp rope, burlap, and oxidized metal were used. Black and dull brown was the dominant color scheme. The design of the set was adapted to PETA's theater space. Contemporary images of barbed wire and searchlights were incorporated without clashing, precisely because the concept was timeless. It was a matter of balancing the prescribed setting, the economic constraints, the use of what is familiar—all in an effort to produce an authentic work that would not in any way be anachronistic. The resulting creation was aesthetic without being opulent.

The design entered into the spirit of the play and showed royalty without having to put on the extravagance of kings. Indeed, with Bennewit, the aesthetics of poverty was explored to the fullest.

THE USE OF INDIGENOUS MATERIALS AND FORMS

Forms or the symbolic use of visual elements such as color or shape is part of the collective unconscious and their use in revitalized forms is important in the vision of a national culture. Where possible, therefore, the PETA designer was urged to draw ideas from folk life and culture. Some productions lent themselves easily to folk forms and materials.

The use of indigenous materials in contemporary plays resulted in a culture based aesthetic. Some examples are the following:

- *Junto al Pasig* (1973) wherein the folk toy *taka* (Papier-mâché animals) were used as hand props, carried overhead by body movers much like the Japanese *bunraku*.
- *Hobe/Job* (1974) used the *parol* (Christmas paper lantern) as the source of form/idea for the giant puppet heads that represented Good and Evil. A sun-face was used as the symbol for Good, radiating its benevolent energy on the people, while a monstrous face in red and silver metallic paper projected Evil. As in the traditional lantern, bamboo, *papel de japon* (Japanese colored tissue paper), and local metallic paper were used.
- Bamboo was again used as the set for both *Si Tatang Atbp. Mga Tauhan Ng Ating Dula/ Tatang and Other Characters in our Play* (1975) and *Langit Langitang Kumunoy/ Heavenly Whirlpool* (1978). The set made out of bamboo actually acted as both backdrop and set props for the actors, taking its cue from Asian theater. Aside from bamboo, inexpensive *katsa* (cheesecloth) was used as costume material for both plays.
- *Dupluhang Bayan/Country Debate* (1975) juxtaposed the traditional *duplo* (debate) and the *alamat* (legend) using folk elements to express

contemporary sentiments. A highly visual play, it combined shadows/silhouettes, color, light, and bodies moving in space. Sounds were produced from non-traditional materials such as shells, stones, crackling paper, and traditional ethnic musical instruments.

- In *Ang Hatol Na Guhit Na Bilog* (1974) suggestive costuming and props thatcrossed sub-cultures were used. In this play, a piece of *banig* (sleeping mat) and a *duyan* (bamboo hammock), commonly used by poor families, marked the setting for the scene in an old couple's hut. Their use immediately established the presence of a child and the social status of the old couple, proving that a single visual idea could explain more than a paragraph. Similarly, the use of the *malong* (tube cloth) as costumes sets the play somewhere in Southeast Asia or in the Muslim Philippines without pinpointing any specific ethnic group.

Designers must take the precaution in the use of cultural forms as symbols. Where the form is non-verbal, there is always the possibility that the audience might find it too abstract, especially if they are used to seeing realistic sets and props. When this happens, it is possible that the artist has failed to select the most appropriate visual symbol for the particular meaning intended. Therefore, it is important for the designer to capture the meaning and select the appropriate combination of elements in order to maximize the use of cultural forms and still be understood. This careful selection of items for its symbolic representation is capturing the gestalt that everyone can understand.

TAKING THE CUE FROM LIFE ITSELF

Genre plays are like period plays. An atmosphere that belongs to a particular period of time or that of a particular setting is captured. The main requirements for designing such productions are the heart and mind of a highly sensitive artist and the internalization of needs and realities. Research is important for this type of design to provide authenticity.

Many themes of PETA plays are about the poor. And so, the costumes and props need not be expensive at all. Props need only to approximate the actual without being naturalistic. One only has to project its essence. If the scene requires a cake, for example, it is not necessary to bake the actual cake each time.

Such a task would be an economic and aesthetic mistake which comes from a lack of understanding about theater work.

In *Juan Tamban* (1979), it was necessary to capture the ambience of the urban poor environment and use lines, color, texture, and rhythmic patterns that express the pulse of life in the slums. To accomplish this, sense-data was observed and gathered through actual visits and immersion in various urban poor communities. This was not difficult as we were working closely with communities, the urban poor included. It was important to capture the essential elements that would project the life of the community—the congestion, squalor, mire, and despair. For this particular production, color was carefully selected for social class representation. The poor were designated earth brown (terracotta) since they are closer to the earth and it is regarded as the color of attrition.

To represent images of squalor, tarnished galvanized iron sheets, plywood that was peeling, discarded rubber tires, metal scraps, plastic pails, etc., were used since these were objects actually used and seen in slum areas. Other than for artistic reasons, props were chosen to express social conditions and problems. For instance, empty plastic pails lined up in rows indicated the lack of water supply as people waited for their turn to get water from one source, which happens in many urban poor communities.

Still in *Juan Tamban*, the scenic design showed the interrelation of static space and dynamic motifs placed within the space: canned goods, plastic toys in *sari-sari* stores, the ubiquitous clotheslines, plants in tarnished fruit juice cans, comic books for rent, plastic curtains, so on and so forth. These provided the visual rhythm and texture that powerfully expressed the life pulse of the people.

During the same year, PETA mounted *Ang Panunuluyan ng Birheng Maria at San Jose sa Cubao, Ayala, Plaza Miranda atbp sa loob at labas ng Metro* (1979) which was a take from the traditional Christmas street play, the *Maytinis*. This reenacts the flight to Egypt of Joseph and Mary but this time, the couple went to strategic places in Metro Manila to give comment on the social apathy of the people. Being a simulated street play, it had minimal sets, using the various stage areas of the Raha Sulayman Theater. The theater space itself was optimized as the setting of the play.

In *Mapait sa Bao/Biter in Shell* (1980), a minimalist approach provided the setting. Included in this design were coconut palm leaves, hung as a wall; bamboos to outline a wall and window, and minimal furniture such as a *banggera* (dish rack) and the *dulang* (low table for dining). This successfully reflected the interior of a rural nipa hut found in the provinces where the play was set.

Still pursuing the goal of making traditional theater contemporary, PETA also did its version of a *sarsuwela*, the *Pilipinas Ca. 1907* (1982). An anti-American period play, the set used thin plywood but captured the time through the use of architectural elements and interior accessories in its furnishing and embellishments. The costumes also provided the color and texture of the period. The point was to capture the period without being cumbersome and realistic in treatment.

And finally, when *Panata sa Kalayaan/Oath to Freedom* (1986) was mounted, the designers had to consider portability since it was going to be a traveling show abroad. To solve the problem of scenery, certain costumes were painted which carried visual meaning, thus the play was not lacking in establishing place or time.

The creation of highly original and unique artistic statements has resulted from these processes and approaches, mainly because of the imperative to eliminate nonessentials. Instead, basic ideas, meaning, and images were the focus, rather than superfluities and ornamentations. The PETA designers realized then that nothing can prevent the artist, who has a rich imagination, to achieve maximum results from simple and inexpensive materials. Non-imitative and original, the resulting aesthetics is from the quality of form and expression that neither ignores nor glosses over conditions of poverty.

The Aesthetics of Poverty stemmed from a social condition and in effect the quality of life found in depressed areas during those depressed times. A highly expressive art has evolved from such conditions. Recognizing this condition of poverty, a Philippine theater aesthetics could evolve as values are reexamined. An imitative colonial culture no longer exists in this particular theater because it does not seek outside models to be able to create. It looks into itself and interprets ideas according to its own perceptions and comprehensions. It continues to explore ideas to strengthen itself. A people's appreciation of beauty is not stunted just because they are poor. In fact, their sense of beauty, coupled with their passion for truth, results in a powerful expression that is part of the process of survival and change. If theater is to be a living tradition, then it must express the life and culture of a people.

To summarize, art is a human experience made manifest in the works of an artist who lives through the experience. The artist sometimes creates objects for use, at other times ideas are explored. In both instances the practitioner belongs to a particular time and space. The art experience is not separate from other life experiences. The artist does not exist in a vacuum, but is surrounded by people and events which are reflected in choices, judgments, and insights.

Since the individual is shaped by culture and the various sub-cultures of a particular society, both artist and percipients are affected by conditions of culture. Moreover, since the individual who creates infuses the work with values, a work of art is the product of insights. At the same time, it becomes a source of insight for the percipient. This makes art a function of value attitudes and value insights, and both the creation and the appreciation of art inherent in social values.

One way of appraising the state of a society is to measure the state of its art, for art contains the ideas, thoughts, feelings, aspirations, spirit, and angst of the people who create it. The artistic achievements reached by a society is a mark of its internal power, a symbol of the worth and quality of life that went on within it. Although the expressive side of art can bring the feelings of innumerable ages about all the major concerns of life, the specific contributions of the arts are not limited to the expressive side alone. It can also arise from materials and form, which may alter the tastes of the people. In our part of the world, people are confronted with problems of survival: economic, social, political, and cultural. The artist of this particular milieu struggles through crises as do fellow members of that society. Together, both artists and percipients develop a particular artistic taste and evolve a peculiar aesthetic sense fashioned by the conditions of their environment.

Because of the culture of material poverty, the artist's taste for color or material is oftentimes limited by what is available. But what is initially a by-product of material poverty becomes an expression which results from sensitivity to the world. The artist begins to choose deliberately particular nuances and tones of color and texture that would express the qualities that are perceived—economic deprivation, cultural pollution, senseless violence. A new art begins to evolve which is authentic, because it expresses life which happens to be in a poor condition, thus the "aesthetics of poverty."

This text was originally published in *Kritika Kultura* 0, no. 15 (2010): 179-194.

On Introvert Liberation

Giulia Loi
in conversation with
Hamja Ahsan

Giulia Loi In 2021, the fifth edition of your book *Shy Radicals: The Antisystemic Politics of the Militant Introvert* (2017) was published. For those who don't know, what is Shy Radicals?

Hamja Ahsan Shy Radicals is the name of a fictional movement of liberation, a narrative for a coalition of shy, quiet, awkward, introverted, autistic spectrum, and neurodivergent people. It's a book as a format but it's also been seen as an art project. It was introduced as a referendum across several galleries at the Ljubljana Biennial of Graphic Arts, Slovenia (2019) curated by the Slavs and Tatars collective. The biennial toured and reexhibited the following year in an expanded exhibition format at the CCA Ujazdowski Castle in Warsaw, Poland (2020). I guess it's a vocabulary and a group of connected identities that transcends borders, generations and nations.

GL Have you coopted many recruits since your book came out in 2017? What kind of crowd are they?

HA Lots of people have told me this is the book that changed their life, empowered them, made them feel less alone or finally articulated the way they felt, and that's gone across everywhere from Mexico City to Australia, like an internationalist thing. I never anticipated the geographical reach or the relatability.

You have teenage fans, like 18- and 19-year-old first year university students and people in their late seventies. There's also a Muslim or Islamic following of it too, some Muslims have their own reading of it. I'm from West Bengal in India, Bangladesh, and I wrote Shy Radicals as someone who was from a British Muslim background who felt oppressed by the domestic war on terror in Britain. I didn't realize it would have such resonances across the world. For example, someone did a little video for "Fora Bolsonaro" against the Bolsonaro government in Brazil. He did a little vlog in Portuguese and basically his understanding of the state of oppression there. There are also vlogs in Spanish, and if I knew the language, I'd speak on them. And I've also got images from Chile and the riots there. I did a talk in Brooklyn in the subway and the entire turnout was female. I've circulated it in Bethlem Royal Hospital, a psychiatric hospital in London, to service users and people with experience of psychiatric care.

There is also the zine festival circuit and DIY publishing. The revival of zine culture has also increased the circulation of the book. I always seem to be recruiting new demographics of people. I just didn't think it would resonate so widely. There's even an extrovert following of Shy Radicals. Some extroverts told me it made them into better people. Someone even told me they'd converted to introversion.

GL Do you think people can read the book as ironic? Not take it seriously? How seriously do you want it to be taken?

HA I mean every word I say. It is taken very seriously, as I say, in these contexts of people in distress. But I also want people to laugh and if people don't laugh when I explain what the book is about, I get really worried. One week I read it at Brixton Hootenanny in South London at Book Jam and it was total rip-roaring laughter, and then I read the exact same series of words in Café Oto in North London, which is an avant-garde music café, and the public was dead silent for the whole set. I don't know how to take it when people go silent like that. If I could choose another job, I'd like to be a stand-up comedian. I think stand-up comedians can tell a lot of truth. There's a stand-up comedian called Aamer Rahman and his work *Fear of a Brown Planet* about racism and the colonial mindset, I wish I was someone like him. There are multiple layers in which Shy Radicals could be read but it is rooted in pain, discrimination, depressive episodes and hopelessness. The film directed by Tom Dream that was released in November 2020 at the Aesthetica Short Film Festival in York, UK, is totally serious. There's no campness, irony, layers of meaning or even much humor; it is actually dead serious.

GL And do you like that?

HA I've had good feedback on it, but I thought that more films and more interpretations could be made. I wanted someone like John Waters to direct it. That could add layers of campness, irony and wit. Posture is everything to the book. I've also presented it in the O Show, with Oriana Fox, which is basically a mental health talk show modeled on Oprah Winfrey and Ricki Lake. That was one of my best interviews, I think—one I'm particularly proud of. I just integrated my biography around suffering from bipolar depressive disorder, colonial understandings of the law and the war against vulnerable people and the welfare state.

GL You seem to have been able to shake off a certain "art world posture" while still being recognized by the art world. What is your relation to the art world?

HA I'm stuck in the art world because the publisher Bookworks is an art world publisher who published many Turner Prize winners and circulates at artist book fairs. Out of the Bookworks catalogue my book is probably the one that has the biggest following outside the art world. It's circulated in Islamic and activist bookshops, also educationally it's taught in lots of disciplines, from Media and Communications at Goldsmiths to the Neurodiversity curriculum at Brown University.

I wanted to actually leave the art world. I was doing DIY Cultures from 2014 to 2017, an annual zine festival, because I felt that zines were generally more authentic and participatory, and a medium that creates a community whereas I don't feel that way about contemporary art. I think contemporary art economies have definitely paved the way for neoliberalism, they definitely recenter New York, London and Berlin. They're not empowering as such and participatory, they're actually more alienating. I had a certain bitterness about it. I realize the power by which art world circles operate and how much bullshit the whole thing is. As well as the culture of pseudo-leftism in the art world, with Slavoj Zizek being very popular. So I was quite cynical. But having said that, I circulated the book at lots of art institutions, such as Tate Modern for Late at Tate during the lockdown. I do appreciate the art world as a structure. It's also got me lots of paid employment. I've been a tutor at Goldsmiths, The Royal College of Art, The Ruskin School of Art at Oxford, multiple art schools across Europe. So, I'm grateful for that employment.

GL In the beautiful chapter "Crisis Voices Oral History Project", you also describe your disappointment with academia. Do you think Shy Radicals will ever get their universities and libraries back? One of the most difficult aspects of living in London for me was the absence of quiet free spaces to dwell in together. Everywhere has been turned into profit-generating spaces. How do we defeat the money-making machine?

HA I guess this is where my project becomes fantasy and not reality. I wish we had a means. If we could become a constituency. Say, for example. there was a newspaper called *Introvert Times* and it got mass circulation in the way, say, *The Pink Paper* did or like *Jewish News* or *Muslim News*. That would make a constituency and in elections people would look to tap into that constituency in order to steer policy. I do think there's a demand for that. I've been asked at some of my public events "How do we campaign for 24-hour café culture?" I felt this frustration and alienation looking for a quiet place to sit, you know, on a high street I can't find one. I think we have to firstly support anti-austerity movements which exist, like the People's Assembly which I spoke at, as an activist. So we keep museums and libraries and non-profit generating spaces open. I think that's vital. But also to build our identity into that. Instead of just seeing it as a neoliberal war against public ownership, we also need to see it as a way of defeating sensitivity—a very productive sensitivity. It's been very fashionable for the conservative government to say "Let's talk about mental health" but we have to challenge that, mental health is more than just doctors. It's also to have access to green spaces, spaces to rest, to recover. I think part of that public conversation is somewhere else where we could insert ourselves.

It's also about how we set ourselves as a force. So, at Jan Van Eyck Academie in Maastricht, the Netherlands, I've given the book to most of my friends, residents, colleagues and the people who run the institute. Still, I feel a sense of alienation. They had a karaoke party outside my window and made me feel very disturbed, particularly with the socialization which caused me a lot of distress. They don't really seem to care, and I don't seem to have a means of asserting my right to just be. There's no respect and no accommodation. Pretty much everyone said, "It's an amazing book" and they really liked the form of it but I worry sometimes of it being thought of as a work of art and literature because it is my grievances outlined, my political program, my collective crying of despair. On Friday there was some sort of big party type gathering and I went, and it made me feel very anxious and distressed, and I don't think anyone recognized the level of stress it caused me. One person, a poet in residency, came after me, saw I was distressed and spoke to me on my own. I was so distressed by the situation that I considered committing suicide. God, in my studio even. I sort of had this rationale, I mean it, if I died, they'd know why I died. And say, if you want to know why this kid committed suicide, it's because of the extrovert supremacy. I have no power. I'm powerless to do anything.

When I won the award at the Ljubljana biennial, for the Aspergistan referendum, the actual award ceremony was exactly like something I hate. That reminded me of my own powerlessness. There needs to be international coalition. Boycott. There needs to be some sort of leverage. I tried to assert myself to have a neurodiverse conversation and for it to be recognized in British art institutions. So Tate has a quiet room, for example, but not all art institutions have a quiet room. Neurodiversity is not evenly recognized everywhere, only at a few art institutes and universities.

GL I have just read an Italian fiction masterpiece from 2008 by Giorgio Vasta titled *Time on my Hands* which follows a group of pre-teens as they get embroiled in armed struggle in 1978 Sicily. You also seem to avoid another great trap of radicalism: violence, but still manage to sound dangerous. In one of my favorite parts of the book, titled "The black power-sensitive white man alliance, or, towards black-black power", you finish by advocating we should become "Sensitive Gs [gangstas]. That is to say sensitive introverts that you dare not fuck with." How do we achieve that? How do we outdo violent extrovert-supremacists?

HA I first have a bit of concern against the ubiquity of security state language. The way radicalization and radicalism have entered the vernacular which we have sort of internalized. To me radicalization is a good thing, it means you understand the system and the structure. Also, in terms of people resisting colonialism, that's the way a lot of historical progress has been achieved, the Brixton riots[1] for the oppressed Black minority in London's Brixton and the Poll tax riots[2] and the Suffragettes smashing things... I also think the Irish Republican movement, Patrick Pearse for example, in the 1916 Easter Rising is very inspiring. I love the power of Bobby Sands, it's still very potent and it still inspires people to take mass hunger strikes whether that's the 2013 Californian hunger strike of almost 30,000 prisoners against solitary confinement or hunger strikes in Palestine today.

My favorite song ever, or one of the many, is called *Song for Marcella* done by Bik McFarlane for Bobby Sands and it sounds like an acoustic ballad. It could almost be one of Nirvana's unplugged or any of The Smith's songs. It's such a sensitive and delicate acoustic song but it is about an Irish Republican militant. I've heard songs sung by women about the Irish anti-colonial struggle which actually combine ultra-sensitivity and tenderness with people you just do not fuck with. That's not to say I endorse the mistakes that were made. You know things like anti-terror legislation and foreign policy... There are power games. What the current British government deems unacceptable in terms of insurgencies and resistance movements aren't necessarily always right and history will eventually bear out what's right. There are the obvious cliché examples that Nelson Mandela was considered a terrorist. I wouldn't take away the right of the African National Congress government under Apartheid to operate. And that goes for a lot of anti-imperialism and anti-colonial movements. I don't know how much this relates to my book, listening to 1990s white sensitive man music. First album I ever bought was Nirvana's *In Utero,* I love Jesus and Mary Chain, I love Eliott Smith, and when I watched *Straight Outta Compton*

1 The Brixton riots were a series of clashes between mainly black British youths and the Metropolitan Police in Brixton, London, then the center of the UK's black community, between April 10 and 12, 1981. It resulted from racist discrimination against the black British community by the mainly white police as well as long term structural racism.

2 The Poll tax riots happened in London and other British towns and cities in 1990 in response to Prime Minister Margaret Thatcher's change of tax legislation and marked the transition to John Major's government which reluctantly scrapped the Poll tax following massive suffrage to subsequently introduce the Council tax, widely regarded as fairer.

at the cinema, I thought it illustrated my entire life and that I could have been a gangster. That's what those meditations were about.

GL You once introduced a panel of yours by saying that having Nina Power write your preface was like Sartre writing Fanon's. Could you introduce Nina Power to us?

HA Nina Power was the editor of the series *Common Objectives*, she's a feminist philosopher and activist. She's now on the receiving end of Cancel Culture. I have a lot of love and respect for her. I don't think the book could have been finished without her, I know what a kind and beautiful person she is, and she helped me through some of my lowest and darkest moments. She wrote a book called *One Dimensional Woman* (2009) and she's also an expert on continental philosophy. The joke on Sartre was suggested by the editor who is now the director of Bookworks. Nina Power actually borrows the first sentence in a parody of Sartre's introduction to The Wretched of the Earth.

GL Do you consider yourself a Fanonist?

HA I'm sympathetic towards Fanon's books, I read them a very long time ago. I read a lot of militant anti-colonial Black literature, some of which was Fanon. Both *The Wretched of the Earth* and *Black Skin, White Masks* have resonances with me, and I also like the way a lot of British Muslims have applied the use of Fanon to thinking about the occupations of Iraq, Palestine, or Kashmir, thinking them through colonialism. I also think there's been an institutionalization of Frantz Fanon by the art world which I feel sort of pacified and domesticated him. I also read Okwui Enwezor's catalogue for the exhibition *The Short Century: Independence and Liberation Movements in Africa, 1945–1994* (2001) which has an anthology of documents from the colonial era, but I think I read Fanon via osmosis anyway. The Black Panthers writings were another big influence on my book. I read an anthology called *The Black Panthers Speak* (1970, edited by Philip S. Foner). The bit where I say "Extrovert Supremacy out of Asia. Extrovert Supremacy out of Africa. Extrovert Supremacy out of the Middle East. Extrovert Supremacy out of the ghetto," that's directly from Emory Douglas and his rhetoric. The Black Panthers use Fanon not to deconstruct the

French Empire but the Afro-American ghettos and that particular struggle in the urban space. So I think that his influence across culture has certainly been absorbed into the book, but the book involved reading a lot of militant literature from different times like Valerie Solanas' SCUM Manifesto and Hezbollah's written documents, so Fanon was absorbed into the rhetoric of the book whilst not necessarily being located as a source as such.

GL You said earlier you were diagnosed with bipolar affective disorder. Has the diagnosis been helpful to you, and if no, why?

HA When I got my diagnosis, I had examples of people I'd read. I knew Virginia Woolf, I knew Nina Simone's music which I liked, it was a nice group to belong to. I found Sinead O'Connor's public breakdown and her diagnosis very helpful. Feeling a sense of common humanity. But I've grown up with some family experiences of this as well. I still re-narrate why I had three manic episodes in my teens and early twenties. In terms of what the cause or factors were. Sometimes I think they might have been caused by the doses of medication I was taking at the time. Then I think lots of things like spiritual narratives and social conditions, including employment and social ostracization. I also think about heartbreak, the way it fucks up your head and soul. All these things. I'm continuously re-narrating and reassessing. I don't take anything, I used to take lithium. I find that actually going to university, at twentythree I went to art school at Central St Martin's, was quite helpful and rehabilitative. When it comes to my experience with therapy, I didn't find it particularly helpful. I quite enjoy some therapists because they tend to be white middle-class people who are very cultured and well-read in philosophy, art and things that I'm interested in, but I can't speak about it with my parents. I had some very full-on discussions with a therapist when I was a teenager, about books, including Fanon, I think. I had relapses whilst in therapy. Via experience I'm actually quite cynical about the public services I had access to. Certainly, I have something, I'm neurodivergent, I've had manic episodes and very depressive episodes.

GL Would you say you're against therapy and medication?

HA Not totally. I haven't found it particularly helpful, but I reflected on it, and there are several people I read, for example the members of the critical psychiatry movement in Britain, like Garry Greenberg's book *Manufacturing Depression: The Secret History of a Modern Disease* (2010), or the work of David Healy who produced a lot of data on SSRIs[3]. Just doing the basic math about people on SSRIs hasn't created a dramatic shift in the suicide rate. I'm very cynical actually. And there's no accountability of the pharmaceutical industry, no accountability of medicine, and there are aspects of British state and economy which are calling for accountability. Because of course various Wall Street crashes, subprime mortgages and similar disasters created by bankers cause all sorts of mental health crises on a mass scale. Of course, insecure workplaces, the zero hour contract, no public houses or public ownership, this causes mental distress. The lack of security. Lots of areas of British governing lack accountability. I was involved in a lot of movements for justice, like the Hillsborough campaign.[4] No one will be held to account, no one. On Bloody Sunday, when the British killed Irish people in the street in 1972, no soldier has been held to account. They're quite extreme examples but especially this non-accountability made me think why we lay so much blame on people on SSRIs.

I know some people find medication and therapy helpful. The one substance I found really helpful is valerian which is over the counter and classified. I've occasionally taken too much of it. That's helped me with sleep, anxiety, feeling refreshed, feeling cleansed. I tried it when I was under a lot of stress with my brother being extradited, it really helped me to restore back to normal sleep. A lot of people have told me to take medication. I thought there are lots of things people just don't want to talk about. I feel like heartbreak actually plays a huge role in someone's

3 Selective serotonin reuptake inhibitors, a widely used type of antidepressant.

4 The Hillsborough disaster was a fatal incident that killed ninety-seven football supporters in 1989 in Hillsborough stadium in Sheffield. The campaign that ensued has been trying to recover justice for the victims against the mistreatment at the hands of the police of the supporters that day.

cognition and someone's mental structure, someone's sense of meaning and trust. It's not necessarily something you can talk about with the GP. I also think we put too much pressure on a GP, they can only do so much, there's very limited scope of intervention. I have no illusions about it, I think there are multiple variables. I'm on the editorial board of *Asylum,* a radical mental health zine, so I get lots of stories. I just find the technocratic understanding of mental health and governmentality not particularly helpful. I'm quite a big fan of Ivan Illich, the catholic anarchist thinker, who wrote *Tools for Conviviality* (1973), *Deschooling Society* (1971) and *Medical Nemesis* (1974) which is a critique of medicine. I think that the critiques of bureaucratic society hold the key to a lot of issues related to mental health.

I've been through hospitalization and now what I do with manic episodes is, I basically just let them run their course. Even depression. Nothing lasts forever. I sort of conceptualize it as processing, or, I don't know, excretion. It takes time. The problem is that the structure of the workday doesn't allow time for things to process or heal. I also think there's a pathology in society where no one has the time to reach out, but people have the time for a Netflix box set. Also, I would like to add that I'm a male bodied person, some of my female friends who experience, say, postnatal depression or a menstrual depressive cycle when they have their period, that's another thing beyond my embodied understanding. I tell my experience as I experience it. And I speak sincerely and honestly but I'm still questioning to what extent my experience could be taken as universal or what is its demographic reach and its potential limits. Much like the book itself.

GL One of the most pervasive aspects of extrovert supremacy is the obsession with productivity. Is Shy Radicals anti-work?

HA That's a really interesting question. I'm part of Artists' Union England so when I lived in England, I was trying to think about making a fairer economy for artist sustainability. I certainly want to change the structure of employment. I've also not been conventionally employed and that's often given me a sense of failure. I read lots of big thick anthologies on work and I've also developed alliances. There's an Italian writer called Silvio Lorusso, who wrote a book called the *Entreprecariat* (2019), he's written some articles on *Shy Radicals*. There's still something in that crossover concern. I also think of the actual act of writing *Shy Radicals* as an economy—I got a £600 advance for something like three to four years of work. It's not exactly a fair representation of my labor or time. There are areas in the book where I'm questioning success. I bought this tee shirt at the anarchist bookshop which says "My value is not determined by my productivity," with a fat cat sleeping, and I wear it in the film as a statement. It's crucial to acknowledge that there are also forms of being such as staring into space, at the sea and at the stars. I think that can offer an answer to your question about whether I'm anti-work.

Who Are We Writing For?

A Feminist Counter-Public Inside and Outside Open Letter

Brigitta Isabella

A writer writes with the shadow of the future reader, the public, in mind. Thinking about it often makes a writer feel rather anxious. Indeed, to write for/against/within the public, one requires not only militant discipline, but also passionate courage. Projecting the problem externally, the writer asks, "Who's going to read my writing? What are they going to think or feel about it? Will they understand me and my ideas?" Internally, the writer asks herself, "What do I want to show to the public? How do I expose the truth of my writerly self to strangers?"

Within the speculative boundaries between the private and the public spheres where an authorship and a readership are being constituted, the art of the open letter has been proven to be a powerful feminist genre to play with. Perhaps because the epistolary form provides, in the first place, the hope for and imagination of interpersonal ties between the writer and her projected feminist reader—a sister in arms who will accompany the writer negotiates the sense of vulnerability at the moment of female self-exposure in a patriarchal public sphere.

"It is not easy writing this letter. It began as a poem, a long poem. I tried to turn it into an essay but the result was wooden, cold. I have not yet unlearned the esoteric bullshit and pseudo-intellectualizing that school brainwashed into my writing. How to begin again? How to approximate the intimacy and immediacy I want? What form? A letter, of course."

So writes Gloria Anzaldua in a 1980's letter addressed to Third World Women Writers—the "mujeres de color," her "companions in writing."[1] Powerful feminist open letters always have a pedagogical appeal, it teaches us how to affirm friendship, how to unlearn a hegemonic language, how to constitute a relational self and a counter-public.

Dear Reader,

Allow me to re-open before your eyes, an open letter written sixty years ago by a female artist named Mia Bustam to her sister in arms, Kartika. It is an open letter which has taught me how to pose a feminist complaint and imagine a community of care. A close reading of her letter—not only of the content but also the paratextual elements—is my detoured open reply, one that hopes for continued correspondence

1 Gloria Anzaldúa, "Speaking in Tongues: A Letter to 3rd World Women Writers," *This Bridge Called My Back: Writings by Radical Women of Color*, eds. Cherríe Moraga and Gloria Anzaldúa (Massachusetts: Persephone Press, 1981), 165.

beyond the borders of histories. At the heart of this re-opening gesture of an open letter as an intimate archive, I want to invite us to think about the concept of the (counter-)public within the social and literary practice of feminist writing. One that encourage us to ponder upon the complexity of the basic question we nervously ask every time we begin and begin again to write, which is: "Who are we writing for?"

A FAILED PLAN, AN OPEN LETTER

Let us step back a moment from the hyper-fast speed of social media and the bias of machine generated algorithms to look at the politics of public communication in the time when writers were humbly dependent upon the post office and printed media. The story of our feminist open letter begins in 1960, when a 26-year-old female painter named Kartika visited all the female artists and aspiring artists that she knew in Yogyakarta city. She invited them to meet to discuss an idea for an association of women artists. On the awaited day, unfortunately, only four women gathered in response to Kartika's invitation. Given the scant enthusiasm and resources, this small group could not imagine how their grand plan could proceed. The proposal, which at that stage had no precedent in Indonesian art history, had run aground.

"Are you disappointed, Tika?
There's no need to be disappointed."

So wrote Mia Bustam, calling her friend by her nickname, in an open letter for the young woman artist, titled "Should Female Artists Separate Themselves from Male Artists?" Mia wrote this letter on January 22, 1960, probably not long after the meeting that Kartika initiated took place. This letter was then published in the newspaper *Harian Rakjat* (People's Daily) a month later, on February 27, 1960. Mia's open letter later won an annual literature prize as an example of the best art essay in that paper. There was no explanation for why *Harian Rakjat* awarded the prize to Mia's open letter. But if I were on the jury, I would have made the same decision. Without Mia's letter, the plan to establish an association of women artists might have left no historical trace. And the history of failed plans can be more interesting than the history of those that succeed. The history of failures holds possibilities; the history of what has yet to be is history awaiting its contemporary actualization.

In the 800 or so words of that open letter Mia did many things, like a woman who has been conditioned by the heteropatriarchal household to cook while doing the dishes while rocking the baby. The letter did its job to reassure Kartika, documenting their cancelled plans for the formation of an association, offering feminist tactics to continue the struggle, and criticizing sexism in the art world. Most importantly, Mia's letter expressed her desire, which was also Tika's desire. The letter is also a political confession, as she firmly stated: "You want to equal and compete with male artists. Great! I feel the same. I feel like I don't want to be left behind and seen as frivolous by men."

A year before she wrote this letter, Mia had divorced a famous artist. Their youngest child, one of eight, was only three years old at the time. Divorce is often painful, and even poverty-inducing in Mia's case, but it's commonly also liberating, like the amputation of a leg that can make a person learn to walk in a different way. Mia's open letter to Tika was the first time that Mia had carved out her writerly public persona. This letter signals how Mia took the courage to put one foot outside of the cage of patriarchal marriage. After her divorce at nearly 40, Mia found the courage to learn to paint amid the burden of domestic care that she had to carry as a single mother. She joined the Sanggar Indonesia Muda (Young Indonesian Artists' Collective–SIM), then began her studies at the People's University, which was supported by the Communist Party of Indonesia, then became an active member of the leftist organization Lembaga Kebudayaan Rakyat (The Institute for the People's Culture–LEKRA). This latter engagement tragically dragged Mia—who had only just begun her new life—down into the jails of the authoritarian New Order regime as a political prisoner for 13 years from 1965.[2] Meanwhile, although she was fourteen years younger than Mia, Kartika also had eight children when she fervently invited her female friends to build a women artist's association. At that time her youngest child had begun to walk, at which time as a mother, she became a little freer to put her hands to canvas and consider herself a painter. Kartika was the only child in a family of artists. Her father was a famous painter, and her

2 Mia had written two memoirs, *Sudjojono and I* (2006) and *From Camp to Camp: The Story of a Woman* (2008). See the translation of a chapter from Mia Bustam's first memoir by Astrid Reza, with introduction by art historian Yvonne Low in "Mia Bustam and Her Memoirs: Speaking for Herself," *Southeast of Now: Directions in Contemporary and Modern Art in Asia* 5, no. 1 (2021): 335–338.

mother Maryati was also an artist, who was steeped in the techniques of embroidery, although she didn't receive the same exposure as her husband. Blessed with this abundance of artistic relatives, Kartika was already familiar with canvas and paint from a young age. She adopted and developed the particular techniques of her father, which was to paint with her fingers and apply the paint straight from the tube. Her family's rising economic status allowed Tika the privilege of studying dance and painting in Santiniketan, India, and sculpture at the Polytechnic School of Arts in London. It was in London, at age 17, that Tika met her first husband, whom she divorced in 1972 because she didn't believe in polygamy and because of her husband's miserly attitude to the materials she needed for painting.[3]

CO-CREAING FEMINIST POLITICAL SUBJECTIVITIES THROUGH CORRESPONDENCE

Overall, Mia and Tika's lived trajectories were very different, but in 1960, after the meeting about the plans for an association of women artists, perhaps Mia saw some of her own desires in Tika's aspirations and reflected a glimpse of Tika's problems in her own daily life. The epistolary framing of Mia's writing allows her to perform the idea of interacting with rather than simply reacting to someone's idea. It responded to, but more importantly, also created correspondence. Mia could have just (and perhaps already had) corresponded with Kartika directly and personally, but she chose to speak through an open letter. Why? I consider this choice of communicative form to be connected with, if not demonstrating, Mia's perspective on the strategy of creating a feminist counter public.

Firstly, Mia's answer to the question of whether female artists should separate themselves from male artists as she proposes in the title of her open letter is "no." She felt the prospect of making an art organization exclusively for women was not aligned with her basic belief that "in art there is no sex, there are no women or men, because art itself has no sex." With this resistance against the simple gender binary, Mia rejects the depoliticization of the female identity.

3 Carla Bianpoen, "Indonesian Women Artists: Transcending Compliance," *Women in Indonesia: Gender, Equity and Development*, eds. Kathryn Robinson and Sharon Bessel (Singapore: Institute of Southeast Asian Studies, 2002), 116.

She writes:

> "What do we want with our art, with our skills, Tika? Just being able to draw, and to develop that practice, for entertainment, for a sideline, and just to say to men: 'look, we can too, whatever you can do!'? Or do we want to devote ourselves to our practice in pure pursuit of art: proclaiming, demonstrating, and defending this truth, anywhere, by any means, without fear, without considering our sex?"

Mia recommended "not considering our sex" in making artwork that "defends the truth," but this doesn't mean she ignores the reality of the gender inequality.[4] Of course she would not write or publish this letter if she believed that the structure of the art world had already liberated women from the confinement of gender based social constructions.

At the end of her open letter, Mia signed off as "Mother" (*Ibu*), not *seniwati* (female artist) or *seniman* (male artist). In contemporary Indonesian language, artists are referred to as *seniman* and the common usage of the term is regarded as gender neutral.[5] However, while male artists can be referred to as *seniman* without any problem, female artists often acquire gendered qualifiers such as *seniwati*, *seniman perempuan* or *seniman wanita* (*perempuan* and *wanita* mean "women"). The usage of the term *seniwati* was circulating in Indonesian feminist-nationalist newspapers in the 1940s, not long after the term *seniman* was coined as a recalibrated term of modern artist.[6] Indonesian language has no distinctions of grammatical gender, yet the need for female art writers to claim the word *seniwati* attests to the difficulty of female artists to occupy an equal position with male artists, even within the realm of language.

Mia's decision to sign off neither as *seniman* nor *seniwati* enabled her to eschew gender binary oppositions—which were debated in her letter—without entirely dismissing her social reality as a woman who bears the burdens of motherhood, and her demand

4 Note that the term "gender" was still foreign to the ears of the educated classes of Indonesia at this time, much less to the larger population. However, consciousness of gender politics, that is the ideology of social justice which questioned the determination of status based on the construct of biological difference, was alive in flourishing social movements even before Indonesian independence in 1945. In other words, when Mia used the term "sex" I believe she was not using it exclusively in a biological sense but in relation to the social constructions of gender.

5 I thank the translator of this text, Elly Kent, who pointed out the need to explain the difference between seniman and seniwati as it has a historical nuance which may not be captured well in English.

6 Heidi Arbuckle, *Performing Emiria Sunassa: Reframing the Female Subject in Post/colonial Indonesia*, dissertation (Melbourne: University of Melbourne, 2011) 112–4.

that women should have an equal opportunity to become artists. The domesticized persona of a mother, whose voice has been constrained in the art world and in dominant public spaces, is fluently displayed through her use of the different types of singular first-person pronouns, which the Indonesian language allows through the use of "*saya*" (formal singular first person), to "*aku*" (colloquial singular first person).

The narrow imagining of social relations embedded in the word "I" in English makes it hard to imagine this subtle difference. In its visual form alone, doesn't the single perpendicular line "I" seem a little Individualistic? With exceptions in variations within literary works, the performance of the writerly self in printed publications in the national language of Indonesian almost always manifests as *saya*. *Saya* demonstrates distance, formality, the public realm. Following the dominant socio-linguistic convention, *saya* is used when Mia is presenting herself as a preaching subject that speaks of the truth that art "does not remember sex." Meanwhile, *aku*, as self-presentation in more intimate and familiar social interactions, was used by Mia as a political subjectivity that aims to distract from her own idealization of art as the reflection of truth. The fluid shift from *saya* to *aku* performs the blurred boundaries between private and public in the literary-social space of her open letter. Revealing another texture of truth based on her lived realities as a mother, Mia poses as *aku* when she complains about the domestic work that prevents women from doing painting:

> "Ah Tika, there are so many things waiting to be painted, so many. And it feels like we have no time to put all of that onto the canvas. We, women with all our difficulties, all our impediments! Objects call: But—wait a while, I (*aku*) must finish in the kitchen, I need to wash up, I have to see to the children, the bedrooms haven't been tidied, the Youngest has a fever—etc., etc."

Here Mia's letter registers an autobiography of complaint, one that is poignantly expressive and excessive. Complaint, as wittily claimed by feminist theorist Sara Ahmed, is a "kill joy genre." Complaint is often dismissed because the complainer is deemed as complaining of unimportant things, or in our present case, the trivial, unserious, non-art thing. But complaint can be a form of feminist pedagogy because the more you share, the more you hear resonances that correspond: yes, me too![7] To complain publicly is to personalize public polemics and to take part in a collective dissatisfaction—something that can be built into a protest or an outcry. The persona of a complaining mother allows the emergence of an affective gender-based tie between Mia, Tika and other women artists who were reached by Mia's open letter. Here the mother's identity is not filled with romanticized imagery of the feminine figure who always willingly sacrifices herself for her family, but rather with the mother who is tired and desiring change.

The emerging ties between women are strengthened as seen in the next part which I quote below. It was the moment when the individual who is in the first person, *aku*, is intertwined with the inclusive "we feminists"—"we" (*kita*) who do not hesitate to share and affirm female fragility while also questioning the male privilege that controls the standards of the art world.

> "We are sometimes close to giving up. We complain: Can I *(aku)* reach what inspires me? Can I stand in line next to those who now have the right to select, critique and reject our paintings?"

"I" and "we" are used interchangeably, indicating the formation of a political subjectivity that is unstable and not fully existing, but imaginable through the recognition of women's shared experiences. The formation of this subjectivity is collective and relational because Mia, Tika and the women who identify with the experience of *aku* are connected in an affective network of the complaining "we." This subjectivity is shaped through a sense of inner self and self-esteem seen through an imagined affirmative relation with other women. One may also argue that Mia's mode of communication offers a feminist alternative to the authoritative-masculine figure of the modern art critic, who generally makes aesthetic judgements within the narrative structure of pretentious monologue and who prioritizes displays of their intellect over building an interpersonal conversation.

The use of *aku* in the middle of the letter, which distracts from the coherence of *saya*, also writes the bodies of women who want to pursue life as artists but are always faced with the distractions of unpaid care work. More than that, the moment of distraction in *aku* and its link to "we feminists" also suggests a spatial

7 Sara Ahmed, *Complaint!* (Durham: Duke University Press, 2021) 1, 9.

politics that creates a temporary safe space in which to complain about domestic work and gossip about the sexism of male artists. This is gossip in the best political sense. As reclaimed by feminist Marxist Silvia Federici, gossip is a social epistemology that is produced and circulated through women's networks of solidarity and friendship—before this informal practice was derided as a waste of time within the economy of the capitalist patriarchy.[8] The circulation of gossip is never entirely private or public. As with the open letter, it moves in two directions, internally (as is fitting for intimate communication among a close circle of friends) as well as externally (indicating a public identity, enabling the formation of social networks). The open letter becomes a space to enact moments of calling *out* sexism and calling *in* feminist solidarity.

IMAGINING A COUNTER-PUBLIC INSIDE AND OUTSIDE AN OPEN LETTER

Mia's letter frames Tika as its explicit addressee and the subtext of friendship enables her to outpour her complaints about personal experiences as a woman, aside from imparting her strategic ideas about the women's movement. But by making the letter public, she creates a bridge between the structures of personal-internal relationships and social-external networks—both imagined and real—of the general readership of the *Harian Rakjat* newspaper. A theorist of the epistolary form has pointed out that the open letter as a genre of political communication always has two addressees. In an open letter addressed to a person close to the writer, the form serves dual functions, that is as an expression of radical intimacy as well as a political public intervention. The conventions of open letter writing complicate the dyadic relationship between the sender and the recipient of a private letter, because the grammatical actors implicated by the circulation of an open letter exist within a triadic relationship between the letter-writer, the explicitly named recipient, and the general community of readers in which the letter is published.[9]

8 Silvia Federici, "How the Demonization of 'Gossip' Is Used to Break Women's Solidarity," *In These Times* (31 January 2019): https://inthesetimes.com/article/the-subversive-feminist-power-of-gossip.
9 Shang-yu Sheng, *Writing for Strangers: Structural Transformations of the Public Letter, 1640–1790*, dissertation (New York: City University of New York, 2017), 2–3.

Mia's letter further complicates this triadic relationship by creating a gendered spatio-linguistic organization in her imagining of readership. This partition is important in the performative work of the open letter because it stages the political self-identity and produces a social network which the writer imagines themselves to occupy. Although imaginary, it departs from the concrete experience of sociability between women in domestic and public spaces. In her letter, Mia recognizes both the individual and collective reader, addressed intimately as a politicized feminine identity.

Meanwhile the reader who is not directly hailed or interpellated—in the Althusserian sense—is positioned as if they are in the next room, eavesdropping on women gossiping about chronic sexism through a wall that fails to muffle the feminist spilling out:

> "We put down our palette and brushes, we shake our heads: —as if to say no!—but we also imagine in front of us the face of painter A, painter B, with a smile that is half sarcastic and half pitying, a patronizing smile—ah women, just mucking around, they have no dedication, no commitment, no determination!—we are irked beyond belief, we grit our teeth—somehow, I must, I must be able to!"

Here the literary sphere of the open letter allows a virtual performance that does not follow the dominant social rules for face-to-face interaction, where usually, when a person is the only woman in a macho environment, there comes a time when she does not want to take the risk and chooses to "grit her teeth." Mia's open letter provides a semi-safe space for women because she constructs an imaginary social space for women to talk intimately inside the male-dominated public sphere of *Harian Rakjat*.

The imagined partition of social space expressed by Mia's language ideology genders the implied third person in the triadic relationship of her open letter. This formation of gendered readership is important because when we publish ourselves, we basically throw our thoughts to invisible people, a community of imagined readers who are networked in what queer theorist Michael Warner calls "stranger sociability."[10] Unlike the concept of an a priori public that the writer generally imagines, Warner proposes an understanding

10 Michael Warner, *Publics and Counter-Publics* (Brooklyn: Zone Books, 2002), 122.

of the public as "something that exists only when it is connected to a text and its circulation" and which "exists only by virtue of being addressed."[11] Warner's theory resembles Ben Anderson's seminal arguments around the "imagined community," which demonstrates how the idea of a national public is circulated through print capitalism. However, Anderson's theory doesn't account for how social identities based on gender and sexuality influence the hierarchy of public space in the imagined community.[12]

Conscious that public spaces are controlled by a regime of heteronormative patriarchy, feminist and queer speech forms a "counter public" by creating alternative affective relations between the writer and reader; relations that are not regulated by the dominant public norms. The public space of *Harian Rakjat* manifested a leftist readership, which no matter how progressive, was still dominated by the centrality of male voices and their revolutionary brotherhood. Mia's open letter created a feminist counter public by speaking to Tika and freely discussing the sexism of men, as if the letter is private, within that male-dominated public space. She enunciated a personal-political speech act which carves out a feminist counter public space by partitioning and rupturing *Harian Rakjat*'s space. This rupturing of course carries risks. When we discuss something personal openly, there are those in its circulation who we don't know and cannot control. But speaking both with people we know and don't know is essential in creating a counter public; speaking by projecting to people we do know enables intimacy and a sense of co-membership, while speaking to those we don't know, apart from the risk, broadens the expectation of collective transformation.[13]

Making and unmaking this partition is a feminist strategy that does not replicate the mode of female seclusion that the patriarchal regime implements, but also doesn't fall into the masculine discourse around gender neutral "universalism." The creation of this gendered space for speaking and listening to women enables criticism of the patriarchy without centering men at the discussion table (or the tea table, which is better for gossip). This strategy is queer as far as it ruptures the simplified gender binary through

11 Ibid. 66–67.
12 Elleke Boehmer, *Stories of Women: Gender and Narrative in the Postcolonial Nation* (Manchester: Manchester University Press, 2005), 7–8.
13 Warner, 91.

a feminist politics of inclusion-exclusion. It also negotiates the dilemma between the need for women artists to create a safe space (with the implication that the patronage of men in the public space will remain undisturbed) as the first choice, or intervention in the macho sociality of men (with the implication of exhaustion in dealing with the privileged mansplaining of the ignorant) as the second. These two dynamics of feminist strategy are still debated today, and each has its own advantages, risks and paradoxes as it as a matter of what women choose to care and not to care about in their contexts.

Rather than making a fixed choice, Mia's open letter negotiates the duality of the inclusive-exclusive space, through which her gendered spatial imagining allows both spaces to co-exist. I believe that our political awareness of the structure, narrative and atmosphere of literature that mediates critical messages to its reader, or what is better termed by Warner as "the poesis of scene making," is important to consider in the practice of art criticism, which has its own form of art to be explored.[14] The intertwining of private and public spaces in Mia's open letter is aligned with Mia's message to Tika and the feminist public, to strategically choose what to care about. Mia's ultimate advice to Tika is to eschew her plans to create an association for women artists, because she believes that organization would make more work for women, who are already burdened with the inconvenience of unpaid care work. She suggests women "break into their spaces, mix in with them [male artist] and join existing associations." In spite of this, Mia doesn't forget the importance of mutual care between women artists, who cannot be left behind because they are occupied in the domestic space, so: "We can try to visit each other occasionally. That way we can see and compare our work."

That is exactly what is done by Mia's open letter to Tika, infiltrating the public space of a national newspaper that is still controlled by men, and visiting the sitting rooms of women artists, including mine, ours, sixty years later.

We can debate whether Mia's suggestion to disband Tika's plan to create a women artist's association is the best feminist strategy or not, both in our particular context of movement in the historical past

14 Warner, 122.

and the present. Here we read and re-read the historical letter from our feminist mothers in order to continue their moving correspondence. By becoming feminist readers ourselves, we let this letter create a new and intergenerational counter public. Perhaps we might also reply to their letter, in writing and through our actions, to progress and problematize the values and strategies of resistance that they have caringly passed down to us.

Translated to English by Elly Kent

Biographies

Hamja Ahsan, London
b. London, United Kingdom, 1981

Hamja Ahsan is an artist, writer, curator, and activist. He is the author of *Shy Radicals: Antisystemic Politics of the Militant Introvert*, a satirical, speculative work of fiction envisioning a revolutionary political movement for shy, quiet, awkward, and autistic people against a neurotypical extrovert-supremacist world order, which he has developed into further art projects. He was awarded the Grand Prize at the Ljubljana Biennial of Graphic Arts 2019 for the artwork *Aspergistan Referendum*, which was based on *Shy Radicals*. The book was adapted into a film in collaboration with director Tom Dream of Black Dog films (part of the Ridley Scott Creative Group), which is currently touring international film festivals. Ahsan is the founder and co-curator of DIY Cultures, an annual festival for zine subcultures and creative activism founded in 2013. He was shortlisted for the Liberty Human Rights Award for the Free Talha Ahsan campaign on extradition and detention without trial under the War on Terror. He was selected to produce an art project on Halal Fried Chicken for Documenta 15.

— Ahsan, Hamja. *Shy Radicals: The Antisystemic Politics of the Militant Introvert*. 5th ed. London: Bookworks, 2021.
— Ahsan, Hamja. "The Library to Come." *Wasafiri*, no. 108 (Winter 2021): 4.

Gwendolyn Albert, Prague
b. Oakland, USA, 1967

Gwendolyn Albert is a human rights activist involved in the issues of dignified remembrance of Romani Holocaust sites, guaranteed access to standard primary school for Romani children in Europe, and helped secure redress for women who have been forcibly sterilized. In August 2020 she was given the Award for Humanity by the Committee for the Redress of the Roma Holocaust in the Czech Republic in recognition of her work on the issue of redress for those who have been forcibly sterilized in the Czech Republic and former Czechoslovakia. She received the Alice G. Masaryk Human Rights Award from the Embassy of the United States of America in the Czech

Republic in 2021, together with Elena Gorolová and Monika Šimůnková, for her work on that same issue.

- Albert, Gwendolyn et. al. *Human Rights of Roma and Travellers in Europe*. Strasbourg: Council of Europe, 2012.
- Albert, Gwendolyn. "Anti-Gypsyism and the Extreme Right in the Czech Republic 2008–2011." In *The Gypsy 'Menace': Populism and the New Anti-Gypsy Politics*, edited by Michael Stewart. London: C. Hurst & Co., 2012.

Dorota Brázdovičová, Prague
b. Trnava, Slovakia, 1993

Dorota Brázdovičová is an interdisciplinary artist and illustrator currently based in Prague. The playful and raw form of her ink drawings usually stands in a high contrast with their content. Situations of power abuse, acts of oppression, or various types of pressure are very present. They depict limbs, bodies, and faces experienc ing desperation and joy, rage and numbness, overstimulation and exhaustion, connection and loneliness, all at the same time. Whether it's her illustrations, minimalistic songs, or DJ sets, she uses her work as a tool to find a way how to function in complex and complicated social structures and overwhelming environments.

- *Scripts of the Shifting Bodies*, group exhibition, Kunsthalle, Bratislava, Slovakia, 2021
- *Stories of the Inflamed Head*, performance, Sensorium Festival, Bratislava, Slovakia, 2021
- *Stories of the Inflamed Head*, performance, ARTWIFE Festival, Liptovský Mikuláš, Slovakia, 2021
- *Obstacle-drawing workshop* (with Dominika Koššová), Pozitif Dej Festival, Spišská Nová Ves, Slovakia, 2020
- *ANTIGOLDRUSH*, group exhibition, OS 17 Gallery, Sczeczin, Poland, 2019

Amanda Carneiro, São Paulo
b. São Paulo, Brazil, 1985

Amanda Carneiro has been an Assistant Curator at Museu de Arte de São Paulo (MASP) since 2018 and a co-editor at the journal *Afterall* since 2020. She worked at Museu Afro Brasil from

2012 to 2017. Carneiro has organized exhibitions and catalogues of Sonia Gomes, Leonor Anuntes, Beatriz Milhazes, and Conecaição dos Bugres at MASP and is interested in the debates related to art and decolonization, afro-Brazilian art, and plural modernisms.

— Carneiro, Amanda, and Fernando Oliva, eds. *Conceição dos Bugres: The Nature of the World*. São Paulo: MASP, 2021.
— Carneiro, Amanda. "Time Will Tell." *Afterall*, no. 50 (Winter 2020): 36–60.
— Carneiro, Amanda. "Rosana Paulino: 'The Sewing of Memory', at Pinacoteca de São Paulo." *Terremoto*, February 14, 2019. https://terremoto.mx/en/online/rosana-paulino-the-sewing-of-memory-at-pina coteca-de-sao-paulo-brazil/
— Carneiro, Amanda. "Who Comes There?: Iconographic Circulation of Hammocks." In *To-and-fro*, edited by Raphael Fonseca. São Paulo: Centro Cultural Banco do Brasil, 2019.

Jana Krejcarová-Černá
b. 1928, Prague; d. 1981, Prague, Czechoslovakia

From 1938, Jana Krejcarová-Černá studied at a secondary school in Prague. Between the years 1942 and 1944, she studied at a two-year graphic school and then, in the years 1946–47, one year at a conservatory. She worked as a writer and took occasional jobs—she worked as a cleaning lady, tram guide, kitchen helper, etc. She was a mother to five children. Krejcarová-Černá was imprisoned in the 1960s in Pardubice. From 1947, she wrote articles for *Svobodné noviny and Kulturní tvorba*, and after 1948, as Honza Krejcarová, she took part in the activities of a surrealist group and from 1950 also in the activities of young writers and artists around Egon Bondy. She was published in the samizdat anthology *Židovská jména* (1949, under the pseudonyms Sarah Silberstein and Gala Mallarmé, reprinted in 1995) and in the samizdat publication *Půlnoc*. Under the name Jana Černá, she published short stories and articles in magazines such as *Květy, Svět v obrazech, Kulturní tvorba,* and *Divoké víno*. She died in a car accident in 1981 at the age of 52.

— Černá, Jana. *Hrdinství je povinné.* Prague: Československý spisovatel, 1964.

— Černá, Jana. *Nebyly to moje děti*. Prague: Naše vojsko, 1966.
— Černá, Jana. *Adresát Milena Jesenská.* Prague: Klub přátel poezie, 1969.
— Krejcarová, Jana. *Clarissa a jiné texty.* Prague: Concordia, 1990.

Brenda Villanueva Fajardo, Quezon City
b. Manila, Philippines, 1940

Brenda V. Fajardo is a painter, printmaker, theater designer, art educator, scholar, and community organizer. She is a professor emerita of the Department of Art Studies at the University of the Philippines (UP) in Diliman. She received a bachelor's degree in agriculture from the University of the Philippines (UP) Los Baños in 1959, a master's degree in art education from the University of Wisconsin–Madison in 1967, and a doctorate in Philippine studies from UP Diliman in 1997. Together with Arceli Dans, Fajardo co-founded the Philippine Art Educators Association (PAEA), which spearheaded training programs and resource development for visual arts teachers in the Philippines. In 1970, she joined the Philippine Educational Theater Association (PETA) as set designer and eventually became the curriculum head for its workshops. Throughout her career, she founded other arts and cultural organizations such as Kababaihan as Sining at Bagong Sibol na Kamalayan (Kasibulan) in 1987, Baglan Art and Culture Initiatives for Community Development in 1993, and Dalubhasaan sa Sining at Kultura (DESK) in 2002. Brenda Fajardo has received the Pamana Award from the Philippine Women's University, the PAEA Lifetime Achievement Award from the Philippine Art Educators Association, the Award for Outstanding Achievement in the Humanities from the Ateneo De Manila University, the Gawad CCP for Visual Arts from the Cultural Center of the Philippines, and the Distinguished Alumni Award from the UP Alumni Association.

— Fajardo, Brenda V. "PETA's Reach In and Out Experience." *In Lakbay Sining*: *Readings on Cultural Development*. Pasig City: CCP and ANVIL Publishing, 2007.
— Fajardo, Brenda V. *Art Education in the*

Philippines, edited by Lindy Joubert. UNESCO Publication, 2005.

— Fajardo, Brenda V. "Contemporary Visual Arts in the Philippines." In *Contemporary Philippine Culture: Selected Papers on Arts and Education.* Manila: The Japan Foundation, Manila Office, 1998.

— Fajrado, Brenda V. "Filipina as Mother and Other Identities." In *Perspectives on the Vargas Museum Collection.* Quezon City: Department of Art Studies, College of Arts & Letters and Jorge B. Vargas Museum & Filipiniana Research Center, 1998.

Robert Gabris, Vienna
b. Hnúšťa, Czechoslovakia, 1986

I describe the content of my work as a critical confrontation with identity issues, especially confrontations of different groups excluded from society. The starting point of my work deals with new experimental forms of drawing as resistance to exclusion and racism. I belong to the Romani ethnic group but don't define myself as a Romani artist. My work shows a much more constant interest in multiple questions of diverse and convertible identity, the queer body, and its existence, possessed in different physical and mental bodies, in relation to normative society and its boundaries. My medium of choice is conceptual drawing and its experimental implementation, the de-construction of forms, and the quest to push all possible limits. My works are mostly autobiographical, imagined as a constant and obsessive search for exact proportion and symmetry.

— *Whiteness as Property*, Künstlerhaus Wien, Vienna, Austria, 2022

— *Jindřich Chalupecký Award Exhibition*, Moravská Galerie, Brno, Czech Republic, 2021

— *STRABAG Artaward International*, Vienna, Austria, 2021

— *Insectopia*, Villa Romana, Florence, Italy, 2021

Ramon Guillermo, Quezon City
b. Manila, Philippines, 1969

Ramon Guillermo is a writer, translator, and scholar of Southeast Asian Studies. He studied at the University of the Philippines Diliman (UPD) and at the University of Hamburg, Germany. He teaches at the Center for International Studies at UPD. He is an active proponent of digital humanities and also makes contributions in translation studies. His current research projects are about the reception, translation, and dissemination of radical ideas and ideologies in Southeast Asia (particularly in the Philippines and Indonesia).

- Guillermo, Ramon, et al. *3 Baybayin Studies*. Quezon City: University of the Philippines Press, 2017.
- Guillermo, Ramon. *Ang Makina ni Mang Turing*. Quezon City: University of the Philippines Press, 2013.
- Guillermo, Ramon. *Pook at Paninindigan: Kritika ng Pantayong Pananaw*. Quezon City: University of the Philippines Press, 2009
- Guillermo, Ramon. *Translation and Revolution: A Study of Jose Rizal's Guillermo Tell*. Quezon City: Ateneo de Manila Press, 2009.

Robin Hartanto Honggare, Jakarta
b. Jakarta, Indonesia, 1989

Robin Hartanto Honggare is a writer, curator, and presently a PhD candidate at Columbia Graduate School of Architecture, Planning and Preservation. He is a visiting scholar within Het Nieuwe Instituut's research team for 2021–2022. He curated the Indonesia Pavilion at the 14th International Architecture Exhibition in Venice in 2014. His articles have been published in *Southeast of Now*, *ARSNET*, *Planning Perspectives*, *Avery Review*, and *Jakarta Post*. In parallel with his broader interest in the architectures of extraction and the histories of colonial modernities in Southeast Asia, his current research explores how buildings and landscapes in the Dutch East Indies shaped, and were shaped by, commodity productions.

- Honggare, Robin Hartanto. "Disease on Display: The First Hygiene Exhibition in the Netherlands Indies Revisited." *Southeast of Now: Directions in Contemporary and Modern Art in Asia* 5, no. 1 (2021): 97–116.
- Honggare, Robin Hartanto and Fauzia Evanindya. "Play, Space, and the Magic

Circle: Reinventing the Game." *ARSNET* 1, no. 2 (2021): 140–151.

— Honggare, Robin Hartanto. "Review: *Southeast Asia's Modern Architecture: Questions of Translation, Epistemology, and Power* by Jiat-Hwee Chang and Imran bin Tajudeen." *Planning Perspectives* 34, no. 5 (2019): 928–930.

— Honggare, Robin Hartanto. "The Shape of Sports Diplomacy: Gelora Bung Karno, Jakarta, and the Fourth Asian Games." *mASEANa Project 2017: Modern Living in Southeast Asia* (2018): 26–29.

— Honggare, Robin Hartanto. "Uncornering Speakers: On Political Speech in Singapore." *Avery Review* (2017).

Filip Herza, Prague
b. Prague, Czechoslovakia, 1986

Filip Herza is a historian and cultural anthropologist. He studied at Charles University in Prague. He has been working as a researcher at the Institute of Ethnology of the Czech Academy of Sciences since 2019. Herza is mainly interested in Eastern and Central Europe in the broader context of modernity and colonial/imperial cultures. His work encompasses histories of popular culture and science in the first half of the 20th century.

— Herza, Filip. *Imaginace jinakosti. Přehlídky lidských kuriozit v Praze 19. a 20. století.* Prague: Scriptorium, 2020.

Jana Horváthová, Brno
b. Brno, Czechoslovakia, 1967

Jana Horváthová is a historian and museologist. She is a co-founder (1991) and the current head of the Museum of Romani Culture, an organization subsidized by the Ministry of Culture of the Czech Republic. Her scholarly work focuses on the history of the Roma in the first half of the 20th century. She is interested in historical Romani groups that had been coming to the Czech lands since the end of the 17th century and during World War II became the subject of Nazi genocide. She mainly focuses on the method of oral history. She lectures on the history and spiritual and material culture of the Romani people.

— Horváthová, Jana. *Kapitoly z dějin Romů.* Prague: Nakladatelství Lidové noviny, 2002.

— Horváthová, Jana. *Devleskere čhave svedectvom starých pohľadníc*. Poprad: Vydavateľsto Region Poprad, 2006.
— Horváthová, Jana. "Fenomén Polansky." *Romano džaniben:* Časopis *romistických studií*, no. 1 (2015): 87–106.
— Horváthová, Jana, ed. *Treasure of the Roma/ Amare somnaka: The Secret of Romani Jewellery*. Brno: Muzeum romské kultury, 2016.
— Horváthová, Jana, et al. *...to jsou těžké vzpomínky: I. svazek*. Brno: Větrné mlýny, 2021.

Brigitta Isabella, Yogyakarta
b. Jakarta, Indonesia, 1989

Brigitta Isabella is a researcher of art history, critical theory, and cultural studies. Her research trajectory engages with the politics of mobility in art practices and the (art) history of transnational solidarity. Since 2014, together with Renan Laru-an, she has been enacting a series of artistic iterations called From Bandung to Berlin, an open and shared immaterial platform of collaboration that revolves around the interval of historical pace and time between the first Asian–African Conference in Bandung in 1955 and the fall of Berlin Wall in 1989. Isabella is part of the self-organized group Kunci Study Forum & Collective and currently serves as the co-editor of the peer-reviewed journal *Southeast of Now: Directions in Contemporary and Modern Art in Asia*.

— Isabella, Brigitta, ed. *UNJUK RASA, Seni–Performativitas Aktivisme*. Jakarta: Yayasan Kelola, 2018.
— Isabella, Brigitta. "The National and The International: Politics of Friendship and Cultural Diplomacy in Indonesia 1950-1965." In *Ambitious Alignment: New Histories of Southeast Asian Art*, edited by Yvonne Low et al. Sydney: Power Institute, Sydney University, 2018.
— Isabella, Brigitta. "Dwelling in Travel as An Aesthetic Practice." In *Interlaced Journeys: Diaspora and the Contemporary in South east Asian Art*, edited by Loredana Parac ciani and Patrick Flores. Hong Kong: Osage Foundation, 2020.

— Isabella, Brigitta, and the Kunci Study Forum & Collective. *Letters: The classroom is burning, let's dream about a School of Improper Education*. Brooklyn: Ugly Duckling Presse, 2020.

Rado Ištok, Stockholm
b. Veľký Krtíš, Czechoslovakia, 1989

Rado Ištok is a curator, editor, and researcher based in Stockholm. Between the years 2018 and 2020 he was the curator of the program *4C: From Conflict to Conviviality through Creativity and Culture* at the Nida Art Colony of the Vilnius Academy of Arts. He is also in charge of *Spaces of Care, Disobedience and Desire* (2018–2022), a research project in collaboration with Marie-Louise Richards and Natalia Rebelo, supported by the Royal Institute of Art in Stockholm. His recent exhibition projects include *Ala Younis: High Dam. Modern Pyramid* (2020) at VIPER Gallery in Prague, *The Spectral Forest* (2020) at the Nida Art Colony in Lithuania, *Black Atlas* (2019) at Július Koller Society in Bratislava, and *Liquid Horizons* at tranzit.sk in Bratislava.

— Ištok, Rado, ed. *The Spectral Forest*. Vilnius: Kirvarpa, 2021.
— Ištok, Rado, ed. *Dwelling on the Threshold*. Nida: Nida Art Colony, 2020. E-publication.
— Ištok, Rado, and Jacqueline Hoàng Nguyễn, eds. *Crating the World*. Bogotá: Athénée Press, 2019.
— Ištok, Rado, ed. *Decolonising Archives*. Ghent: L'Internationale Online, 2016. E-publication.

Tarek Lakhrissi, Paris
b. Châtellerault, France, 1992

Tarek Lakhrissi is a French artist and poet with a background in literature. He works across installation, performance, film, text, and sculpture, engaging with political and social issues around transformative narratives within language, magic, codes, and affects. His background in literature draws influence from feminist and queer writers such as Elsa Dorlin, Jean Genet, Monique Wittig, and José Esteban Muñoz, providing his work with a romantic and critical atmosphere. He currently teaches in the CCC

Research Master Program of the Visual Arts Department at HEAD (the Geneva School of Art and Design).

— *I wear my wounds on my tongue*, Kunstverein Kevin Space, Vienna, Austria, 2021
— *Perfume of Traitors*, Vitrine Gallery, London, United Kingdom, 2021
— *Anticorps*, Palais de Tokyo, Paris, France, 2020
— *NIRIN 22nd Biennale of Sydney*, Museum of Contemporary Art Australia, Sydney, Australia, 2020

Renan Laru-an, Sultan Kudarat/Manila
b. Sultan Kudarat, Philippines, 1989

Renan Laru-an is a researcher and curator. He creates exhibitionary, public, and research programs that study "insufficient" and "subtracted" images or subjects at the juncture of development and integration projects. His ongoing projects include *But Ears Have No Lids* (2021) and *Promising Arrivals, Violent Departures* (2018). Since 2017, Laru-an has been the Public Engagement and Artistic Formation Coordinator at the Philippine Contemporary Art Network (PCAN). He has curated and co-curated many biennales and festivals, including the 6th Singapore Biennale in Singapore, the 8th OK.Video—Indonesia Media Arts Festival in Jakarta, and the 1st Lucban Assembly in Quezon. His other recent exhibitions include *Sourcebook: Mandy El-Sayegh and Helena Hunter* at LUX in London (2022), *Motions Of This Kind* at SOAS in London (2019), *A Tripoli Agreement* at Sharjah Art Foundation in Sharjah (2018), and *The Artist and the Social Dreamer* at Forecast Festival at Haus Der Kulturen Der Welt in Berlin (2017). Laru-an's scholarship has been supported by the Foundation for Arts Initiatives, the National Commission for Culture and the Arts, and other curatorial fellowships. Between 2012 and 2015, he directed the self-organized, multi-disciplinary platform and "virtual" organization DiscLab|Research and Criticism. He is the Curatorial Advisor to the 58th Carnegie International in Pittsburgh.

— Laru-an, Renan. "Centers of the World." In *Meridians of Region: Writing Art History*

and Curating Contemporary Culture in the Philippines and Taiwan, edited by Patrick Flores and Chiang Po-shin, 36–49. New Taipei: Ministry of Culture of Taiwan, 2021.
— Laru-an, Renan. "General Nourishment: The Aga Khan Museum of Islamic Arts in Marawi." In "Extreme." Special issue, *OnCurating* 50 (2021): 38–54.
— Laru-an, Renan, ed. *Writing Presently*. Quezon City: The Philippine Contemporary Art Network, 2020.

Giulia Loi, Marseille
b. Rome, Italy, 1983

Giulia Loi is a writer based in France whose practice started with poetry and performance, first in French and then in English after she moved to London to study fine art. In the UK, she ran a performance night and a radio show on NTS radio. In 2021, she curated a translation of early vignettes by Katherine Mansfield with the Italian publishing house Elliot, and she has now started collaborating with Bruit du Monde, a Marseille-based publishing house looking for fresh voices from around the world. She translates from French, Italian, English, and Russian into French and English. She has been published in *Salt* (when it was still a zine), *Hysteria*, *Different Skies*, and others, and she has performed at DIY Cultures, Dangerous Times, and on every stage she could find for a long time.

— Loi, Giulia, trans. *Katherine Mansfield. Il Pino, I Passeri, Io e Te*. Rome: Elliot Edizioni, 2021.
— Loi, Giulia. "A Filmmaker of Our Time." *Different Skies*, no. 3 (September 2014).
— Loi, Giulia. "My Own." *Hysteria* (2014).
— Loi, Giulia. "Holy." *Salt* (2010).

Dorota Jagoda Michalska, London/Warsaw
b. Rome, Italy, 1988

Dorota Michalska is an art researcher, writer, teacher, and curator based in London and Warsaw. She is currently a doctoral student at the Ruskin School of Art of the University of Oxford, where she is working on a dissertation on the relationships between class, subalternity, materiality, and art in post-war Poland. Between 2013 and 2015, she was an assistant researcher at the Museum of Modern Art in Warsaw. Her recent exhibitions include *Passo Dopo Passo* at Fondazione Sandretto Re Rebaudengo in Turin, *The Shape Left by the Body* at The Sunday Painter in London, and *The House of the Spider* at Gdansk City Gallery in Gdansk. Michalska's writings have appeared in a number of art jounals such as *ARTMargins*, *L'Internationale*, *Afterall*, and *Kajet Journal*, and she wrote one of the texts for the Polish Pavilion of the 2019 Venice Biennale. Her research currently focuses on questions of race and decoloniality within the context of Eastern and Southern Europe as well as on global, decolonial histories of surrealism(s).

— Michalska, Dorota Jagoda. "Degraded Objects, Harrowed Bodies: Roman Stańczak and Shock Therapy in Poland, 1990–1996." *ARTMargins* (June 2022).
— Michalska, Dorota Jagoda. "Have We Really Never Been Colonisers? A Decolonial Perspective on Ethnographic and Archaeo logical Collections in Poland." *L'Internationale Online*, August 18, 2021.
— Michalska, Dorota Jagoda. "Vertigo. A Decolonial Biennial at the Edge of Western Europe." In *Returning to the Future*. Zielona Góra: BWA Zielona Góra, 2020.

Ábel Ravasz, Bratislava
b. Dunajská Streda, Czechoslovakia, 1986

Ábel Ravasz is a sociologist, activist, and politician. He studied at Eötvös Loránd University and Corvinus University of Budapest as well as Columbia University in New York City. He is the founder of several NGOs, such as the pro-Roma organization PURT (2013) and the Mathias Bel Institute (2014). Between 2016 and 2020, he worked as the plenipotentiary of the Slovak government for Roma communities. His research interests include ethnic minorities, minority rights, social integration, and regional development. He is currently the president of the Mathias Bel Institute.

— Ravasz, Ábel, Ľuboš Kovács, and Filip Markovič. *Atlas rómskych komunít 2019*. Bratislava: Veda, 2020.
— Ravasz, Ábel. "Alternatives to Multiculturalism: Why Saying It has Failed is not Enough." In *Unity in Adversity*, edited by

Vít Novotný, 99–107. Brussels: Wilfried Martens Centre for European Studies, 2017.

— Ravasz, Ábel. "A multikulturalizmus-bumeráng." In *50 könyv, amit minden baloldalinak ismernie kell*, edited by Balázs Böcskei and Miklós Sebők, 223–227. Budapest: Kossuth, 2015.
— Ravasz, Ábel. *A multikulturális jogrend lehetőségei Magyarországon*. Budapest: ELTE, 2011.

Anna Remešová, Prague
b. Prague, Czechoslovakia, 1990

Anna Remešová is an editor of the Czech-Slovak online art magazine *Artalk*. In the past, she worked as a curator of etc. gallery in Prague, where she led a long-term research project dedicated to documentary in the contemporary moving image. She studied art history and theory of modern and contemporary art at the Academy of Arts, Architecture, and Design in Prague and was a member of Studio Without Master. Since 2020, she has been studying in a doctoral program at the Academy of Fine Arts in Prague, where she is dedicated to the research of ethnographic exposition in relation to discussions on decolonization in the Eastern European context. Her long-term research interests include the institutional conditions of the art scene in relation to feminist and ecological criticism.

— Remešová, Anna. "Kdo se směje nejvíc." *Artalk.cz*, January 17, 2022. https://artalk.cz/2022/01/17/kdo-se-smeje-nejvic/.
— Remešová, Anna. "Kde vzal Robinson svůj meč." *Kapitál*, no. 10 (October 2021). https://kapital-noviny.sk/kde-vzal-robinson-svuj-mec/.
— Remešová, Anna. "An Insecure Shelter Against the Imagination of the West. *Revista-ARTA*, October 23, 2017. https://revistaarta.ro/en/an-insecure-shelter-against-the-imagination-of-the-west/.

Sráč Sam, Česká Bříza
b. Plzeň, Česká Republika, 1969

Sráč Sam's work involves the reassessment of the linguistic, visual, and social models that grow out of power relations. She founded the sam83 gallery, organizes residencies Artist in Cottage, publishes the independent magazine Pižmo, and is the author the books *Vanda* (2011), *Kuniba Likes Things in Threes* (2011), and *My Husband's Fear* (2017). By adopting a sense of socio-economic responsibility, she was among those artists who consciously anticipated the ethical shift in art. The situations that Sam creates are environments in which she exposes the various aspects of manipulation and approaches to reality. In differing proportions, these scenarios move from the distinctly artificial, as explicit performances, to the completely natural, indistinguishable from reality. In every case the result is a new experience for the participant, even when it only concerns the recollection of memories.

Františka Schormová, Prague
b. Prague, Czechoslovakia, 1991

Františka Schormová is an Americanist and literary critic who currently teaches at the University of Hradec Kralové. Last year, she finished her PhD at Charles University Prague. She has been a Visiting Fellow at IWM Vienna and the Davis Center for Russian and Eurasian Studies at Harvard University and a PhD Fellow at CEFRES Prague. Her fields include critical race and whiteness studies, especially in Cold War contexts, transnational literature, and translation in a broad sense. She is currently working on a monograph on the allegiances within the 1950s internationalist network with a focus on the contacts between African American poets and Czechoslovakia.

— Schormová, Františka. *Prague, Red and Black: Early Cold War Journeys, Networks, and Poems* (upcoming).
— Schormová, Františka. "Stalinův černý apoštol: Paul Robeson v Praze. *Soudobé dějiny* 28, no. 1 (2021): 183–213.
— Schormová, Františka. "Hlasy z Harlemu: Transkontinentální solidarita v poezii Noémie de Sousy". In *Zamyšlení nad africkými identitami zobrazenými v básnickém prostoru*, edited by Vojtěch Šarše. Prague: FFUK, 2020.

Piotr Sikora, Prague
b. Krakow, Poland, 1986

Piotr Sikora is a critic and curator of contemporary art. He earned his master's degree at the Institute of Art History of the Jagiellonian

University in Krakow. He is a member of the Polish Section of the AICA. He explores the connections between pop culture, politics, and the art world. His curatorial practice focuses on developing methods of deconstructing great narratives based on the concepts of irony, exaggeration, and provocation. As curator of the MeetFactory AiR Program in Prague, together with Lucia Kvočáková he initiated the platform The New Dictionary of Old Ideas. He is also a lecturer at the Anglo-American University in Prague. Sikora is an ardent player of bike polo and father of two sons, Bořivoj and Otakar. He lives and works in Prague.

— *Hussites at The Baltic Sea*, Rondo Sztuki, Katowice, Poland, 2021
— *An Out of This World Event III.*, Karlin Studios, Prague, Czech Republic, 2019
— *Slav Squatting and Its Discontents*, Meet Factory, Prague, Czech Republic, 2018
— *Goodbye AiWeiWei*, INI Project, Prague, Czech Republic, 2018
— *Swag and Threat*, TRAFO Art Center, Szczecin, Poland, 2017

Markéta Soukupová, Prague
b. Prague, Czechoslovakia, 1992

Markéta Soukupová is a Prague-based artist in whose illustration practice meets interactive media. Her socially critical artworks focus on topics such as gender stereotypes, work relationships, or other contemporary social problems. In her work, Soukupová uses a variety of media, from illustration, through textiles, to digital games or object installations. Consequently, she never gives up her strong stylization, and she dismantles the conventions of exhibition architecture. Markéta Soukupová is part of the artistic duo Pink Flamingos and the group No Fun Collective.

— *Těch 10 minut se v 8 hodinách ztratí*, City Surfer Office, Prague, Czech Republic, 2022
— *Bad Joke*, Galerie Panel, Prague, Czech Republic, 2020
— *After New Media*, Galerie NTK, Prague, Czech Republic, 2019
— *Bauhaus: The Stress Simulator*, Ideal Prostor, Prague, Czech Republic, 2019

Tereza Stejskalová, Prague
b. Prague, Czechoslovakia, 1981

Tereza Stejskalová is a curator and researcher focusing on (post)socialist visual culture from a feminist and postcolonial perspective. In recent years, she has been researching the film production of students from the Global South in Czechoslovakia between the years 1948 and 1989. The results of this research have been exhibited in various places, including tranzit.sk (2016), National Gallery Prague (2017), Framer Framed in Amsterdam (2017), and Kunstraum Kreuzberg/Bethanien (2017). She teaches at FAMU in Prague and is a program director at tranzit.cz. She was the co-curator of the first edition of Biennale Matter of Art.

— Stejskalová, Tereza. "No Creation Without Destruction: Images of Child Birth and Candice Breitz's *Labour*." *Journal of Visual Art Practice* 20, no. 1–2 (2021).
— Stejskalová, Tereza. "We Do Not Know Ourselves: How Global South Filmmakers Exposed Racism in Czechoslovakia." *ARTMargins Online*, January 28, 2021.
— Stejskalová, Tereza. "Online Weak and Poor Images: On Contemporary Feminist Visual Politics." In *Photography Off the Scale: Technologies and Theories of the Mass Image*, edited by Jussi Parikka and Tomáš Dvořák. Edinburgh: Edinburgh University Press, 2021.
— Stejskalová, Tereza, ed. *Filmaři všech zemí, spojte se! Zapomenutý internacionalismus, československý film a třetí svět.* Prague: tranzit.cz, 2018.

Olúfẹ́mi O. Táíwò
b. 1990

Olúfẹ́mi O. Táíwò is an assistant professor of philosophy at Georgetown University. His theoretical work draws liberally from the Black radical tradition, anti-colonial thought, German transcendental philosophy, contemporary philosophy of language, contemporary social science, and histories of activism and activist thinkers. He is currently writing a book entitled *Reconsidering Reparations*, which offers a novel philosophical argument for reparations and explores links with environmental justice. He also engages in public philosophy, including articles exploring the intersections of climate justice and colonialism.

- Táíwò, Olúfẹ́mi O. *Elite Capture: How the Powerful Took Over Identity Politics (And Everything Else)*. Chicago: Haymarket Books, May 2022 (upcoming).
- Táíwò, Olúfẹ́mi O. *Reconsidering Reparations*. New York: Oxford University Press, March 2022 (upcoming).

Zai Xu, Prague
b. Prague, Czech Republic, 1998

Zai Xu is many things. From an outside perspective, he seems quite sure about the off-space SVĚTOVA 1, which he established, and which is still open today. One of the main activities of the space is that it continually focuses on young artists and experiments with different ways of supporting and finding the optimal scheme of sustainability. It is not just for the artists nor the space. His own art practice also reflects the burdens that come with it. His projects in various media and forms usually reflect his own personal struggles, such as stress, anxiety, or becoming an adult. For example, he is now very over-worked and struggling with his studies at the Academy of Fine Arts in Prague. He is very fascinated by the complexity and structure of the issues—how everything is connected. In his practice, he goes deeper into each component, such as racism, drugs, or feelings of exhaustion, while discoveing how shared these experiences sometimes are.

- Director and curator at SVĚTOVA 1, Prague, Czech Republic
  First solo show titled *Smažené nudle* in Galerie města Třince, Czech Republic, March 2022
- He is primarily a gallerist, curator, artist, organizer, student, and model, but he also occasionally writes and experiments with music